Library of
Davidson College

DEVELOPMENT OF THE MONETARY SECTOR, PREDICTION AND POLICY ANALYSIS IN THE FRB-MIT-PENN MODEL

Development of the Monetary Sector, Prediction and Policy Analysis in the FRB-MIT-Penn Model

J. PHILLIP COOPER
University of Chicago

Lexington Books
D.C. Heath and Company
Lexington, Massachusetts
Toronto   London

Library of Congress Cataloging in Publication Data

Cooper, Jerome Phillip, 1943
  Development of the monetary sector, prediction and policy analysis in the FRB-MIT-Penn Model.

  1. Monetary policy—Mathematical models.
  2. Monetary policy—United States—Mathematical models. 3. Economics—Mathematical models.
  I. Title.
  HG221.C7413   332.4'6   72–13279
  ISBN 0–669–85704–1

Copyright © 1974 by D.C. Heath and Company

All rights reserved. No part of this publication may be reproduced or transmitted in any form or by any means, electronic or mechanical, including photocopy, recording, or any information storage or retrieval system, without permission in writing from the publisher.

Published simultaneously in Canada.

Printed in the United States of America.

International Standard Book Number: 0–669–85704–1.

Library of Congress Catalog Card Number: 72–13279.

To my parents,
ARTHUR *and* ROSE COOPER

Table of Contents

LIST OF FIGURES ix
LIST OF TABLES xi
PREFACE xiii
INTRODUCTION 1
   Outline 1
   FMP Model Overview 7
   Model-Building Strategy in General 11

CHAPTER 1. DEVELOPMENT OF THE MONETARY
   SECTOR (with F. Modigliani and R. H. Rasche) . . . 15
   1.1 The Money Supply Mechanism 15
   1.2 Relation of the Money Supply Model to the Federal
       Funds Market 40
   1.3 The Demand for Money 44
   1.4 System Estimation: The Joint Determination of the
       Rate of Interest and the Stock of Money 58
   Appendix 1A Comments on the Orr and Mellon Model 72
   Appendix 1B Gauss-Seidel Solution Method 80

CHAPTER 2. EX POST AND EX ANTE PREDICTIVE
   PERFORMANCE (with C. R. Nelson) 97
   2.1 One–Quarter–Ahead Sample–Period Predictive Performance and Comparison with Time Series Models 97
   2.2 Composite Predictions: Single Equation and Joint
       Estimates 107
   2.3 Policy Implications of Composite Predictions . . . 113
   2.4 Post–Sample Predictive Performance 115

CHAPTER 3. STOCHASTIC SIMULATION 121
   3.1 Reasons for and Description of Stochastic Simulation Techniques 121
   3.2 Dynamic Simulation Results 126
   3.3 One–Period Simulation Results 146
   3.4 Estimation of Reduced–Form Equations 163

CHAPTER 4. POLICY ANALYSIS: SIMULATION OF
  MONETARY RULES (with S. Fischer) 177
  4.1 Constant–Growth–Rate, Proportional, and Derivative Rules 177
  4.2 Sensitivity Analysis, Conclusions, and Caveats . . 190
  4.3 Experimental Design and Explanation of Tests for Stochastic Simulation 194
  4.4 Results and Conclusions 197
  Appendix 4A The Use of the Secant Method in Econometric Models 205

REFERENCES 211
INDEX 219
ABOUT THE AUTHOR 227

List of Figures

1–1a	Hypothetical Graph of $\Phi(x)$	21
1–1b	Graph of $\Phi^{-1}(-\overline{FR})$ and Determination of $\widehat{FR}$, Given $(i-r_S)/(r-r_S)$	21
1–2	The Relationship Between Desired Free Reserves and the Bill Rate, for Fixed Discount Rate	29
1–3	Relation among the Three Variables: FR, S, B^*	41
1–4	Relation among B, FFB, and r	43
1–5	Currency–Demand-Deposit Ratio	57
1–6	Flow Chart for Demand-Deposit Component of Money Supply	60
1–7	Dynamic Simulation of Demand Deposits: Least Squares Coefficients	63
1–8	Dynamic Simulation of Free Reserves: Least Squares Coefficients	64
1–9	Dynamic Simulation of Treasury Bill Rate: Least Squares Coefficients	66
1–10	Dynamic Simulation of Demand Deposits: Two-Stage Coefficients	68
1–11	Dynamic Simulation of Treasury Bill Rate: Two-Stage Coefficients	69
1–12	Profit-Risk Opportunity Locus	76
1–13	Effect of Damping on Real Roots	85
1–14	Effect of Damping on Complex Roots	85
2–1	Visual Display of Composite Regression: FMP and ARIMA (1956: I Through 1966: IV) Short-Term Interest Rate	110
3–1a	Mean, Standard Deviation, Minimum, and Maximum of Stochastic Dynamic Solutions: Nominal GNP	128
3–1b	Actual, Deterministic Dynamic Solution, and Mean Stochastic Dynamic Solution: Nominal GNP	129
3–2a	Mean, Standard Deviation, Minimum and Maximum of Stochastic Dynamic Solutions: GNP Deflator	130
3–2b	Actual, Deterministic Dynamic Solution, and Mean Stochastic Dynamic Solution: GNP Deflator	131
3–3a	Mean, Standard Deviation, Minimum, and Maximum of Stochastic Dynamic Solutions: Real GNP	132

3–3b	Actual, Deterministic Dynamic Solution, and Mean Stochastic Dynamic Solution: Real GNP	133
3–4a	Mean, Standard Deviation, Minimum, and Maximum of Stochastic Dynamic Solutions: Long-Term Interest Rate	134
3–4b	Actual, Deterministic Dynamic Solution, and Mean Stochastic Dynamic Solution: Long-Term Interest Rate	135
3–5a	Mean, Standard Deviation, Minimum, and Maximum of Stochastic Dynamic Solutions: Short-Term Interest Rate	136
3–5b	Actual, Deterministic Dynamic Solution, and Mean Stochastic Dynamic Solution: Short-Term Interest Rate	137
3–6a	Mean, Minimum, and Maximum of Stochastic One-Period Solutions: Nominal GNP	148
3–6b	Actual, Deterministic One-Period Solution, and Mean Stochastic One-Period Solution: Nominal GNP	149
3–7a	Mean, Minimum, and Maximum of Stochastic One-Period Solutions: GNP Deflator	150
3–7b	Actual, Deterministic One-Period Solution, and Mean Stochastic One-Period Solution: GNP Deflator	151
3–8a	Mean, Minimum, and Maximum of Stochastic One-Period Solutions: Real GNP	152
3–8b	Actual, Deterministic One-Period Solution, and Mean Stochastic One-Period Solution: Real GNP	153
3–9a	Mean, Standard Deviation, Minimum, and Maximum of Stochastic One-Period Solutions: Long-Term Interest Rate	154
3–9b	Actual, Deterministic One-Period Solution, and Mean Stochastic One-Period Solution: Long-Term Interest Rate	155
3–10a	Mean, Standard Deviation, Minimum, and Maximum of Stochastic One-Period Solutions: Short-Term Interest Rate	156
3–10b	Actual, Deterministic One-Period Solution, and Mean Stochastic One-Period Solution: Short-Term Interest Rate	157
3–11	Estimated Lag Structures for ΔM and ΔE	168
3–12a	Distribution of Estimated Lag Coefficients for ΔM	170
3–12b	Distribution of Estimated Lag Coefficients for ΔE	171
4–1	Mean Quarterly Rates of Inflation and Unemployment for Simulations 1 to 20	182
4–2	Standard Deviations of the Quarterly Rates of Inflation and Unemployment for Simulations 1 to 20	183
4–3	Time Paths of Demand Deposits	187
4–4	Time Paths of the Quarterly Rate of Inflation	188
4–5	Time Paths of the Rate of Unemployment	189

List of Tables

1	Breakdown of Equations in the FMP Model (Version 4.1)	9
1–1	Standardized Bank Balance Sheet	17
1–2	Free Reserve Estimates	36
1–3	Demand Deposit Estimates: 1955: I to 1966: IV	49
1–4	Currency Demand Estimates: 1955: I to 1966: IV	55
1–5	Equations of the Monetary Sector	58
1–6	Root Mean Square Errors of Single Equations and Dynamic Simulations	62
1–7	Optimal Values of D under Uncertainty Compared with Traditional Values	77
1–8	Sensitivity of $\hat{D}$ and α to Changes in M and Other Parameters	78
1–9	Sensitivity of $\hat{D}$ to Parameters when $R=1.0$	80
2–1	ARIMA Models for FMP Variables, Fitted Through 1966: IV	100
2–2	Summary Statistics for Ex Post and Ex Ante Sample-Period Errors of the FMP Model: 1956: I Through 1966: IV	103
2–3	Correlations Between Ex Post, Ex Ante and ARIMA Sample-Period Errors: 1956: I Through 1966: IV	105
2–4	Serial Correlation Coefficients for Sample Period FMP Ex Post, Ex Ante, and ARIMA Prediction Errors: 1956: I Through 1966: IV	106
2–5	Estimated Weights for the Composite Predictions $\beta \cdot FMP + (1-\beta) \cdot ARIMA$: 1956: I Through 1966: IV	109
2–6	*Jointly* Estimated Weights for the Composite Predictions $\beta \cdot FMP + (1-\beta) \cdot ARIMA$: 1956: I Through 1966: IV	111
2–7	Summary Statistics for Post-Sample Errors: 1967: I Through 1968: IV	116
2–8	Summary Statistics for Post-Sample Errors from the Composite Regressions: 1967: I Through 1968: IV	117
3–1	Dynamic Simulation Summary: Nominal GNP	138
3–2	Dynamic Simulation Summary: GNP Deflator	139
3–3	Dynamic Simulation Summary: Real GNP	140
3–4	Dynamic Simulation Summary: Long-Term Interest Rate	141
3–5	Dynamic Simulation Summary: Short-Term Interest Rate	142
3–6	One-Period Simulation Summary: Nominal GNP	158
3–7	One-Period Simulation Summary: GNP Deflator	159

3–8	One-Period Simulation Summary: Real GNP	160
3–9	One-Period Simulation Summary: Long-Term Interest Rate	161
3–10	One-Period Simulation Summary: Short-Term Interest Rate	162
3–11	Estimated Lag Coefficients for ΔM and ΔE	172
4–1	Simulations	180
4–2	Simulation Results for Two Subperiods	192
4–3	Parameter Values for Policy Rules	194
4–4	Results of Stochastic Simulations	198
4–5	Summary Standard Deviations of Target Variables	199
4–6	Better-Worse-Tied Comparaisons	199
4–7	Two-Way Analysis of Variance	200
4–8	Simultaneous Confidence Intervals on Differences in All Means	202
4–9	Simultaneous Confidence Intervals for Comparing Means of III and IV with I	203
4–10	Range of Ratios of Standard Deviations	204

Preface

This book reports the results of several research studies with a large, quarterly, macroeconometric model of the U.S. economy. The studies involve the various aspects of modeling including specification of economic structure, predictive performance, model methodology, and policy analysis. The model common to each of these studies is the Federal Reserve Board-MIT-Pennsylvania (FMP) model. Primary research tools are econometric regression techniques and especially simulation analysis, both deterministic and stochastic. The Introduction presents a brief overview of the model and discusses the interrelationship between model building and some of the uses of econometric models. The remaining four chapters are each devoted to specific areas of economic investigation with the FMP model.

Chapter 1 begins with a detailed specification of the supply of money based on the portfolio behavior of individual, profit-maximizing commercial banks. Problems associated with aggregation within the banking system and over time are treated explicitly. An aggregate demand function for money, in the spirit of the modern transactions demand theorists, is also developed. Supply and demand elements are combined and the monetary sector, in which the stock of money and the short-term interest rate are jointly determined, is simulated to investigate its performance as a dynamic system. Estimates are then refined to handle econometric problems of simultaneity and autocorrelated errors.

Chapter 2 investigates the predictive performance of the FMP model inside and outside its estimation sample period. One-quarter-ahead forecasts are analyzed not only for the situation in which exogenous variables are known without error but also for the more realistic case in which they must also be predicted. The benchmarks of prediction accuracy are time-series models of the Box-Jenkins autoregressive moving-average variety. Mean square error is shown to be reduced by the estimation of linear composites of the different predictors available for endogenous variables. These composite equations also have interesting policy applications.

Chapter 3 explores some of the dynamic and single-period system properties of the FMP model using the technique of stochastic simulation. The additive disturbances of the stochastic equations of the model are drawn from a multivariate normal distribution with zero mean and appropriate covariance matrix; the technique and its motivations are discussed in detail. Investigation centers on the relationship between the mean of stochastic simulations and a deterministic solution, the distribution of the time paths of stochastic simulations about their mean, and the behavior of various functions of simulated endogenous variables, including regression equations based on simulation output. Some comments are offered on the practice of neglecting nonlinearities in econometric models.

The final chapter presents evidence against the well-known but controversial suggestion that the supply of money be expanded at a steady rate. In the context of the FMP model and over a thirteen-year period, it is shown that variation in the rates of inflation and unemployment can be reduced by adjusting the rate of growth of money in accordance with simple, mechanical rules. The rules tested are members of the class of feedback control rules and utilize proportional and derivative control. Deterministic and stochastic simulations are carried out followed by a battery of statistical tests. Some sensitivity checks are also performed on the specificity of results to the monetary growth rate selected, the sample period and the path of fiscal policy.

We all have become accustomed to glowing acknowledgments. This book will be no exception; the sincerity of my expressions of gratitude, however, could be really apparent only to me. Franco Modigliani, as the head of my thesis committee and a coauthor of Chapter 2, has been a true inspiration; I would be happy to have absorbed at least a small part of his deep, insightful knowledge of economic processes. (I still expect his voice on the other end of the line if the phone rings early Sunday morning.) A second member of my committee, Edwin Kuh, tried to teach me econometrics in and out of the classroom and was in many areas an invaluable adviser. Robert Solow also read the manuscript and provided many helpful suggestions. To my collaborators—Stanley Fischer, Charles R. Nelson and Robert H. Rasche—I owe substantial debts for their patience and the rewarding experience of working with them. (Certainly all spelling mistakes must remain their responsibility.)

My other teachers at M.I.T., especially Franklin Fisher, deserve and receive my grateful thanks. Many colleagues, first as a student at M.I.T., then as a faculty member at the University of Chicago, have been extremely helpful with comments on the various essays here and answers to my many questions. Merton Miller of the University of Chicago deserves a special extra nod for giving me the necessary boost to compile this volume. Preparation of the manuscript was expertly supervised by Mrs. Ilene Haniotis.

Acknowledgment is also given for the use of the following: "Central Bank Policy, the Money Supply, and the Short-Term Rate of Interest," by Franco Modigliani, Robert Rasche, and J. Phillip Cooper, and "Simulations of Monetary Rules in the FRB-MIT-Penn Model," by J. Phillip Cooper and Stanley Fischer, are reprinted, in substantially edited form, from the *Journal of Money, Credit, and Banking*. Copyright © 1970, 1971 by the Ohio State University Press. "The Use of the Secant Method in Econometric Models," by J. Phillip Cooper and Stanley Fischer, is reprinted, in substantially edited form, from the *Journal of Business*. Copyright © 1973 by The University of Chicago Press. "Stochastic Simulation of Monetary Rules in Two Macroeconomic Models," by J. Phillip Cooper and Stanley Fischer, is reprinted, in substantially edited form, from the *Journal of the American Statistical Association*. Copyright © 1972 by the American Statistical Association.

My final acknowledgment is to my wife, Ellen, who has endured all with me, has understood all, and never nagged—not even a little bit.

J. PHILLIP COOPER

Chicago, October, 1972

DEVELOPMENT OF THE MONETARY SECTOR,
PREDICTION AND POLICY ANALYSIS IN
THE FRB-MIT-PENN MODEL

Introduction

Outline

This volume is a collection of four essays, the themes of which include the three primary reasons economists build econometric models —specification of economic structure, forecasting, and policy analysis. The model common to each of the essays is the Federal Reserve Board-MIT-Pennsylvania Macroeconometric Model (hereafter called the FMP model).[1] Perhaps, one of the most unusual features of this model is that it can be considered useful to those whose interests in and requirements of a model may be very different. The second reason that economists build models—that is, to use in forecasting—was not an especially important consideration to the FMP model builders; yet we will see that the model has definite utility in this area. The background and a brief overview of the model are presented in the next section; and the interrelationship between model building and its various applications is discussed in the final section of this Introduction. The remainder of this first section is devoted to outlining the four essays comprising Chapters 1 through 4.

Chapter 1, entitled "Development of the Monetary Sector," contains the theoretical and empirical specification of the kernel of the model's financial sector, the monetary sector. Though it would be in no way logically independent of either the rest of the financial sector or the rest of the model if one were to analyze the causal structure of the model, it is nevertheless useful to describe the monetary sector loosely as comprising those equations which interact to jointly determine the stock of money and the short-term rate of interest. In other words, the equations represent the supply of and the demand for money and the money market equilibrium condition. The monetary sector, or more properly subsector, is an especially sensitive area of the model, since it is here that the immediate impact of monetary policy—open-market operations, and the setting of discount and reserve requirement rates—is felt. The following section ("FMP Model Overview") and especially the references cited there go to some length to explain the transmission of monetary policy out of that subsector and into and throughout the rest of the model. The body of this chapter is a result of a lengthy collaboration with Franco Modigliani of M.I.T., the head of my doctoral thesis committee, and Robert H. Rasche of Michigan State University.[2]

The first section of Chapter 1 describes our approach to formulating a money supply model for the U.S. economy. In particular, we concentrate on the factors contributing to the banks' demand for earning assets, assigning important roles to exogenous changes in bank reserves, and the behavior of commercial and industrial loans. The theoretically optimal investment portfolio for a single profit-maximizing bank in an uncertain environment is developed. Based on the result obtained by aggregating this investment behavioral equation across banks and adding a second relation obtained from the bank balance sheet identity, an equation for the supply of deposits is developed. This supply equation, however, contains some unobservable variables. After a brief incursion into the Federal Funds market, a relationship, which is normalized with free reserves as the dependent variable, is obtained containing only observables. Since this relation is applicable to the decision period of the banking system, we aggregate over time to the final operational specification which is fit to quarterly data.

The brief incursion into the Federal Funds market referred to above is amplified in section 1.2 with a description of the demand for and supply of Federal Funds. The main purpose is to investigate the relation between the cost of borrowing from the Fed (one of the theoretical constructs used in the portfolio discussion of section 1.1), the discount rate, and the level of free reserves. This analysis allows us to eliminate a key unobservable variable and to identify precisely the relationship between the coefficients estimated in our operational equation and the parameters of our model.

Section 1.3 is a brief description of the demand-for money function necessary to complete the monetary sector. The basic model rests on the modern transactions approach to the demand for money. Both long-run (stock) demand for money and short-run (flow) relations are developed and the relationship to a number of competing hypotheses indicated. This model is then applied to both demand deposit and currency components of the money supply. A few variations in the basic hypothesis are discussed and empirical results summarized.

In the final section, the supply and demand parts of the sector are brought together and the severe econometric problems of a non-linear model with serially correlated disturbances *and* simultaneity recognized. The single-equation estimates are used in dynamic simulations of the sector and the interaction of the equations is analyzed. A somewhat ad hoc two-step least squares estimator is applied and the results of dynamic simulations are again analyzed. These latter simulation results indicate definite improvement relative to the single-equation estimates in tracking over the sample period and in extrapolating over the next five quarters. The structural coefficients, themselves, are more in line with a priori expectations. The section concludes with a brief discussion of the problem of defining exogenous policy variables.

There are two appendices to Chapter 1. The first presents comments on the well-known Orr and Mellon model of optimal credit expansion by a bank faced with stochastic reserve losses.[3] The model is closely related to the *microeconomic* one in section 1.1. The main difference is that the Orr and Mellon model has been numerically parameterized so that we may infer the pattern of bank behavior; our model in the text is specified only so far as functional form and arguments so that we can choose the appropriate specification for estimation of aggregate relationships. The comments presented have to do with Orr and Mellon's misleading parametric tabulation of the optimal solution, misspecification of the bank's expected profit function, and lack of consideration of global optimality.

Appendix 1B discusses the Gaus-Seidel simulation method used in section 1.4. It is included here for a number of reasons. First, when the study was being conducted, there was no expository presentation of the technique at all in literature available to the economist; the method itself had only recently been applied to economic models. Second, many problems in obtaining solutions were encountered during the study. The source of these problems and a modification of the technique that was always helpful are discussed in this appendix. Third, the remaining chapters in this volume are also based on simulation; it seems essential that the primary computer tool used be documented here, especially since, as just noted, it is fairly new to economic research.

Chapter 2 is an attempt to measure the one-quarter-ahead prediction performance of the FMP model. There are five features of this essay which add special flavor to what has to be an otherwise unappetizing diet of tables of numbers and descriptions of tables of numbers. First, the standard of accuracy used is the one-quarter-ahead forecasts of a set of single-variate time-series models which, though statistically sophisticated, are completely naive from an economics standpoint. In particular, we compare FMP predictions with those of integrated mixed autoregressive moving-average form, the so-called "Box-Jenkins models." Secondly, the time-series models are used to extrapolate key exogenous variables of the model so that we can analyze impersonal ex ante predictions of the model as well as the more traditional ex post predictions which are conditioned on the true values of exogenous variables. Knowledge of the true values of the exogenous variables is, of course, a luxury never bestowed upon the operational forecaster. Both kinds of forecast provide useful information about the potential usefulness of a model as a predictor. Third, linear composites are formed from the FMP and time-series model predictions which yield minimum mean square error forecasts given the availability of both models. This is a useful tool with which to evaluate the marginal contribution of one predictor given the other, and examples are presented which show that it would be inefficient to use only one predictor, chosen on the basis of lower individual mean quare error. Fourth, the linear composites are estimated jointly across variables using the Zellner across-equation generalized least squares technique. We are then able not only to increase the efficiency of our estimates but also to test—and reject—a particularly interesting notion that the weights of individual predictors in linear composites of the type we employ are to be interpreted as applying to the models as a whole rather than individual economic variables. Fifth, we work with the composites to learn what usefulness a policy maker might find in the naive time-series models. It is shown that information from the time-series models can be incorporated with that from econometric models in a systematic and appealing way. This chapter is based on work with Charles R. Nelson of the University of Chicago.[4]

Section 2.1 details most of the statistical aspects of the chapter. Included are goodness-of-fit tests on FMP (ex post and ex ante) and time-series predictions and correlations of errors across predictive method and across time. In section 2.2, the notion of the linear composite is developed and estimates tabulated. Equations are estimated using single-equation ordinary least squares and joint generalized least quares, and some tests are performed. The policy implications of linear composites of different predictors are explored in section 2.3 and the post-sample errors of the various predictors (including composites) are analyzed in section 2.4.

Chapter 3 explores some of the dynamic and single-period system properties of the FMP model using the technique of stochastic simulation.[5] This technique is considerably more expensive than the more common deterministic simulation since each stochastic simulation consists of a number of replications of ordinary simulation runs. In a deterministic simulation, the additive disturbances are set at their mean value, zero; in each replication of a stochastic simulation experiment, the disturbances are pseudorandom numbers with "appropriate" properties. Section 3.1 discusses the various reasons why stochastic simulations are desirable. Among them are considerations of statistical inference from experimental results, reproduction of the actual environment of policy makers, and problems raised by the nonlinearity of modern econometric models such as the FMP model. The section also includes a detailed description of the technique, including the generation of uniform pseudorandom numbers, the transformation to produce normality, a futher transformation to produce an appropriate across-equation covariance matrix, and the implementation of the technique in a system solved by the Gauss-Seidel method.

Sections 3.2 and 3.3 are devoted to discussing results of dynamic and one-period simulations, respectively. In each section, the time patterns of a number of key economic variables are displayed along with a number of other pertinent paths. These include: paths of statistics calculated over twenty-five replications such as mean, mean plus and minus one standard deviation and the maximum and minimum; the deterministic path; and the actual or historical path. Various statistics of goodness-of-fit are tabulated and discussed. The main aspects of the results analyzed are: the relationship among the paths of the stochastic mean, a deterministic solution, and historical data; the dispersion in the stochastic solutions over time; and the behavior of functions of endogenous variables over time. The motivation behind much of the analysis is to find out the extent to which the FMP model might be considered approximately linear in its behavior.

The stochastic solutions of the FMP model actually constitute twenty-five realizations of sets of data generated by a particular economic system. In other words, a by-product of the simulation experiments is the material for a Monte Carlo experiment of the type econometricians have recently been finding useful in studies of econometric methodology. And the model is much more general and realistic than those designed specifically for a particular Monte Carlo application. Section 3.4 presents an example of one such use to which these data might be put. A so-called reduced-form equation, relating a key endogenous variable to current and past policy variables, is estimated for each available data set. The many problems of this approach, popularized by the St. Louis Federal Reserve Bank, are outlined; and some evidence is provided on one of the most important of these—namely, the improper declaration of a regressor as exogenous when it is, in reality, endogenous.

Chapter 4, entitled "Policy Analysis: Simulation of Monetary Rules," investigates in the context of the FMP model the question of whether or not monetary rules of a mechanical, feedback-control type would be preferred to less active policies. In other words, we are interested in an issue which is logically part of the "rules versus discretion" controversy of monetary economics. In particular, if a rule is to be adopted, should the rule be of the constant-growth-rate-of-the-money-supply variety widely recommended by the so-called "monetarists" or could some of the class of automatic control rules produce marked gains in stability. The usual contention is that the latter would not be the case primarily because of the long and variable lags in the effect of monetary policy on economic aggregates like the rates of inflation and unemployment. The FMP model is useful for such a study since it has a detailed specification of monetary processes, because it exhibits rather long lags in the effects of monetary policy, and because the structure of these lags varies with the stage of the business cycle and the values taken on by other exogenous influences. This chapter is based on papers written with Stanley Fischer of the University of Chicago.[6]

The problem is stated in section 4.1 and a brief survey of previous literature is used to motivate the approach taken. A class of control rules for the rate of growth of the money supply—which includes the constant-growth-rate rule—is discussed along with the simulation design. Our criterion function allows us to select a preferred rule from among the members of the class. Essentially, a particular rule dominates another if it lowers a measure of variability of either the rate of inflation or the unemployment rate without increasing variability in the other target. A search is then conducted for the "optimal" form of the rule, the process providing extremely useful information on the relative merits of different subclasses of rules.

Since there are a large number of qualifications in the approach of section 4.1, the next section makes some of these explicit and also presents the results of some sensitivity experiments. First, we check that the improvement exhibited by a feedback-control rule over a constant-growth-rate rule is relatively independent of the growth rate selected. Second, the sample period was divided into two parts and the performance of our preferred rule over each subperiod analyzed. Third, the path of exogenous fiscal policy was altered in such a way that, loosely speaking, the Korean War was moved into the sample period and the Vietnam War out; again, the monetary rule is evaluated.

One of the main caveats expressed in section 4.2 is that the stochastic specification of the model has been suppressed. In section 4.3, therefore, the design of some stochastic simulation experiments is outlined and the battery of tests to be applied to the results is explained. Some of these tests are intuitive but rather ad hoc, others have more sound statistical bases including analysis of variance and multiple comparison techniques by both Tukey and Dunnett. Results and conclusions of these tests are presented in section 4.4.

Chapter 4 concludes with an appendix which borrows a rather old method from numerical analysis and applies it to a problem in the study of policy in econometric models. Tinbergen's method for solving a model for the values of policy instruments which lead to desired values of target variables cannot be used in today's nonlinear models. Instead we have found a rather robust and efficient method of accomplishing the same goal which interfaces very neatly with the Gauss-Seidel solution method.

FMP Model Overview

The FMP model is a closed quarterly econometric model of the post-Korean War economy, designed to improve understanding of the workings of tools of monetary and fiscal stabilization policy. Research was begun in the autumn of 1966 by a group of academic economists at M.I.T. under the direction of Albert Ando and Franco

Modigliani and by economists of the Research Department of the Board of Governors of the Federal Reserve System under the direction of Frank de Leeuw. The main concern of the project was to produce a structural model which emphasized the role of policy instruments; further, special attention was given to modeling of financial markets. A decision was also made that the specification of the model should follow closely the existing body of economic theory, with due consideration paid to institutional factors; the primary goal was not maximizing goodness-of-fit.

To describe adequately the structure of the FMP model in a brief section of a chapter is impossible. The whole of Chapter 1, the longest in this volume, explains the theoretical and empirical basis of *one* subsector of the model, containing *less than 5 percent* (i.e., 3) of the sixty-six stochastic equations of the model. The simple listing of equations, coefficients, and a glossary of variables would run easily fifty typed pages. The appropriate thing to do is to reference the more important material and allow the interested reader to immerse himself there. The following publications and mimeographed working papers should be noted: de Leeuw and Gramlich [26, 27], Rasche and Shapiro [68], Ando and Modigliani [7], Zellner [85], and Gordon [40]. These are all of a rather general nature and will point to detailed works on specific sectors or subsectors, such as Modigliani, Rasche, and Cooper [57] for the money market; Jaffee and Modigliani [44] for the commercial loans market; Modigliani [55] for consumption, and so on. There are in addition a number of mimeographed unpublished working papers and equation listings avalable from those actively involved with the FMP project.

The version loosely identified as 4.1 appearing circa the summer of 1969 is the one containing the monetary equations developed in Chapter 1 and the one used in all of the experiments reported in Chapters 2, 3, and 4. Table 1 gives a breakdown of the number of stochastic and nonstochastic equations in parts of the model.[7] It is immediately evident that the FMP model builders focused their efforts quite differently from their predecessors.

Monetary policy works through three main channels. In the first instance, changes in the money supply affect interest rates. These in turn affect the rates of various categories of investment through *cost of capital* variables; the rate of consumption directly and through *wealth* variables; and housing expenditures directly and through *credit rationing* variables. Fiscal variables can affect the cost

TABLE 1   Breakdown of Equations in the FMP Model (Version 4.1)

	Stochastic	Nonstochastic
I. Final Demand Equations		
Consumption	3	3
Investment in plant and equipment	10	9
Housing	7	3
State and local government expenditures	3	3
Inventory investment	1	
Imports	1	1
	25	19
II. Distribution of Income		
Definition of outputs		5
Net national product and national income		2
Labor income		1
Nonlabor income		1
Corporate profits, cash flows, and dividends	3	4
Personal income and disposable income		2
Inventory valuation adjustment	1	1
Saving and net worth		2
Miscellaneous items	1	3
	5	21
III. Taxes and Transfers		
Corporate income taxes	2	
Indirect business taxes	2	2
Personal income taxes	2	2
Contributions to social insurance	3	2
Transfer payments	3	1
Net deficit of government		2
	12	9

Table 1 (continued)

		Stochastic	Nonstochastic
IV.	*Labor Market*		
	Demand for manhours, hours/man, and employment	2	5
	Supply of labor and unemployment	1	5
		3	10
V.	*Prices*		
	Wage rate	1	
	General price level	1	1
	Other prices		20
	Current-to-real-dollar transformations		9
		2	30
VI.	*Financial Sector*		
	Money market	5	5
	Term structure	1	
	Commercial loan market	2	
	Municipal bond rate	1	
	Mortgage rate	1	
	Time deposits at commercial banks	3	7
	Savings and loan associations	2	1
	Mutual savings banks	2	1
	Life insurance reserves	1	1
	Dividend-price ratio	1	
	Savings flows for housing starts		1
		19	16
	Complete Model	66	105

of capital and level of disposable income. The lag patterns for the effects of monetary policy vary with the values of other exogenous variables in the model and are presented at some length in de Leeuw and Gramlich [26].

To amplify somewhat on the cryptic description of the previous paragraph we should map the causal structure of the model. We start at the monetary subsector of the next chapter and imagine the factors behind the demand for and supply of money (including exogenous monetary policy variables) interacting to "determine" the level of demand deposits and the rate on three-month treasury bills. We might then trace the flow of causation through the commercial paper rate to other longer maturity market rates. These in turn affect the demand for other types of deposits and the holdings of assets of financial intermediaries. We can trace the financial effects further and find them associating with fiscal policy variables in the determination of the levels of real expenditures. Proceeding further, the implied level of real output leads into an employment sector determining wages and prices and, in turn, the nominal level of GNP.

This is all too simple, of course. The model does *not* have this recursive structure. There are important feedbacks at all levels. Real GNP is both input and output to the area of the model determining consumption and investment expenditures. Some of these expenditures influence the demand for financial instruments supplied by intermediaries, particularly commercial and industrial loans by the banking system. These, in turn, feed farther back into the monetary subsector itself and are instrumental in the demand-for-free-reserve equation, thereby affecting the supply of money. Because of the transactions approach to the demand for money, nominal GNP is an important variable in the monetary subsector, too. On top of all this, the net wealth of households is a key endogenous variable in many parts of the model, and it has been neglected in the above discussion. The model is essentially fully simultaneous with no meaningful decomposability.

Model-Building Strategy in General

In addition to the FMP model itself, another essential element common to the essays in this volume is the use of simulation techniques to study the system and dynamic properties of an economic model. These techniques are also employed in most of the references cited in the previous section. The growing use of simulation is due largely to two factors: models have become more complex as we try to get closer to our view of the true economic process; and computer technology, machines *and* programs, have progressed to the point where most economists could be in the position of running their own model simulations. With regard to the first of these factors, "complex" does not necessarily mean "large." Tinbergen was building models, medium size even by today's standards, in the 1930s that did not need simulation capability to permit understanding. The difference was the linearity of his models and those that followed it. Until recently, given a model with estimated parameters we could, because of the linearity, calculate its reduced form and learn all we needed to know about its system properties;[8] or we could calculate its characteristic equation and learn most of what we needed to know about its dynamic properties. As for computer technology, we can now solve a large, nonlinear, difference-equation model like the FMP model for 50 quarters for about $ 10, depending upon the nature of the simulation run and the type of output desired. A run takes less than a minute on computers such as the IBM 360/65.

But in addition to the need to use simulation for an understanding of our models that goes deeper than individual equations and our capability to do so, we *ought* to be doing so for another important reason. Simulation is an important activity in model building itself; it should not be confined to a postpartum kind of role. What is intended here is a recommendation for an iterative strategy to model building as opposed to, say, a straight progression from model specification through estimation to application.[9]

We can think of the ith iteration in model building as involving a model, formulated, estimated, and mathematically complete. The model may be an initial prototype or the output of the $(i-1)$th iteration. Computer simulation in a wide range of experiments and checks using old and new data lead to new research findings and ultimately a reformulation of the model. This is the end of iteration i; and so on. The information about the characteristics of the model by the experimentation with the *dynamic system* cannot be gleaned from our practice of fitting single equations using historical data for the endogenous variables, current and lagged, appearing on the right-hand side of the equal sign. It was, of course, awareness of the danger in the practice of overemphasizing the standard goodness-of-fit criteria—the possibility of "mining" the data to produce equations with absurd economic implications—that led those directing the FMP research projects to eschew explicitly maximizing R^2's and to elevate theoretical considerations.

It is also possible, in the author's view, to pay too much attention to single-equation properties of the model, even if they are single-equation theoretical considerations. I do not believe the directors of FMP model research are guilty of this, but at the same time the scope of simulation experiments by "insiders" was a lot narrower than the class of experiments we see being performed with models today. Naturally, their interests are bound to be more limited than those of the profession as a whole. It is with this in mind that Chapters 2, 3, and 4 are offered as sources of, we believe, valuable information to the model builders. I and my collaborators on those essays were in a real sense "outsiders"; we provide objective and different views of the model as seen in the light of a number of varied applications of the model—the model as a predictor, ex post and ex ante; the model as a nonlinear, stochatic system; and the model as a test environment for rules of stabilization policy. Occasionally, we make our model-specific observations explicit, and more often we do not. There is a lot of information there; some of it should be very useful in revision of the model, at least in knowing where to concentrate resources. We believe, in any case, that these experiments were useful in their own right, in the purpose for which they were intended, be it forecasting performance, model methodology, or policy analysis.

Notes

[1] The model has been known by many aliases, among them the FRB-MIT-Penn, Fed-MIT, MIT-Fed, MIT, and Fed Model. More recently, a new version has appeared entitled the MPS Model (MIT-Pennsylvania-Social Science Research Council).
[2] The product of that collaboration is reported in Modigliani, Rasche, and Cooper [57]. Chapter 2 represents Section III, IV, and the Appendix of that article and includes a portion of Section II.
[3] A slightly condensed version of Appendix 1A has been published; see Cooper [18].
[4] See Cooper and Nelson [23], a paper prepared for the 1971

Econometric Society Meetings in New Orleans; the paper also included analysis of and comparisons with the St. Louis Federal Reserve Bank Model which are not presented here.

[5] Some of the material in the first three sections of this chapter was presented by the author at a Midwest Model Users Conference at the Chicago Federal Reserve Bank, December 1969.

[6] The body of Chapter 4 is extracted from Cooper and Fischer [20, 21], who also include some experiments, not reported here, with the St. Louis Federal Reserve Bank Model. The appendix to the chapter is also the result of that collaboration [22]. The second of the above papers was presented at the 1970 Econometric Society Meetings in Detroit.

[7] Source for this breakdown is FMP model (version 4.1, 4/15/69) mimeographed equation coding sheets which correspond very closely to the operating model used in all experiments reported in the text.

[8] This includes the multiplier effects of changes in coefficients in equations, such as tax rates; this ability was not widely perceived, though. All that is needed is the expression for the derivative of an element of an inverse of a matrix with respect to an element of the original matrix; see, for example, Theil [73], p. 33.

[9] For a detailed description of an iterative strategy see Zellner [86].

1 Development of the Monetary Sector

1.1 The Money Supply Mechanism

The Basic Approach

The total money supply in the FMP model consists of the sum of currency and demand deposits. The supply of currency in our framework is entirely controlled by the demand for currency (see section 1.3). Therefore, to understand the total money outstanding, we must understand the determinants of the stock of demand deposits, namely, the interaction of the central bank, the commercial banking sector, and the public's demand. Also, since in the present American system the bulk of demand deposits is created by the member banks and the behavior of their deposits in turn largely controls the total (at least in the short run), in the rest of this section we deal explicitly with only this component.

Our approach to the supply of deposits by member banks differs somewhat in spirit, as well as in operational details, from the most recent empirical studies which endeavor to handle the problem by focusing on the "demand" for excess reserves and for borrowing from the Federal Reserve.[1]

We start instead from the notion that to account for the supply of demand deposits we need to understand the forces controlling banks' demand for earning assets. Furthermore, in developing the short-run dynamics of the supply equation, we assign a crucial role to the behavior of commercial loans. This role, which has already been recognized by other authors (e.g., Goldfeld [38]), arises from the fact that, in the case of commercial loans, as distinguished from most other assets, the initiative lies largely with the customers, rather than with the bank. More specifically, we hypothesize that, in the

---

The body of this chapter is an edited version of an article, by Franco Modigliani, Robert Rasche, and J. Phillip Cooper, that first appeared in *Journal of Money, Credit and Banking* (May 1970), 166–218.

face of an upsurge in commercial loan demand, banks will endeavor to accommodate this demand because of the importance of their commercial loan customers as a source of deposits, as well as other business. On the other hand, in the face of a decline in demand, there is little banks can do to prevent borrowers from reducing their indebtedness.

Thus, in the short run, fluctuations in the volume of commercial loans will tend to reflect variations in customers' demand. Given enough time, these variations will give rise to movements in the opposite direction in the portfolio of other assets and/or to actions designed to control the volume of commercial loans. However, since these actions require time, within a period as short as one quarter, we should expect changes in the level of commercial loans to give rise to significant changes in the same direction in the level of total assets and of demand deposits, even though this may require corresponding short-run changes in borrowings and opposite changes in excess reserves.

Determinants of Investment Portfolio for a Single Bank

In order to derive formally our money supply hypothesis, it is convenient to start out from the condensed balance sheet of a member bank set out in Table 1–1, which also serves to introduce the needed notation. We add the following definitional identities:

Unborrowed reserves $\quad RU \equiv R - B^*$ $\hfill (1.1)$

Free reserves $\quad FR = S - B^* \equiv (R - B^*) - (R - S) \equiv RU - RR$
$\hfill (1.2)$

These identities in turn imply:

$$FR = D(1 - \delta) + T(1 - \tau) - CL - I + CA \qquad (1.3)$$

Proceeding along lines analogous to those suggested by, for example, Orr and Mellon[2] [64] or Tobin [76], we visualize the bank as holding anticipations as to the level of deposits, both demand and time, and as to the volume of commercial loan demand that will prevail over the coming "decision" period, but realizing that these anticipations are subject to error. This notion can be formalized

TABLE 1–1 Standardized Bank Balance Sheet

Assets		Liabilities	
Reserves total	R	Demand deposits	D
Required[a]	RR	Federal government	Dg
against demand		All others	Dp
deposits	δD	Time deposits	T
against time deposits	τT	Borrowing (from FRB	
Surplus (excess reserves		and Federal funds	
and loans in		market)	B*
federal funds		Miscellaneous liabilities	
market)	S	and capital	CA + MA
Commercial loans	CL		
Other investments	I		
Miscellaneous assets	MA		

[a] δ and τ are required reserve ratios against demand and time deposits, respectively.

by assuming that the bank regards the above three variables as random variables, $\tilde{D}$, $\tilde{T}$, and $\tilde{CL}$ subject to a known (subjective) probability distribution. Let the $\bar{D}$, $\bar{T}$, $\overline{CL}$ denote the mathematical expectations of the three random variables and define

$$\tilde{x}_D \equiv \tilde{D} - \bar{D}, \qquad \tilde{x}_T \equiv \tilde{T} - \bar{T}, \qquad \tilde{x}_{CL} \equiv \tilde{CL} - \overline{CL} \qquad (1.4)$$

The problem of the bank can now be formalized as that of choosing the most profitable level of its investment portfolio, I. To a given choice of I, there will correspond an uncertain outcome in terms of free reserves, since that outcome depends on the realization of the three random variables, $\tilde{D}$, $\tilde{T}$, and $\tilde{CL}$. By means of (1.3) and (1.4) the relation between $\tilde{FR}$, the chosen I, and the three random variables can be expressed as follows:[3]

$$\begin{aligned}\tilde{FR} &= \tilde{D}(1-\delta) + \tilde{T}(1-\tau) - \tilde{CL} - I + CA \\ &= [\bar{D}(1-\delta) + \bar{T}(1-\tau) - \overline{CL} - I + CA] \\ &\qquad + [\tilde{x}_D(1-\delta) + \tilde{x}_T(1-\tau) - \tilde{x}_{CL}] \qquad (1.5) \\ &= \overline{FR} + \tilde{x}\end{aligned}$$

where

$$\overline{FR} \equiv \mathscr{E}(FR) = \overline{D}(1-\delta) + \overline{T}(1-\tau) - \overline{CL} - I + CA \qquad (1.6)$$

and

$$\tilde{x} \equiv [\tilde{x}_D(1-\delta) + \tilde{x}_T(1-\tau) - \tilde{x}_{CL}] \qquad (1.6a)$$

The assumed probability distribution for variables D, T, and CL implies a probability distribution for the variable $\tilde{x}$, which we shall denote by $\phi(x)dx$; the corresponding cumulative distribution will be denoted by $\Phi(x)$. (Note that there is no reason why the three components of x are independently distributed; on the contrary, if the volume of loans affects the volume of deposits as it is usually assumed, $\tilde{x}_D$ and $\tilde{x}_{CL}$ will be positively correlated. Similarly, $\tilde{x}_D$ and $\tilde{x}_T$ may be negatively correlated.) Clearly, the probability distribution $\Phi(x)$ will be different for different banks. In particular, we should expect that its dispersion, as measured, say, by the standard deviation, would tend to grow with the size of the bank as measured, e.g., by its deposits, though presumably less than in proportion because of the operation of the "law of large numbers." This in turn means that the slope of $\Phi(x)$ may be expected to be smaller, the larger the bank, at least in the neighborhood of $x=0$.

Equation (1.6) brings out the fact that, for given anticipations about D, T, and CL, the mathematical expectation of free reserves is controlled by the decision variable I (which, in the short run, is also the only decision variable on the reasonable assumption that the net capital account, CA, can be regarded as given).

We note in particular that (1.6) implies

$$\frac{d\overline{FR}}{dI} = -1$$

i.e., an increase in I reduces the expected value of free reserves by an equal amount.[4]

We assume that the bank endeavors to choose I so as to maximize expected returns from its portfolio. Since this implies that a bank will not normally plan to simultaneously borrow and hold surplus reserves, we can identify negative free reserves with borrowing and will denote by r the cost of borrowed funds. Similarly, positive free reserves may be identified with surplus reserves and the return thereon will be denoted by r_S (which may, of course, be zero). Finally, we denote by i_{CL} and i, respectively, the return on commercial loans and on I. Under these conditions, expected profits (P) can be expressed as follows:

$$P = K + r_{CL}\overline{CL} + iI + r \int_{-\infty}^{-\overline{FR}} (\overline{FR} + \tilde{x}) d\Phi(\tilde{x}) + r_S \int_{-\overline{FR}}^{\infty} (\overline{FR} + \tilde{x}) d\Phi(\tilde{x})$$

$$= K + i_{CL}\overline{CL} + iI + r_S\overline{FR} + (r - r_S) \int_{-\infty}^{-\overline{FR}} (\overline{FR} + \tilde{x}) d\Phi(\tilde{x}) \quad (1.7)$$

In the expression following the first equality sign, K denotes those components of profits which are independent of portfolio composition (operating costs, interest on time and demand deposits, etc.); the next two terms represent the expected returns from commercial loans and the investment portfolio;[5] the first integral term is the expected cost of borrowing if the realization of the random variable $\tilde{x}$ is sufficiently small to make borrowing necessary; and, finally, the second integral is expected return from surplus reserves, if positive free reserves should arise. By adding and subtracting

$$r_S \int_{-\infty}^{-\overline{FR}} (\overline{FR} + \tilde{x}) d\Phi(\tilde{x})$$

and rearranging terms, one also readily derives the expression on the right of the second equality. The result is an expression for profits in terms of the two variables I and $\overline{FR}$, which in turn are tied to each other through equation (1.6). To find the optimum level of I, we therefore need to differentiate (1.7) totally, with respect to I, taking into account (1.6). This yields the first-order maximum condition

$$\frac{dP}{dI} = i + r_S \frac{d\overline{FR}}{dI} + (r - r_S) \int_{-\infty}^{-\overline{FR}} \frac{d\overline{FR}}{dI} d\Phi(\tilde{x}) = i - r_S - (r - r_S) \Phi(-\overline{FR}) = 0$$

(1.8)

Here $\Phi(-\overline{FR})$ is the probability that $\tilde{x}$ will not exceed $-\overline{FR}$, or equivalently, the probability of $\tilde{FR}$ being negative. As one should expect, this probability rises as I increases and hence $\overline{FR}$ falls.

Let us at this point use a subscript j to characterize a specific bank j. Then condition (1.8) can be rewritten as

$$\widehat{FR}_j = -\Phi_j^{-1}\left(\frac{i-r_s}{r-r_s}\right) \tag{1.8a}$$

where $\widehat{FR}_j$ is the profit-maximizing value of $\overline{FR}$ for bank j, and Φ_j^{-1} is the inverse of the cumulated distribution $\Phi_j(x)$. The determination of $\widehat{FR}_j$ and its relation to $\Phi(x)$ is shown graphically in Figure 1–1. Clearly, Φ_j^{-1} is a monotonically nondecreasing function of its argument and its slope (at least in the relevant neighborhood) may be expected to be larger, the larger the size of the bank. Substituting now from (1.8a) into (1.6), and solving for I, we finally obtain

$$\hat{I}_j = \overline{D}_j(1-\delta) + \overline{T}_j(1-\tau) - \overline{CL}_j + CA_j + \Phi_j^{-1}\left(\frac{i-r_s}{r-r_s}\right) \tag{1.9}$$

which expresses, for bank j, the profit-maximizing value of the size of its investment portfolio $\hat{I}_j$, in terms of its expectations $\overline{D}_j$, $\overline{T}_j$, $\overline{CL}_j$, $\Phi(x)$ and the rates i, r, and r_S.

Note that for finite maximizing values $(\widehat{FR}_j, \hat{I}_j)$ to exist, it must be assumed that markets and/or institutional forces ensure that $0 < (i-r_S) < (r-r_S)$; under these conditions, we find

$$\frac{\partial \hat{I}_j}{\partial i} = -\frac{\partial \widehat{FR}_j}{\partial i} > 0 \qquad \frac{\partial \hat{I}_j}{\partial r} = -\frac{\partial \widehat{FR}_j}{\partial r} < 0$$

Investment Portfolio and the Supply of Deposits for the Aggregate Banking System

Equation (1.9) exhibits the investment portfolio decision of an individual bank. It is clear, however, that if all banks face the same rates (and assuming for the present that they are subject to the same reserve requirements), we can describe the aggregate demand for investments by the banking system as a whole by simply summing (1.9) over all member banks, obtaining

$$\hat{I} = \overline{D}(1-\delta) + \overline{T}(1-\tau) - \overline{CL} + CA - \widehat{FR} \tag{1.10}$$

where

$$\overline{D} = \sum_j \overline{D}_j$$

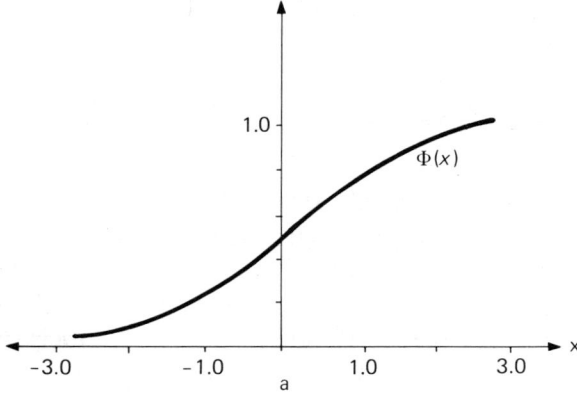

Figure 1-1a. Hypothetical graph of $\Phi(x)$ (the probability that $\tilde{x}$ is less than x).

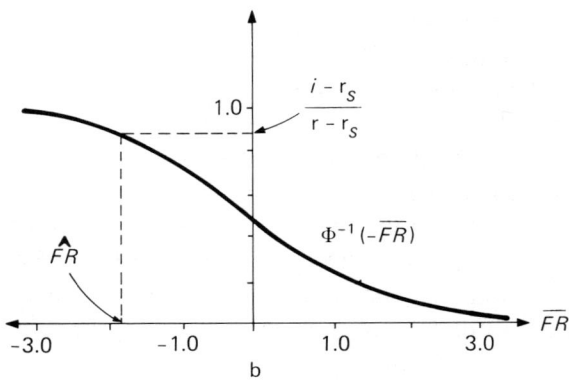

Figure 1-1b. Graph of $\Phi^{-1}(-\overline{FR})$ (the probability that $\tilde{x}$ is less than $-\overline{FR}$, i.e., that $\tilde{FR}$ is negative for given $\overline{FR}$) and Determination of $\hat{FR}$, given $(i - r_S)/(r - r_S)$.

21

is the aggregate expectation of deposits and similarly for the remaining variables. In particular,

$$\widehat{FR} = \sum_j \widehat{FR}_j = -\sum_j \Phi_j^{-1}\left(\frac{i-r_S}{r-r_S}\right) = -\Psi\left(\frac{i-r_S}{r-r_S}\right) \quad (1.11)$$

where Ψ still exhibits the properties of Φ_j^{-1}.

Equation (1.10) assumes that aggregate investment is entirely determined by beginning-of-period anticipations. A somewhat more general formulation is to assume that banks are willing and able to adjust in part their portfolios to errors of anticipations which emerge during the period itself, and, at the same time, to allow for the possibility that a portfolio adjustment to bring free reserves to the optimum level, $\widehat{FR}$, might occur only gradually in time. To take into account these two possibilities, we rewrite (1.10) in the form

$$I = \bar{D}(1-\delta) + m_D(1-\delta)(D-\bar{D}) + \bar{T}(1-\tau) + m_T(1-\tau)(T-\bar{T})$$
$$-\overline{CL} - m_{CL}(CL - \overline{CL}) - [n_F \widehat{FR} + (1-n_F) FR_{-1}] + CA \quad (1.12)$$

Here D is the actual level of deposits and hence $(D-\bar{D})$ is the error of anticipation and similarly for T and CL. The reaction coefficients m_D, m_T, and m_{CL} measure the extent to which the investment portfolio responds (on the average) to errors of anticipations emerging within the decision period. They may thus be expected to be positive but to fall short of unity for two reasons. First, banks may be unable to adjust the portfolio fully on short notice; but, in addition, they may not find it worthwhile to respond fully to the extent that the difference between the realization and the expectation may be deemed to be in the nature of transient fluctuations. For this second reason, the three coefficients might well have different values. In particular, m_T might be larger than the remaining two because of the lower volatility of time deposits. Finally, the coefficient n_F measures the speed with which banks plan to adjust their portfoilio (on the average) to meet the free reserve target.

In (1.12) the expected values $\bar{D}$, $\bar{T}$, and $\overline{CL}$ are not directly observable. Hence, if we are to test and estimate our model, we must approximate these nonobservable anticipations in terms of observables. The most elementary and commonly used expectation model is the "static" hypothesis

$$\bar{Z} = Z_{-1} \quad \text{for} \quad Z = D, T, \text{ or } CL$$

In the present instance, however, it seems more reasonable to suppose that banks do endeavor to anticipate change and have enough information to do so with some success on the average. This hypothesis can be formulated in the form

$$\bar{Z} = Z_{-1} + m'_Z(Z - Z_{-1}) \quad \text{or} \quad (Z - \bar{Z}) = (1 - m'_Z)(Z - Z_{-1}) \quad (1.13)$$
$$Z = D, T, \text{ or } CL$$

Here again m'_Z may be expected to lie between zero and unity, being closer to unity for those variables which are more accurately forecasted. On a priori grounds, one would conjecture that, of the three components, changes in D would probably be the hardest, and those in T the easiest, to predict, implying that

$$m'_D < m'_{CL} < m'_T$$

Substituting (1.13) into (1.12), rearranging terms, and making use of identity (1.3), we deduce

$$\Delta I = n_D(1-\delta)\Delta D + n_T(1-\tau)\Delta T - n_{CL}\Delta CL - n_F(\widehat{FR} - FR_{-1}) + \Delta CA \quad (1.14)$$

where $\quad n_Z = 1 - (1 - m_Z)(1 - m'_Z) \quad Z = D, T, CL$

These coefficients, it will be noted, measure the extent to which the investment portfolio responds to changes in D, T, and CL within the decision period. They should fall between an upper limit of unity if the changes are fully predicted ($m'_Z = 1$) or banks are able and willing to adjust perfectly to forecast error ($m_Z = 1$), and a lower limit of zero if banks are on the average totally unsuccessful in predicting change ($m'_Z = 0$) and equally unable to adjust to forecast error ($m_Z = 0$). On a priori grounds, we might expect $n_T > n_{CL} > n_D$, with n_D itself rather close to zero.

Equation (1.14) expresses the change in I in terms of changes in D, T, and CL. For the purpose of the present essay, we may regard T and CL as exogenously given though they are endogenous to the entire FMP model.[6] However, D, cannot be treated similarly, since our task is precisely that of accounting for D. The apparent impasse can be resolved by observing that, for the system as a whole, there is a second relation between I and D that can be inferred from the balance sheet identity of Table 1–1, after summing over all banks in the system, namely

$$\Delta D = \Delta RU + \Delta CL + \Delta I - \Delta T - \Delta CA \qquad (1.15)$$

This second equation is seen to relate the money supply explicitly to central bank policy by way of unborrowed reserves, RU. By solving (1.14) and (1.15) simultaneously for I and D, we can thus express D and I in terms of the policy variable RU, the "exogenous variables," T and CL, and of $\widehat{FR}$, which in turn depends on the relevant interest rates. In particular, the solution for the money supply D can be expressed as

$$\Delta D = \frac{1}{(1-n_D)+\delta n_D}[\Delta RU+(1-n_{CL})\Delta CL-(1-n_T+\tau n_T)\Delta T \\ -n_F(\widehat{FR}-FR_{-1})] \qquad (1.16)$$

Equation (1.16) is a key result and deserves close scrutiny and interpretation. To this end, it is helpful to consider two limiting cases. Suppose first that the system is able to forecast perfectly, or to adjust fully to any forecast error, so that $n_D=n_T=n_{CL}=n_F=1$. Since, under this assumption, $FR_{-1}=\widehat{FR}_{-1}$, (1.16) reduces to the well-known formula

$$\Delta D = \frac{\Delta RU - \tau \Delta T - \Delta FR}{\delta} \quad \text{implying also} \quad D = \frac{RU - \tau T - RF}{\delta}$$
$$(1.16a)$$

i.e., the change (level) of deposits is equal to the change (level) of reserves available to support demand deposits, divided by the required reserve ratio. This is a generalization of the elementary textbook "equilibrium" (or monopoly bank) formula, $D=RU/\delta$, which allows for reserve requirements against time deposits and for an "optimum" level of free reserves. Suppose, at the opposite extreme, that banks are totally unable to forecast and adjust to forecast error, so that $n_D=n_T=n_{CL}=0$. Them (1.16) reduces to

$$\Delta D = \Delta RU - n_F(\widehat{FR}-FR_{-1})+\Delta CL-\Delta T \qquad (1.16b)$$

If we put ΔCL, ΔT, and $\widehat{FR}$ equal to zero, $n_F=1$, disregard borrowing so that FR equals excess reserves, then (1.16b), together with the second half of identity (1.2) in differenced form, describes analytically the textbook version of the step-by-step expansion of deposits. That is, equation (1.16b) implies that a given increment in RU will generate an expansion of D through time, which asymptotically approaches the equilibrium value given by (1.16a), with the disequilibrium gap after t periods proportional to $(1-\delta)^t$. The two additional terms in $\varDelta CL$ and $\varDelta T$ in (1.16b) come from the fact that, if all changes come as a surprise, and banks do not adjust at all to errors, then an expansion of loans will produce an equal expansion of deposits while a shift from demand to time deposits will reduce D and increase T by equal amounts.

The expansion of D implied by (1.16) is, of course, somewhere in between these limiting cases. The adjustment is gradual, but at a rate faster than implied by (1.16b). The key reason for a less than instantaneous response, even if $n_F \approx 1$, is that n_D is likely to be rather close to zero. If so, the adjustment of any one bank tends to create surprises and thus throw other banks out of adjustment, thereby causing delays in the complete adjustment of the entire system. This delay will tend to be greater the less concentrated the banking system—for a monopoly bank, one might well expect a speedy adjustment, though even here the difficulty of forecasting $\varDelta RU$, $\varDelta CL$, and $\varDelta T$ suggests that all the adjustment coefficients would still be less than one.

Target-Free Reserves, the Cost of Borrowing and the Return from Lending

Before we can test and estimate (1.16) we must express $\widehat{FR}$ in terms of interest rates. To this end we can rely on equation (1.11), but we need to establish an appropriate parametric representation for the function Ψ and an appropriate empirical counterpart for the rates i, r_S, and r, that appear as arguments of that function. We shall deal first with this second issue.

Insofar as i is concerned, since the relevant decision period is presumably rather short, say, of the order of the averaging period for reserve requirements (one to two weeks), the choice at the margin can be visualized as between free reserves and short-term market instruments; hence, a rate such as the three-month treasury bill rate seems a reasonable choice (one might prefer returns on bills of even shorter maturity except for the difficulty of obtaining equally reliable data).

The problem of the remaining two rates is considerably more complex. Since no interest is received on excess reserves, one might be inclined to set r_S at zero, and to equate r with the discount rate, hereafter denoted by d. Under these condition, equation (1.8) would reduce to

$$\widehat{FR} = -\Psi\left(\frac{i}{d}\right)$$

In reality, the identification of r with d is subject to serious objection. For one thing, it would imply that whenever the bill rate exceeds the discount rate, a rather frequent occurrence in recent years, free reserves would tend to become indefinitely large in absolute value! The point is that d is a very biased measure of the true opportunity cost of making up reserve deficiencies because, in the present American system, borrowing at the window is a "privilege" subject to many constraints.

Accordingly, there is ample reason to suppose that the true opportunity cost of borrowing at the window is generally higher than d, and the more so the larger the volume (and average duration) of outstanding borrowing. This hypothesis is strongly supported by the evidence of recent years which shows that as borrowings grow, the rate of the Federal Funds market in which banks can borrow freely tends to be bid up to a growing premium over the discount rate. Equally serious objections can be raised against taking r_S as zero. Indeed, since positive free reserves include loans in the Federal Funds market as well as excess reserves in the conventional definition, it would appear that r_S itself must be related to the Federal Funds rate.

The above considerations suggest that a really adequate analysis of the determinants of $\widehat{FR}$ would require explicit treatment of other markets, notably the Federal Funds market. Unfortunately, this line of approach would take us far afield. We shall rely instead on a shortcut which makes no explicit reference to the Federal Funds market, though it is in fact derivable from a fuller analysis of that market.

First, it is shown in section 1.2, by an explicit analysis of demand and supply in the Federal Funds market, that the equilibrium conditions in that market imply a relation between the rate r, the discount rate d, and the level of free reserves, say

$$r = R(d, FR) \qquad (1.17)$$

with the properties $R_d \geq 0$, $R_{FR} \leq 0$, and R_d probably less than, but close to, unity.

Second, we suggest that (1.11) can be approximated as follows:

$$\widehat{FR} = -\Psi\left(1 + \frac{i-r}{r-r_S}\right) \approx F(i,r) \approx f(i-r) \qquad (1.11a)$$

The approximation is supported by the consideration that $r - r_S$ should tend to remain relatively constant, reflecting basically costs associated with transacting in the Federal Funds market (see also section 1.2). From (1.9), we can also infer that

$$F_i \approx f' \approx \frac{\partial \widehat{FR}}{\partial i} < 0 \qquad F_r \approx -f' \approx \frac{\partial \widehat{FR}}{\partial r} > 0$$

The two equations (1.11a) and (1.17) involve three endogenous variables—$\widehat{FR}$, r, and FR—in addition to the two "exogenous" variables d and i; to close the system we need one additional equation. This equation can be derived from the deposit supply equation (1.16) by restating it in terms of free reserves, relying on the identity (1.2) and the definition of required reserves. First, from the second equation in (1.2) (neglecting for the moment the possibility of changes in reserve requirements) we infer that

$$\Delta FR = \Delta RU - \Delta RR = \Delta RU - \delta \Delta D - \tau \Delta T$$

Substituting now for ΔD from (1.16) and solving for FR, the result can be expressed as

$$FR = \mu \widehat{FR} + \left\{(1-\mu) FR_{-1} + \frac{\mu}{n_F}\left[(1-n_D)\frac{1-\delta}{\delta}\Delta RU - (1-n_{CL})\Delta CL + n_T^* \Delta T\right]\right\} \qquad (1.18)$$

where

$$\mu = \frac{\delta n_F}{(1-n_D) + \delta n_D} \qquad n_T^* = (1-n_T) + \tau(n_T - n_D) - \frac{\tau}{\delta}(1-n_D) \qquad (1.18a)$$

We note here for later reference that μ, and hence the coefficients of all variables except that of ΔT should fall between zero and unity. In the case of ΔT, the sign of the coefficient implied by the model cannot be established a priori, since n_T^* could be negative if n_T is sufficiently greater than n_D, that is, if I responds more to time deposits than to demand deposits changes within the period—whether because T is easier to forecast or because of greater response to forecast errors.[7]

We could at this point endeavor to estimate the parameters of the three equations listed above and think of the supply of deposits as generated by the simultaneous solution of this system plus the identity

$$D = \frac{RU - \tau T - FR}{\delta} \qquad (1.19)$$

We shall not pursue this approach because it presents some serious difficulties.[8] We shall proceed instead to derive and estimate directly a free-reserve equation representing the "reduced" form of the above "structural" system. That is, we can conceptually solve the system to yield reduced forms relating each of the three endogenous variables, $\widehat{FR}$, FR, and r, to the exogenous variables. In particular, if we denote by Q the linear combination of variables appearing inside the braces in the right-hand sode of (1.18), the solution can be expressed as

$$FR = g(i, d, Q) \qquad (1.20)$$

or to a linear approximation as

$$FR = a_0 + a_1 i + a_2 d + a_3 Q = a_0 + a_1 i + a_2 d + a_3 (1-\mu) FR_{-1}$$
$$+ a_3 \frac{\mu}{n_F}\left[(1-n_D)\left(\frac{1-\delta}{\delta}\Delta RU\right) - (1-n_{CL})\Delta CL + n_T^* \Delta T\right] \qquad (1.21)$$

Furthermore, by relying on the model's specifications about the properties of the partial derivatives of the equations (1.11a) and (1.17), we can derive inferences about the sign of a relation between the parameters a_1, a_2, and a_3. In particular, it can be shown that these specifications imply:

$$a_1 < 0 \qquad a_2 > 0 \qquad 0 < a_3 \leq 1$$

and also $|a_1| > |a_2|$, i.e., an increase in i tends to reduce free reserves by more than an equal change in d.[9]

A word of caution, however, should be entered concerning the appropriateness of the linear approximations (1.21) to the function g of (1.20). The considerations set forth in formulating the equation (1.11a) and deriving (1.17) in section 1.2 suggest that $\widehat{FR}$, and thus FR, are definitely not linear functions of i and d in the large. In particular, the relation between FR and i, for given d (and Q) is likely to exhibit the shape represented in Figure 1–2. Accordingly,

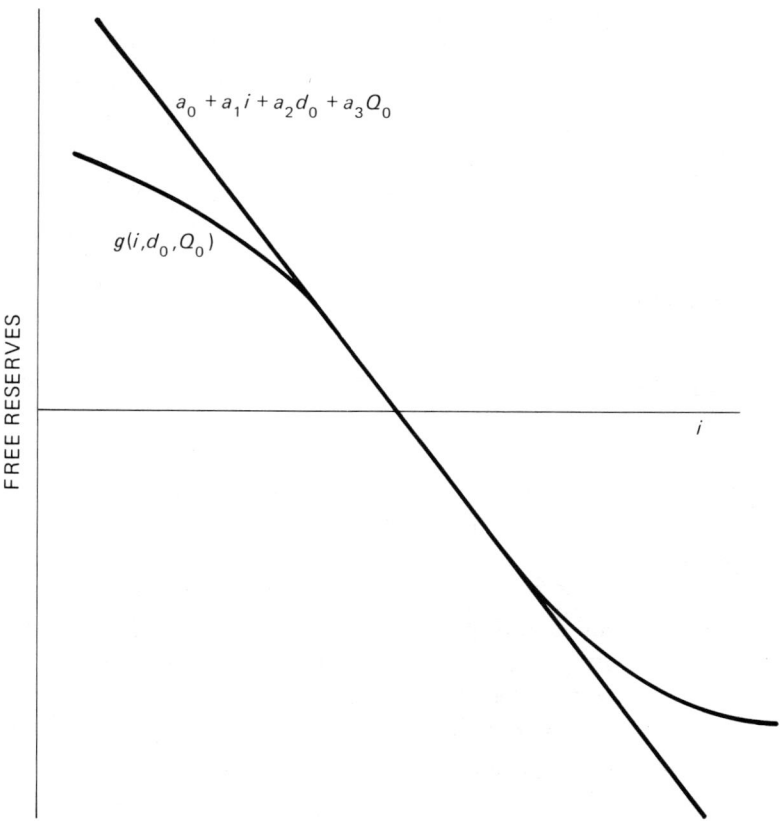

Figure 1–2. The Relationship between Desired Free Reserves and the Bill Rate, for Fixed Discount Rate.

the linear approximation (1.21), also exhibited in the figure, can only be valid as long as the spread $(i-d)$ remains within reasonable limits. This condition was probably roughly satisfied over the period of observation, since the spread has generally remained inside 100 basis points, a range within which the linear approximation should, we hope, prove bearable.[10] However, the empirical results reported below should be regarded as valid only within a range of spreads of the indicated magnitude.

Subject to the above qualifications, we could proceed to estimate equation (1.21). Unfortunately, before we can do so, we must face another hurdle. Equation (1.21) applies directly to a "decision period." In practice, however, because of data availability and convenience of analysis, as well as the fact that the decision period is best regarded as a theoretical rather than an operational construct, the time unit we wish to employ will not coincide with the "decision period." In our specific case, for example, the time unit for the entire FMP model is a calendar quarter, which presumably extends over several decision periods. We must therefore stop to inquire how our analysis can be extended to cover an arbitrary time period.

Generalization to a Unit Period Including
a Number of Decision Periods

The method by which our results can be generalized depends somewhat on the specific definition of the variables. For our present purpose, we wish to define all stock variables as relating to the end of the period, and therefore all increments as relating to the change in stock between the beginning and the end of the chosen unit period.

Then let $Z(t)$ ($Z = FR$, RU, CL, T) denote the stock of each variable at the end of unit period t and $\Delta Z(t)$ the change in stock in the course of unit period t. Similarly, let $\Delta Z(t, \alpha)$ denote the change in the course of the αth decision period of period t, and let the number of decision periods within the unit period be m (which, we assume, can be represented by an integer). We propose to show that from (1.21) we can, under appropriate conditions, derive an approximation in terms of $Z(t)$ and $\Delta Z(t)$. To this end, we first use (1.21) recursively to substitute m times for the lagged dependent variable. The result can be expressed as

$$FR(t) = \sum_{\alpha=1}^{m} [a_3(1-\mu)]^{m-\alpha}$$
$$\times \left\{ a_0 + a_1 i(t,\alpha) + a_2 d(t,\alpha) + \frac{a_3 \mu}{n_F} \left[(1-n_D)\frac{1-\delta}{\delta} \Delta RU(t,\alpha) \right. \right.$$
$$\left. \left. - (1-n_{CL})\Delta CL(t,\alpha) + n_T^* \Delta T(t,\alpha) \right] \right\} + [a_3(1-\mu)]^m FR(t-1)$$
(1.22)

The interpretation of $i(t, \alpha)$ and $d(t, \alpha)$ is evident from the context. Now, on the condition that RU, CL, and T grow relatively smoothly within each period, we can use the approximation

$$\Delta Z(t,\alpha) = \frac{\Delta Z(t)}{m} \qquad \alpha=1,\ldots,m \quad Z=FR, RU, CL, T \qquad (1.22a)$$

Similarly, on the condition that i and d remain reasonably constant within each period, we can approximate $i(t, \alpha)$ by the mean value of i in period t, say, $i(t)$, and, similarly for d. With these approximations, we deduce the following basic hypothesis to be tested empirically:

$$FR(t) = A_0 + A_1 i(t) + A_2 d(t) + B_1[(1-\delta)\Delta RU(t)]$$
$$+ B_2[\delta \Delta CL(t)] + B_3[\delta \Delta T(t)] + CFR(t-1) \qquad (1.23)$$

The meaning of (1.23) can be more readily understood by rewriting it in the difference form

$$\Delta FR(t) = C'[A'_0 + A'_1 i(t) + A'_2 d(t) - FR(t-1)]$$
$$+ B_1[(1-\delta)\Delta RU(t)] + B_2[\delta \Delta CL](t) + B_3[\delta \Delta T(t)] \qquad (1.23a)$$

whose coefficients are related to those of (1.23) and to the various parameters introduced earlier as follows:

$$C' = 1 - C = 1 - [a_3(1-\mu)]^m$$
$$A'_j = \frac{A_j}{1-C} = \frac{a_j}{1-a_3(1-\mu)} \qquad j=0,1,2$$
$$B_1 = (1-n_D)B \quad B_2 = -(1-n_{CL})B \quad B_3 = n_T^* B$$
$$B = \left(\frac{C'}{1-a_3(1-\mu)}\right)\left(\frac{\mu a_3}{m\delta n_F}\right)$$

According to (1.23a), the change in free reserves in the unit period involves four distinct components: (i) the first term in square brackets results from the adjustment of free reserves toward their equilibrium value $\widehat{FR}$. Indeed, the quantity $A'_0 + A'_1 i(t) + A'_2 d(t)$ can be shown to be an estimate of $\widehat{FR}$, corresponding to the prevailing values of i and d.[11] C' is the proportion of the gap between $\widehat{FR}$ and the initial value, $FR(t-1)$, that is made up within the unit period. It is therefore a measure of the speed of adjustment toward equilibrium. This speed is seen to be an increasing function of μ; and from (1.18a) in turn, we see that μ is an increasing function of n_F, the speed of portfolio adjustment at the level of the individual bank, and of n_D, the speed of response to changes in deposits. In addition, C' is seen to increase with m, the number of decision periods per unit period, and thus with the length of the unit period. But note that while C' should accordingly tend to approach unity as we lengthen the unit period, the approximation (1.22a) becomes less tenable. (ii) The second component reflects the response to a change in unborrowed reserves. This response, measured by B_1, could be as low as zero if n_D were unity, in which case the portfolio would expand enough to absorb ΔRU fully into required reserves. On the other hand, for values of n_D and n_F approaching zero B_1 approaches unity, since the only effect of ΔRU would then be to increase D by an equal amount and hence to increase FR by $(1-\delta)RU$. (iii) The third component is the response to a change in CL and its coefficient should again fall between zero and -1. However, we should expect $|B_2| < B_1$ on the ground that n_{CL} is likely to exceed n_D.[12] (iv) Finally, the last term is the response to a change in time deposits and its coefficient B_3 is of uncertain sign, for reasons expounded earlier.

It should be recognized that since μ depends on the reserve ratio δ, in principle all the coefficients (1.23) should vary in time if δ changes, even if all other behavior coefficients were stable. It can be verified, however, that variations in δ of the order of magnitude observed in the relevant post-war period should be expected to have rather minor effects on the coefficients. It would therefore appear that they can be treated as constant to a good approximation.[13]

*Final Specification of the Hypothesis and
Operational Definition of Variables*

Equation (1.24) below completes our operational formulation of the money supply hypothesis.

$$FR = A_0 - A_1 i(\bar{D}_{-1}) + A_2 d(\bar{D}_{-1}) + A_3 FR_{-1}$$
$$+ A_4(1-\delta)\Delta RU - A_5 \delta \Delta CL + A_6 \delta \Delta T + A_7(RL) \qquad (1.24)$$

This equation follows from (1.23) with two modifications.[14] First, the interest rates are scaled by $\bar{D}_{-1}$ where $\bar{D}_{-1}$ is a four-quarter moving average of demand deposits ending with the previous quarter. In examining the interest rate coefficients A_1 and A_2, we must remember that the function F (derived by aggregating the individual bank inverse probability distribution functions) and its partial derivatives are going to depend on the scale of the system. These coefficients, with F_i and F_r entering multiplicatively in their respective numerators, would thus exhibit a strong dependence on the size of the banking system.

The second modification is the addition of the last term, $A_7(RL)$, which will be called the "reserve release term." This term originates from the consideration that there are two distinct ways in which the central bank can change the amount of demand deposits that can be supported by unborrowed reserves: (i) by changing directly RU through open market purchases (although RU can also change through in- or outflow of currency); (ii) by changing the required reserve ratio against either demand or time deposits. If we denote by $\Delta\delta$ and $\Delta\tau$, respectively, the difference between the required ratios in the current and the previous period, it is clear that the change in δ and τ is equivalent to an increase in RU amounting to

$$RL = -(\Delta\delta D_{-1} + \Delta\tau T_{-1})$$

Indeed, RL, just like RU, measures the change that would occur in free reserves if all other bank assets and liabilities (except D itself) were unchanged. The only difference is that, under the assumed conditions, a change in RU must be accompanied by an equal change in D and, hence, in the final analysis, FR would change only by $(1-\delta)\Delta RU$, whereas in the case of changes in reserve requirements, D would be unchanged and hence FR would change by the full RL.

The above considerations suggest that the effect of changes in reserve requirements could be handled by simply adding RL to $(1-\delta)\Delta RU$ and treating the sum as a single variable whose coefficient should be A_4. This approach, however, is not quite consistent with the derivation of (1.24) for, as we have seen, the coefficients of the three increments are related in part to the ease with which banks can foresee such changes and respond to them if foreseen. From this point of view, reserve releases generated by changes in reserve requirements may be rather different from those generated by addition to unborrowed reserves. In particular, changes in RU basically affect individual banks through changes in deposits and their effect is not distinguishable from that of any other source of deposit changes. Thus the predictability of, and response to, changes in RU is unlikely to differ appreciably from that of deposit changes in general, as summarized in the coefficient n_D. On the other hand, legal reserve releases occur in one shot, and there can be little question about their permanence (and furthermore, each bank can anticipate the response of the rest of the system). We should therefore expect that, even if their occurrence is not easier to forecast, the response to them would be faster; this means that A_7 can be expressed as $(1-n_{RL})B$ with $n_{RL} \geq n_D$, implying $A_7 \leq A_4$.

Strictly speaking, this conclusion applies only to reserve releases through changes in reserve requirements. In the present American system, however, reserve releases occur not only through changes in legal reserve requirements but also, to some extent, through shifts in deposits between classes of banks or between types of deposits subject to different reserve requirements. Such shifts, which occur continuously and more or less haphazardly, might best be lumped together with RU rather than with RL. Since such releases are typically quite small, and because of the difficulty of separating the contribution of the source of changes in δ and τ, we have actually included under RL all changes regardless of source. (These releases are quantitatively very unimportant in those quarters for which there were *legal* reserve releases.)

For the empirical test reported below, FR and RU (which are subject to considerable short-run variability) have been defined as the daily average value in the two months surrounding the end of each quarter. Similarly, FR_{-1} is the same average for the preceding quarter. On the other hand, CL is the end-of-quarter stock of commercial and industrial loans. Ideally, it should include only commercial loans at member banks, but considerations of data availability as well as consistency with the rest of the FMP model have led us to approximate this quantity by commercial loans at all commercial banks. Finally, all monetary variables are measured in billions of dollars and interest rates in percentage points per year.

Empirical Results

Row 1 of Table 1–2 exhibits the parameters of equation (1.24) estimated by ordinary least squares, after "normalization" by dividing both sides by the scale variable $\bar{D}_{-1}$. We note immediately that the estimated coefficient of T is only slightly positive, which we have seen to be consistent with the model. Its value is, in fact, well within the range implied by the model.[15] It is, however, of quite negligible magnitude, implying that a $1 billion change in time deposits would increase free reserves by only 4 million—insignificantly different from zero. It seems, therefore, preferable to drop this variable of little empirical relevance, especially since a few other tests relying on other methods of estimation pointed consistently in the same direction. When this is done, one obtains the estimates exhibited in row 2. These results, on the whole, are quite favorable to the hypothesis. All the coefficients have the sign implied, and have fairly significant t ratios despite the large number of variables—six plus the seasonal dummies and constant—and the substantial collinearity among several of them (e.g., the bill rate and the discount rate). The standard error (adjusting roughly for the scale variable whose mean value is 105 billion) is about 80 million, equivalent to just over half a billion when expressed in terms of money supply (since $\delta \approx 0.15$).

Before taking a closer look at individual coefficients and their consistency with our model, we should like to touch briefly on some refinements of the basic hypothesis which did not prove too worthwhile.

Timing of the Legal Reserve Release. While changes in unborrowed reserves should tend to occur randomly through the quarter, legal reserve releases generally occur in bulk at a specified date, and typically with advance warning ranging from a couple of weeks up. Under these conditions, one should expect that the extent to which banks can take advantage of the release by the end of the quarter

TABLE 1-2 Free Reserve Estimates

Row	Sample Period	1	2	3	4	5	6	7	8	9	10	11	12	13	14	15	16	17
			A_0			A_1	A_2	A_3	A_4	A_5	A_6		A_7					
		Constant	S_2	S_3	S_4	$-i$	d	$\frac{FR_{-1}}{D_{-1}}$	$\frac{(1-\delta)ARU}{D_{-1}}$	$\frac{-\delta ACL}{D_{-1}}$	$\frac{\delta AT}{D_{-1}}$	$\frac{RL}{D_{-1}}$	$\frac{X \cdot RL}{D_{-1}}$	Time	ρ	R^2	σ_u	$D-W$
1	1955-66	.00100 (1.07)	−.00198 (−3.13)	−.00231 (−4.08)	−.00210 (−2.10)	.00125 (2.34)	.00144 (2.38)	.692 (10.2)	.639 (7.93)	.508 (5.09)	.0284 (.24)	0.381 (3.94)	—	—	—	.952	.000792	2.07
2	1955-66	.00100 (1.03)	−.00204 (−3.53)	−.00237 (−4.84)	−.00223 (−2.67)	.00122 (2.39)	.00144 (2.41)	.705 (16.0)	.646 (8.13)	.502 (5.23)	—	0.394 (5.00)	—	—	—	.952	.000782	2.09
3A[a]	1954-66	.00120 (1.13)	−.00219 (−3.31)	−.00249 (−4.29)	−.00267 (−2.78)	.00108 (1.95)	.00129 (1.46)	.712 (14.2)	.664 (7.08)	.485 (4.45)	—	0.459 (3.15)	.00557 (.024)	—	—	.945	.00089	1.92
3B[a]	1954-66	.00107 (.839)	−.00225 (−2.82)	−.00230 (−3.41)	−.00308 (−2.68)	.00022 (.356)	.00045 (.597)	.768 (13.2)	.701 (6.24)	.393 (3.05)	—	1.0	.809 (5.08)	—	—	.913	.00107	2.04
4	1955-66	.00091 (.97)	−.00192 (−3.25)	−.00230 (−4.59)	−.00185 (−1.94)	.00169 (2.27)	.00143 (2.40)	.612 (5.53)	.604 (6.49)	.531 (5.21)	—	0.347 (3.63)	—	.00003 (.87)	—	.953	.000785	1.99
5[b]	1955-66	.00172 (1.73)	−.00290 (−4.45)	−.00267 (−5.02)	−.00366 (−4.34)	.00126 (2.24)	.00145 (2.21)	.700 (14.4)	.649 (7.37)	.511 (3.99)	—	0.348 (3.92)	—	—	—	.942	.000962	2.39
6	1955-66	.00268	−.00205	−.00233	−.00219	.00158	.00133	.648	.657	.512	—	0.346	—	—	.227	—	.000931	2.07

[a] For row 3A, $X \equiv \theta$; for row 3B, $X \equiv (\theta - 1)$.
[b] Data for CL in this test were seasonally adjusted.

would depend on the timing of the release. A release occurring say very close to the end of the quarter, should largely show up in free reserves at the end of that quarter, while a release occurring at the very beginning might be largely used up and leave little trace in free reserves. With this thought, we added to the variables of row 2 (Table 1–2) an additional variable measuring the timing, θRL where θ is the proportion of the quarter elapsed before a legal change in reserve requirements becomes effective. Experimentation included using the announcement dates in lieu of effective dates and constraining the proportion of RL left in FR when legal changes occur at the end of a quarter to unity. These constraints were implemented by setting $A_7 = 1$ and adding in terms of the form $(\theta - 1)RL$ or $(e^{\theta - 1})RL$ which vanish when $\theta = 1$ and are expected to be negative otherwise for positive RL. While these trials yield coefficients with the appropriate signs, in no case did they improve the fit significantly. Note that θ was set at 0.5 whenever no legal changes in reserve requirements occurred.

Growing Aversion to Borrowing. The recent study of the discount window by Bernard Shull [71] reports some evidence that, from 1955 to 1966, banks showed increasing reluctance to make use of the window, whether as a result of the way the window was administered or for other reasons. As a crude test of this hypothesis, we have added a linear time trend and the results are shown in row 4 (Table 1–2). It is seen that the trend has the anticipated positive sign. It can be interpreted as implying that the constant term of the free-reserves equation has increased at the rate of $.000029 \times 105 = .003$ or some 3 millions per quarter. This is quite negligible relative to quarterly changes, but over a ten-year period it amounts to a sizable 120 million. However, as one can see from the t ratio, the estimate of the coefficient is very unreliable and the variable adds negligibly to the explanation (indeed, after adjustment for degrees of freedom, the standard error rises). For this reason, and furthermore, because one would always hesitate in extrapolating mechanically a time trend, we feel that omission of the variable is likely to yield a more reliable estimate of the money supply mechanism.

Having thus been led back to row 2 as providing the most reliable estimate of the coefficients of our model, we may proceed to a closer inspection of their magnitude and the reactions among them in the light of our model. Specifically, from row 2 and equation

(1.24) we can infer the following equilibrium demand for free reserves:

$$FR = A_0\bar{D}_{-1} - \bar{D}_{-1}\left(\frac{.00122i - .00144d}{1 - .705}\right) \approx A_0\bar{D}_{-1} + .54d - .46i$$
$$= A_0\bar{D}_{-1} - .54(i-d) + .082i$$

where we have assigned to $\bar{D}$ the value 110, roughly its mean value for the 1960s, and the constant A_0 is left unspecified because it varies seasonally. Now the coefficient of the spread is of a credible order implying a reduction of free reserves of 540 millions per 100 basis points of spread. But contrary to our expectations, the coefficient of the bill rate is less than that of the discount rate in absolute value, though the difference is quite small and not significantly different from zero. The interpretation of the remaining coefficients of row 2 is straightforward. They imply that only about one-third of an increase in unborrowed reserves is utilized for the expansion of assets and deposits within the same quarter while the remaining two-thirds goes temporarily to swell free reserves. In the case of reserves provided by a legal reserve release, the response is, as expected, somewhat faster, as only some 40 percent remain unused by the end of the quarter. The contribution of the commercial loan term is seen to be highly significant and quantitatively impressive; the coefficient implies that $n_{CL} > n_D$, as expected. But even so, it suggests that only around one-half of the increase in commercial loans is offset within the period by liquidation of other assets while the remaining one-half shows up as an increase in demand deposits.

Generally, these coefficients imply a rather slow speed of adjustment, reflecting, according to our model, error of forecast plus failure to adjust to errors; but, it should always be recalled that these errors of forecast result in part from the fact that as individual banks adjust to their errors they change the deposits of other banks contributing to their error. That the result is a rather slow adjustment to "disturbances"—changes in reserves and in commercial loans—is confirmed by the coefficient of the lagged dependent variable. As can be seen from (1.23), this coefficient, C, equals $[a_3(1-\mu)]^m$ where

$$\mu = \frac{\delta n_F}{(1 - n_D) + \delta n_D} \qquad 0 \leq a_3 \leq 1$$

and m is the number of "decision periods per unit time." Thus, for $n_F=1$, even assuming that n_D is very close to zero as seems plausible, $[a_3(1-\mu)]$ cannot exceed $(1-\delta)$ or roughly 0.85. Since our estimate of A_3 is 0.7, the implied value of m would be in the order of 2 to 3. This is rather low since on a priori grounds, we should have expected a figure closer to 6 (implying a two-week decision period). However, if we allow n_F to range below unity, implying a less than immediate adjustment of actual to target reserves, more plausible values for m are implied. The presence of a_3, of course, acts in the other direction.

In assessing these results, we observe that two coefficients do not quite check with the implications of the model, namely the coefficient of i which is too low relative to that of d, and the coefficient of the lagged dependent variable that seems somewhat too high. These coefficients are precisely those that are most subject to least squares bias. Furthermore, the direction of this bias is such that the result could produce the observed inconsistencies with the theoretical model. This is most easily seen in the case of the coefficient of the lagged dependent variable. It is well known that if the true error component of the equation has positive serial correlation, a most likely situation when dealing with quarterly data, the ordinary least squares estimate of that coefficient is upward biased.[16] In the case of the bill rate, on the other hand, the bias may be expected to come from the simultaneity problem mentioned again in section 1.3 in connection with the demand equation: This simultaneity may be expected to lead to a positive correlation between the error component and short-term market yield as measured by the bill rate, which would impart an upward bias to our estimate, pushing it toward zero. Before we can pass final judgement on the consistency of our model with the data we therefore need to consider procedures for minimizing the bias in the estimates and the results obtained from following such procedures. This is the task to which we turn in the final section 1.4. In the process, we shall also be able to assess how well our money demand and supply mechanisms together account for the behavior of demand deposits and short-term interest rates.

1.2 Relation of the Money Supply Model to the Federal Funds Market

We propose to exhibit here the derivation of equation (1.17) of section 1.1 from an explicit model of the Federal Funds market. To this end, we identify the borrowing rate r with the Federal Funds rate—which we regard as appropriate as long as there are no extraneous constraints on the behavior of the Federal Funds rate.

Next, we can visualize the supply of loans in our market as coming from banks which end up with a reserve surplus for the period, and the demand as coming from banks which end up with a reserve shortage and thus have to borrow. Denote by S the aggregate surplus (and free reserves) of all banks with a surplus and by B^* the aggregate borrowings of the banks with negative free reserves. We can then express aggregate free reserves as

$$FR = S - B^* \qquad (1.25)$$

Now S and B^* will vary with FR and the relation that may be expected to hold, on the average, between the three variables is sketched in Figure 1–3. In this figure, S is measured on the ordinate from the origin up, while B^* is measured from the origin down. When FR is zero, some banks will have positive free reserves, and their aggregate reserve position S is represented by point b on the ordinate; this aggregate will be just balanced by the aggregate negative position B^* of the remaining banks, shown by b'. As FR rises, we may expect a growing proportion of banks to have positive free reserves and a declining number to have a negative position. Accordingly, B^* may be expected to decline and approach asymptotically zero (or at least some small positive number as shown by the curve $b'c'$ graphed in the southeast quadrant). By the same token, in view of (1.25), S will approach asymptotically FR (i.e., the dotted 45° line with equation $S = FR$) as shown by curve bc. Conversely, as FR declines, S will approach zero, as shown by ab, and B^* will approach the 45° line, as shown by $a'b'$. All this can be summarized by the fundamental relation:

$$S = S(FR) \qquad 0 < S' < 1 \qquad (1.26a)$$
$$B^* = S(FR) - FR = B^*(FR) \qquad 0 > B^{*\prime} > -1 \qquad (1.26b)$$

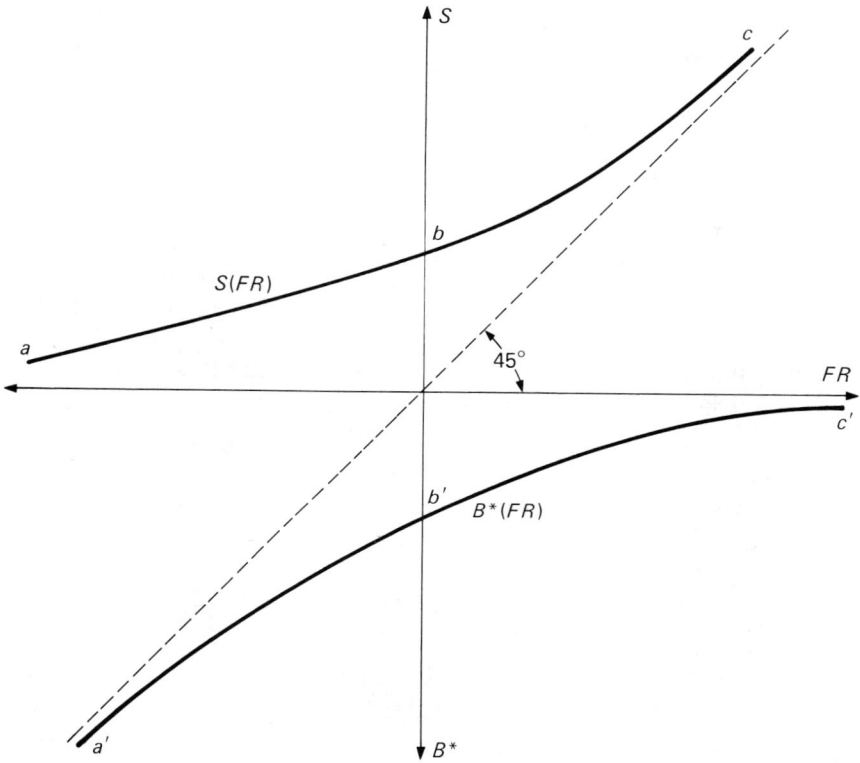

Figure 1-3. Relation among the Three Variables: FR, S, B^*.

The supply of loans in the Federal Funds market, *FFL*, can now be expressed as the difference between the aggregate surplus, S, and that part of the surplus that banks choose to hold in the form of excess reserves, E, i.e.,

$$FFL = S - E \qquad (1.27)$$

But as suggested in section 1.1, the portion of S kept in the form of E may be expected to depend on the return from lending, namely the rate r, or

$$E = \eta(S, r) \qquad 0 \leq \eta_s \leq 1 \quad \eta_r \leq 0 \qquad (1.28)$$

Furthermore, making use of (1.26) to express S in terms of FR, we can also write

$$E = E(FR, r) \qquad E_{FR} = \eta_S S' \geq 0 \qquad E_r = \eta_r \leq 0 \qquad (1.29)$$

The *supply function* for Federal Funds can now be finally expressed as

$$FFL = S - E(FR, r) = l(FR, r) \qquad 0 \leq l_{FR} = S'(1 - \eta_S) \leq 1$$
$$l_r = -\eta_r \geq 0 \qquad (1.30)$$

Similarly, the demand for borrowing in the market will be $FFB = B^* - B$, where B is borrowing at the window. Considerations similar to those unsed in deriving (1.28) suggest that FFB should be an increasing function of B^*, and a decreasing function of $r - d$, the spread between the cost of securing Federal Funds and that of obtaining funds at the window, or

$$FFB = b^*(B^*, r, d) \qquad 0 < b^*_{B^*} \leq 1 \quad b^*_r \leq 0 \quad b^*_d \geq 0 \qquad (1.31)$$

The relation between FFB and r for given B^* might be expected to look somewhat like curve bb in Figure 1–4. The distance between the curve and the horizontal line of height B^* equals borrowing at the window B. When r falls below d, the use of Federal Funds is cheaper even in terms of cash cost; the use of B would tend to be limited to smaller banks and/or possibly, seasonal needs. As r rises above d, B rises and FFB shrinks, though eventually limitations on the use of the window would cause B to flatten out. Changes in B^* should lead to roughly parallel shifts in the curve, except for the fact that FFB can never become negative. This means that $b^*_{B^*}$ should be positive and generally close to, but not higher than, unity in the relevant range indicated in (1.31) above. Note also that since FFB should depend basically on the spread $r - d$, we can infer that $b^*_r \approx -b^*_d$. Now, making use of (1.25) and (1.26), we can express B^* as a function of FR, $B^* = S(FR) - FR$, and therefore, substituting in (1.31), we can write, the *demand function* as

$$FFB = b(FR, r, d) \quad \text{with} \quad b_r = b^*_r \leq 0$$
$$b_d = b^*_d \geq 0 \qquad (1.32)$$
$$b_{FR} = -b^*_{B^*}(1 - S') < 0$$

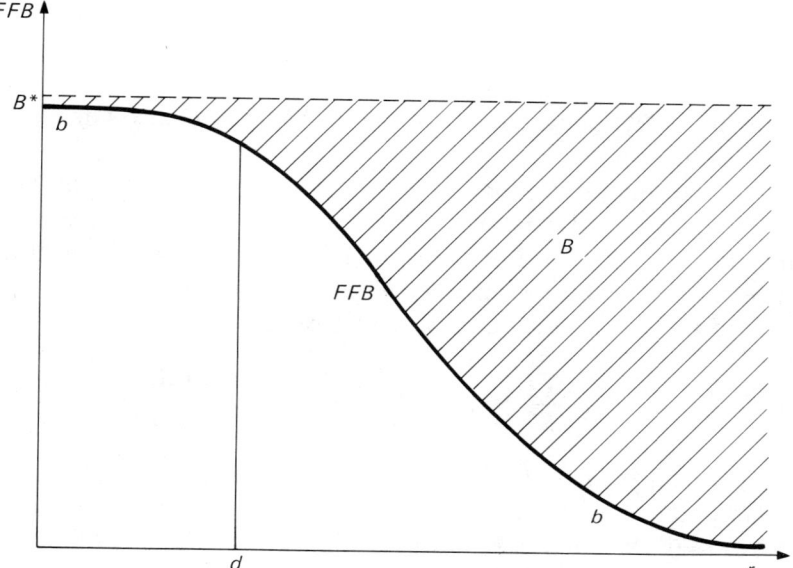

Figure 1-4. Relation among B, FFB, and r.

The description of the market can now be completed by the *market clearing condition*:

$$FFB = FFL \qquad (1.33)$$

Substituting in (1.33) from (1.32) and (1.30), we find that equilibrium implies

$$b(FR, r, d) = l(FR, r) \qquad (1.34)$$

an equation which can be solved for r in terms of FR and d to yield

$$r = R(FR, d)$$

which is equation (1.17) in section 1.1. The properties of R_{FR} and R_d can be inferred by the differentiation of (1.23) and the properties of the functions l and b, stated in (1.30) and (1.32) above. We find:

$$R_{FR} = \frac{b_{FR} - l_{FR}}{l_r - b_r} < 0 \qquad R_d = \frac{b_d}{l_r - b_r} > 0$$

Furthermore, if, as suggested above, $b_d \approx -b_r$, we can also infer that R_d is less than unity.

The above analysis is also useful in clarifying the relation between (1.11) and the approximation (1.11a). Equation (1.11) involves not only r but also the return from lending r_S. But this variable in turn can be expressed as an average of r and r_E, the return on excess reserves weighted by the proportion of S kept in each form, or

$$r_S = r_E\left(\frac{E}{S}\right) + (r-c)\left(\frac{FFL}{S}\right) = (r-c)\left(\frac{FFL}{S}\right) = (r-c)\frac{l(FR, r)}{S(FR)} \qquad (1.35)$$

Here c is an approximation to transaction costs in the Federal Funds market, and the second equality follows since, under present arrangements $r_E = 0$. Once more, r_S can be eliminated from (1.11) by using the last equality in (1.35). The resulting expression is analogous to (1.11a), except that in the approximation we have dropped the variable FR from the list of arguments of F.

1.3 The Demand for Money

In this section we review the theory of the demand for money, and present estimates of two demand functions, one for currency outside banks, and the other for publicly held demand deposits at commercial banks. For the purposes of the broader FMP model, we feel that it is necessary to disaggregate currency, the quantity of which is determined by the demand of the public, from demand deposits, whose behavior results from the interaction of the demand of the public sector and the portfolio adjustment process of the commercial banking sector.

The Basic Hypothesis

Our point of departure in specifying the demand for money is the "Neo-Fisherian" model.[17] According to this hypothesis, the demand for money is basically related to the flow of transactions and arises from a lack of synchronization between receipts and payments, coupled with the transactions costs involved in exchanging money for short-term assets. In this model, the ratio of money demand to transactions, the Cambridge K, or the reciprocal of "velocity," is controlled by the interest obtainable on short-term assets relative to transactions costs. Assuming that real transactions costs per real dollar have not significantly and systematically changed over the period of observation, and neglecting for the moment transactions on asset account, we are led to a demand equation of the Pigou-Latane form:[18]

$$M = K(i)Y \qquad \frac{\partial K}{\partial i} < 0 \qquad (1.36)$$

Here M denotes money demanded, i stands for a vector of available returns on short-term assets, and Y denotes a broad measure of the flow of transactions, such as GNP, in current dollars.

We must, however, think of (1.36) as representing the "long-run" demand equation which need not be satisfied instantaneously because we expect that time is required for the public to respond to changes in interest rates as well as to adjust cash balances to the optimum level. To stress this point, we rewrite (1.36) as

$$M^* = K(i)Y \qquad (1.37)$$

where M^* is the demand for money corresponding to "indefinitely" maintained values for i and Y.

We next hypothesize that the actual demand for money, M, adjusts gradually toward the equilibrium level given by (1.37).[19] This gradual-adjustment hypothesis can be approximated either by the arithmetic form

$$\Delta M = \gamma'(M^* - M_{-1}) = \gamma'[K(i)Y - M_{-1}] \qquad (1.38a)$$

or by the logarithmic form

$$\Delta m = \gamma''(m^* - m_{-1}) = \gamma''[k(i) + y - m_{-1}] \qquad (1.38b)$$

where lower case letters denote the logarithm of the corresponding capital letters. Equations (1.38a) and (1.38b) are roughly equivalent to each other and both can be directly estimated, once we specify the functional form and arguments of $K(i)$ or $k(i)$.

Relation of the Basic Hypothesis to the Friedman and Allais Models

Before we present the evidence that (1.38), with the appropriate specification for $K(i)$ or $k(i)$ fits the data for the United States in the post-war period remarkably well, it is useful to point out the consistency of our hypothesis with the so-called "permanent income" model of Friedman [32], with the model of Brunner and Meltzer [15] and with the model of Allais [2].

To establish the relation to Friedman's model, we first solve (1.38a) for M to obtain

$$M = \gamma' KY + (1-\gamma')M_{-1} \quad \text{where} \quad K \equiv K(i) \tag{1.39}$$

Recursively substituting for the lagged value of M yields

$$M = \gamma' \sum_{\tau=0}^{\infty} (1-\gamma')^{\tau} K_{-\tau} Y_{-\tau} \tag{1.40}$$

If we now follow Friedman in neglecting the effect of interest rates on the demand for money (even though this specification is shown below to be inconsistent with the evidence),[20] then K can be taken as a constant, $\bar{K}$, and (1.40) becomes

$$M = \gamma' \bar{K} \sum_{\tau=0}^{\infty} (1-\gamma')^{\tau} Y_{-\tau}$$

The summation on the right-hand side is readily recognized as an exponentially weighted average of past income, entirely analogous to Friedman's "permanent income." There are, to be sure, some differences in specification, since (1.40) implies an average of past *aggregate money income,* whereas Friedman averages *per capita real income* and then multiplies it by permanent prices and population. But these are rather minor differences, especially with a sluggish series like income. Furthermore, as will soon be apparent, our empirical estimate of γ' based on quarterly data, turns out to imply a weighting factor for annual data, which is not very different from that used by Friedman to construct this "permanent income."

The relation of our model to the Brunner and Meltzer generalization of the Friedman model can be most conveniently established by starting from the approximation (1.38b) and expressing $k(i)$ as a linear function of the logarithm of i. Again solving the equation

46

recursively for m, one can readily establish that our hypothesis implies that m can be expressed as an exponentially weighted average of past incomes and of the short-term rates that appear as arguments of k, except that the average is now of the geometric rather than of the arithmetic variety. Since the weighted average of past incomes can again be identified as a variant of Friedman's permanent income, the main difference between our formulation and Brunner-Meltzer's reduces to the fact that they measure the return on money substitutes by the current long-term interest rate, whereas our model implies an exponentially weighted average of current and past short-term rates. Even this difference in specification can be largely reconciled in the light of results suggesting that long-term interest rates are closely related to a weighted average of past short-term rates (though the weighting structure is not strictly of the monotonically declining form implied by (1.38b).[21]

Allais' basic proposition is that the velocity of circulation is an exponentially weighted average of past changes in money income. Solving (1.38b) for m, subtracting y from both sides of the equation, and rearranging terms, we obtain

$$m - y = \gamma'' k + (1 - \gamma'')(m_{-1} - y) =$$
$$\gamma'' k + (1 - \gamma'')(m_{-1} - y_{-1}) - (1 - \gamma'')(y - y_{-1}) \qquad (1.41)$$

Remembering the definition of velocity $V \equiv Y/M$ or $v = y - m$, we can rewrite (1.41) as

$$v = -\gamma'' k + (1 - \gamma'') \Delta y + (1 - \gamma'') v_{-1}$$

or, by substituting recursively,

$$v = (1 - \gamma'') \sum_{\tau=0}^{\infty} (1 - \gamma'')^\tau \Delta y_{-\tau} - \gamma'' \sum_{\tau=0}^{\infty} (1 - \gamma'')^\tau k_{-\tau} \qquad (1.41a)$$

Treating k as a constant instead of a function of interest rates, the second term reduces to a constant. Thus, (1.38b) is seen to imply that velocity is a weighted average of past rates of change in Y, though again the detailed specifications of Allais' weighted average differ somewhat from those implied by (1.38b).[22]

The Demand for Demand Deposits

The basic hypothesis (1.38) has been applied to demand deposits and currency with somewhat different specifications of the independent variables.

For demand deposits, denoted by *Md* (or *md* in log form), the vector (i) should include rates on those financial instruments that, in the given institutional setting, are the closest alternatives to holding demand deposits unneeded for very short time intervals (which themselves may be partly random). Since our demand equation includes households as well as firms, we need to consider the relevant instruments for each. In the case of large firms and wealthy households, the relevant substitute may be taken as a short-term market instrument like treasury bills or commercial paper and, more recently, certificates of deposit. In the case of other households, the closest substitute can be taken as savings deposits, and the relevant rate is therefore the rate offered on this instrument, which we denote by r_s.

The first two rows of Table 1–3 show the results of the test of hypothesis (1.38) in each of its two variants, (1.38a) and (1.38b). In both cases, the dependent variable was taken as M/Y (or its log, $m-y$), the reciprocal of velocity. For (1.38a) we have approximated $K(i)$ linearly in the two rates, and thus, the equation estimated has the form

$$\frac{M}{Y} = \gamma'(a_0 - a_1 i - a_2 r_s) + (1-\gamma')\frac{M_{-1}}{Y} + u$$

$$= a'_0 - a'_1 i - a'_2 r_s + a'_3 \frac{M_{-1}}{Y} + u \qquad (1.42a)$$

which is derived by dividing both sides of (1.39) by Y. This form was deemed to yield more reliable estimates of the structural coefficients by making the error component u more nearly homoscedastic, and by reducing the collinearity among all the "independent" variables which would have resulted from the trend-like behavior of both M and Y. In the case of (1.38b), the form estimated is that given by the first equality of equation (1.41), but with $k(i)$ specified to be linear in the logarithms, i.e.,

$$m - y = \gamma''(\alpha_0 - \alpha_1 \log i - \alpha_2 \log r_s) + (1-\gamma'')(m_{-1} - y) + u'$$

$$= \alpha'_0 - \alpha'_1 \log i - \alpha'_2 \log r_s - \alpha'_3 (m_{-1} - y) + u' \qquad (1.42b)$$

The last seven columns of Table 1–3 provide measures of goodness of fit based on various characteristics of the estimated error compo-

TABLE 1-3 Demand Deposit Estimates: 1955: I–1966: IV

Row	Form	1 i	2 r_s	3 Md_{-1}/Y	4 N^*P/Y	5 r^*_{cd}	6 STK/Y	7 Const.	8 η_i (S.R.)	9 η_{rs} (S.R.)	10 η_i (L.R.)	11 η_{rs} (L.R.)	12 Total L.R. Interest Elast.	13 ρ	14 σ_ε	15 R^2	16 D-W	17 Relative Error (%)	18 σ_u	19 Relative Error (%)
1	Ratio	−.00214 (−6.04)	−.00411 (−2.50)	.8414 (18.4)	—	—	—	.0536 (3.57)	.03	.05	.18	.32	.50	.58	.00090	.999	2.01	.41	.00110	.52
2	Log	−.0180 (−4.32)	−.0163 (−1.20)	.9259 (28.2)	—	—	—	−.0733 (−2.03)	.018	.016	.24	.22	.46	.52	.0047	.999	1.84	.47	.0055	.55
3	Ratio	−.00212 (−5.44)	−.00428 (−2.08)	.8330 (10.6)	.0046 (.12)	—	—	.0542 (3.48)	.03	.05	.18	.30	.48	.58	.00091	.999	2.01	.41	.00112	.52
4	Ratio	−.0021 (−5.70)	−.0048 (−2.48)	.8163 (13.9)	—	−.0006 (−.65)	—	.0610 (3.30)	.03	.06	.16	.26	.42	.60	.00091	.999	2.04	.41	.00113	.52
5	Ratio	−.00218 (−6.23)	−.0039 (−2.40)	.856 (18.8)	—	—	.00005 (1.44)	.0486 (3.24)	.03	.05	.19	.33	.52	.56	.00089	.999	2.09	.40	.00108	.51
6	Ratio	−.0047	−.0098	.658	−.0298	—	—	.127	.07	.12	.20	.35	.55	.68	.00132	—	1.68	.59	.00187	.88

49

nent. Since there was evidence of significant serial correlation in the error term, both equations have been estimated using the autoregressive transformation. Column 13 shows the estimated value of the autoregression coefficient, i.e., of the coefficient of the equation

$$u_t = \rho u_{t-1} + \varepsilon_t$$

The next three columns show for the error term ε of the above equation the standard deviation, R^2, and the Durbin-Watson statistic. Column 17 provides an estimate of the relative or percentage error. For the logarithmic form, this figure is the same as that of column 14, while for the ratio form we have estimated the relative error by dividing the figure of column 14 by the mean value of the dependent variable, Md/Y (which is 0.221 for the period of observation). It should be noted that these statistics are not an adequate measure of the explanatory power of the hypothesis per se, since ε only measures the error in any quarter given u_{-1}, the actual error in the quarter before. Since this error can only be known after the quarter has elapsed, ε can best be characterized as a measure of the "one-period" forecast error.

A more useful measure of how well the hypothesis explains the phenomenon under investigation is provided by the standard deviation of the error term u, which is given in columns 18 and 19. It can be verified readily that σ_u depends on σ_ε, as well as the serial correlation of the ε: if the ε are serially independent, then asymptotically

$$\sigma_u = \frac{\sigma_\varepsilon}{\sqrt{1-\rho^2}}$$

Note that when the equation does not involve the lagged dependent variable, u can be looked upon as measuring the error of a "dynamic" simulation, in which the computed value of the dependent variable is computed, except for initial conditions, entirely from the values of the independent variables. When the independent variables include the lagged dependent variable, however, the error of a dynamic simulation is more complex, being also an increasing function of the coefficient of the lagged dependent variable.

It is apparent that there is little difference between the fit of the two variants of our hypothesis. For (1.38a) the relative "one-period" error is only four-tenths of one percent, implying an error in Md of about half a billion dollars (since the mean value of Md in the period is some 120 billion dollars). For (1.38b) the one-period error is somewhat higher, but the difference in terms of the u error is less pronounced because of the lower serial correlation. However, the two forms do have somewhat different implications about the role of interest rates. In both cases the coefficient of the bill rate is highly significant, but (1.38a) implies a short-run elasticity almost twice as high (cf. column 8). The difference is even more pronounced in the case of the savings deposit rate, with (1.38a) implying an elasticity three times higher (column 9). Closer examination reveals that these differences can be traced in large measure to differences in the coefficient of the variable Md_{-1}/Y, which is an estimate of $(1-\gamma)$. Equation (1.38b) implies a speed of adjustment of less than 9 percent per quarter, while (1.38a) yields an estimate of 16 percent. If we use these estimates of γ' and γ'' to compute the long-run elasticities (columns 10, 11, and 12) we find that the two versions have similar implications. In particular, the long-run elasticity of demand with respect to a simultaneous change in both rates is substantial, around one-half. This estimate implies, e.g., that an increase in both rates from, say, 3 to 4 percent would eventually increase velocity by some 15 percent. However, (1.38a) assigns a relatively larger role to the savings deposit rate r_s and, even more important, it implies a considerably faster response.

Despite similarities, we are inclined to question the reliability of the estimates provided by logarithmic version (1.38b). A speed of adjustment of less than 10 percent per quarter seems hardly credible. Even the estimate implied by (1.38a), 16 percent per quarter, or roughly half the full effect within the first year, may appear on the low side; but it is not altogether unreasonable when one recalls that the delay we are measuring reflects in part the time it takes for the public to change the effort devoted to economizing money in response to changes in interest rates. Since (1.38a) seems to fit the data slightly better, we are inclined to conclude that this version provides a better approximation to the money demand mechanism over the sample period and shall primarily rely on it in what follows. Some caution is required in that the linear approximation to $K(i)$ may become poor for values of i very much outside the range of observation, say, 1 to 6 percent. This is especially true at the low end, for a linear form is incapable of capturing significant liquidity trap effects.

Refinements of the Basic Hypothesis

A number of tests have been carried out to assess the empirical significance of certain refinements of the basic hypothesis (1.38) which have been proposed by various authors. Since these tests were not very successful, we shall review them very briefly.

Real Income Effects. Several authors have suggested that the proportionality factor K of equation (1.36) might be systematically affected by real per capita income. In particular, Friedman [32] has maintained, partly on the strength of his own empirical analysis, that money is a luxury, the demand for which rises proportionately faster than real income. This would imply a positive elasticity of K with respect to real per capita income. On the other hand, the inventory-theoretic analysis of Baumol [9], Tobin [75] and others suggests that there should be some economies of scale in cash holdings, implying that the elasticity of K with respect to real income should be negative, possibly as low as -0.5. Others, such as Ando and Modigliani [6], have suggested that both effects might well be present, but to a minor and largely offsetting extent, resulting in no significant net effect. These hypotheses can be most easily tested for version (1.42b) by adding the logarithm of real per capita income to the set of independent variables listed in row 2 (Table 1–3); its coefficient should be positive under the "luxury" hypothesis and negative if there are significant economies of scale. It should be noted, however, that the findings of a significant coefficient for this variable could not be unambiguously interpreted as supporting either position because, over the period, real per capita income is basically a secular trend and hence, the variable could proxy for other slowly changing forces, such as changes in transaction costs, payment habits, and the like. In practice, the problem of interpretation did not arise because the coefficient of the variable, though negative, as implied by the economy of scale hypothesis, is quite small (-0.05) and its t ratio was less than one.[23] A similar test was repeated for version (1.42a) by adding to the independent variables the *reciprocal* of real per capita income; its coefficient should thus be negative to be consistent with Friedman's hypothesis. The outcome reported in row 3 confirms the above results, in that the coefficient of the variable is positive but totally insignificant, while the remaining coefficients are basically unchanged. These results can also be interpreted as indicating absence of significant trend-like forces acting on the demand for money.

The Effect of Transactions on Wealth Account. These were neglected in the basic hypothesis (1.37), which would be justified insofar as the ratio of transactions on wealth account to transactions on GNP account remains roughly stable.[24] Such stability is plausible in view of the well-known stability in the wealth-income ratio, yet it cannot be taken for granted. Unfortunately, it is very hard to get a measure of transactions on wealth account. As a crude approximation, we have tried the ratio of the value of stock transactions on all exchanges[25] to current dollar GNP. According to the model the coefficient of such a variable should be positive, since transactions on wealth account should increase the demand for money relative to income, or equivalently, reduce income velocity. The results are reported in Table 1–3, row 5. The variable turned out to have the expected positive coefficient, but the implied elasticity of Md with respect to this variable was negligible. It was therefore decided to let this small systematic effect be impounded in the error term.

Effect of Certificates of Deposit. As noted earlier, this instrument is likely to be a relevant substitute for money for large transactors. Accordingly, the rate on certificates of deposit deserves testing. There is one difficulty—certificates of deposit did not become a significant factor until around 1962–1963. To get around this difficulty, we use as an additional variable r_{CD}^*, defined as the spread between the certificates of deposit rate, and r_s when this spread is positive, and otherwise zero.[26] As can be seen from the results reported in row 4 (Table 1–3), the coefficient of this variable has the anticipated negative sign, but it is statistically insignificant and the implied effect on Md is negligible.

Effects of the Rate of Change of i. One might conceive that the rate of change of i could exert some influence on Md by way of expectation effects. If short-run interest expectations are prevailingly regressive, then a rise in i might be regarded as providing an exceptionally favorable opportunity to invest short-term balances and thus would have a negative effect on (Md/Y). If, on the other hand, short-term expectations were prevailingly extrapolative—as some recent evidence might suggest (see, e.g., Modigliani-Sutch [58]—then Δi should have a positive sign in (1.42a) and (1.42b).[27] Tests of the rate-of-change hypothesis were limited to the bill rate (there being little ground for expectational effects in the case of a sluggish rate like r_s), and did not prove very conclusive. The coefficient of Δi is generally negative, but is not significant and is not robust with respect to minor changes in specifications.

Stock Adjustment Delay Versus Learning and Expectational Effects. In the equations of the forms (1.42a) and (1.42b), which underlie the test presented so far, the coefficient, γ' or γ'', is meant to reflect two types of delay which, in principle, are distinguishable. The first type of delay is the usual stock adjustment, reflecting the time it takes for the public to adjust the cash balance to the *desired* level. A second source of delay might be expected to reflect the time it takes for the desired cash balance, or more precisely, for the desired ratio of money to transactions, to respond to changes in interest rates. This decomposition is investigated in detail in Modigliani, Rasche, and Cooper [57] and is not reported here.

In conclusion, the above battery of tests suggested that the demand for money may be affected by variables other than those appearing in (1.42a), but only to a minor extent, and that the effect of past values of the independent variables could be somewhat more complex than the Koyck type of distributed lag structure implied by (1.42a). Nevertheless, pragmatic considerations have led us to adopt (1.42a) for the present as an operationally acceptable approximation to the demand for money to be used in the model.[28] It should be noted here, too, that the coefficients of this equation presented in row 1 of Table 1–3 were estimated by ordinary least squares, a method likely to lead to significant simultaneous equations bias in view of a second relation connecting the short-term rate to the stock of money via the money supply mechanism. We come back to this question in section 1.4 but note here that this bias is likely to cause an underestimation of the elasticity of demand, particularly with respect to the short rate i, and probably also the speed of adjustment.

Demand for Currency

Here we again rely on a model of type (1.38), but we replace Y by consumers' expenditure, C, on the ground that the use of currency (Mc) largely arises out of such transactions. However, we should expect interest rates, especially i, to be less important in this case.

TABLE 1-4 Currency Demand Estimates: 1955: I–1966: IV

Row	Form	1 r_s	2 Mc_{-1}/C	3 Const.	4 η_{r_s}(S.R.)	5 η_{r_s}(L.R.)	6 ρ	7 σ_ε	8 R^2	9 D–W	10 σ_u
1	Ratio	−.0014 (−1.89)	.8369 (13.60)	.0190 (2.57)	.04	.25	.78	.00031	.999	2.42	.00058
2	Log	−.0395 (−2.09)	.8324 (14.70)	.3590 (3.01)	.04	.24	.71	.0034	.999	2.31	.0050

The results of the estimation are presented in Table 1–4 for both the linear (row 1) and logarithmic (row 2) forms of our specification. It should be noted that in both of these equations the only interest rate which appears is r_s; in each case we tried the treasury bill rate as an additional regressor, but its coefficient was always small and insignificant. Again, the "fits" are quite close and the results are reasonable. The estimated speed of adjustment in both equations is remarkably close to that which we found when we estimated the demand for demand deposits in the linear form, and which we regard as more sensible than that produced by the logarithmic form for Md. The elasticities with respect to r_s are of the same order of magnitude as those of demand deposits, but the total interest elasticity of currency demand is considerably lower than that of demand deposits, since i has no significant contribution in this case. A characteristic of both results in Table 1–4 is the very high serial correlation as indicated by estimated autoregression coefficient, ρ, in excess of 0.7. In this respect the logarithmic form is superior to the linear one.

In carrying out the test we have to face one special difficulty. At the end of World War II, the currency–deposit ratio was unusually high by historical standards, a phenomenon widely held to be related to (i) black market operations under price controls and rationing, and (ii) the hoarding of U.S. currency in foreign countries. These unusual sources of demand were presumably gradually eliminated over the early post-war years. Accordingly, we would expect the model which we fit over the years 1955–1966 to underestimate the currency–deposit ratio when extrapolated back into the Korean War years.

In Figure 1–5 we have graphed the actual currency–deposit ratio and that computed from the linear forms in Table 1–3 and 1–4. This ratio, which is frequently supposed to be rather stable, has actually exhibited a surprising amount of variation in the post-war period falling from over 30 percent at the end of the war, down to a low point just over 25 percent in the mid-fifties, and rising back up to over 29 percent by the end of 1966. These movements have in part a cyclical character, with the currency–deposit ratio tending to rise in expansions (1951–1953, 1955–1957, 1959–1960, and 1962–1966), and to fall during contractions. It is appearent that our model accounts fairly well for the observed movements, though, of course, it would systematically underestimate the level of the ratio in the early post-war years. In particular, it catches rather well all major turning points.

The swings in the ratio, and, in particular, its cyclical features are accounted for in our model by (i) movements in interest rates—since demand deposits are more interest-elastic than currency, a rise in interest rates tends to raise the ratio; (ii) movements of the market i relative to the more sluggish rate r_s—since Md responds much more to i than does Mc, cyclical swings in short-term market rates cause similar procyclical swings in the currency ratio; and (iii) the fact that C is less cyclically variable than Y, which tends to moderate the cyclical tendency resulting from (i) and (ii).

Refinements of the Currency Demand Model

Real Income Effects. As in the case of demand deposits, it is conceivable that the ratio Mc/C could be affected, either way, by an increase in real per capita permanent income. We thought this variable could well be approximated by real consumption per capita, but this measure did not contribute significantly when added to the specifications in Table 1–4.

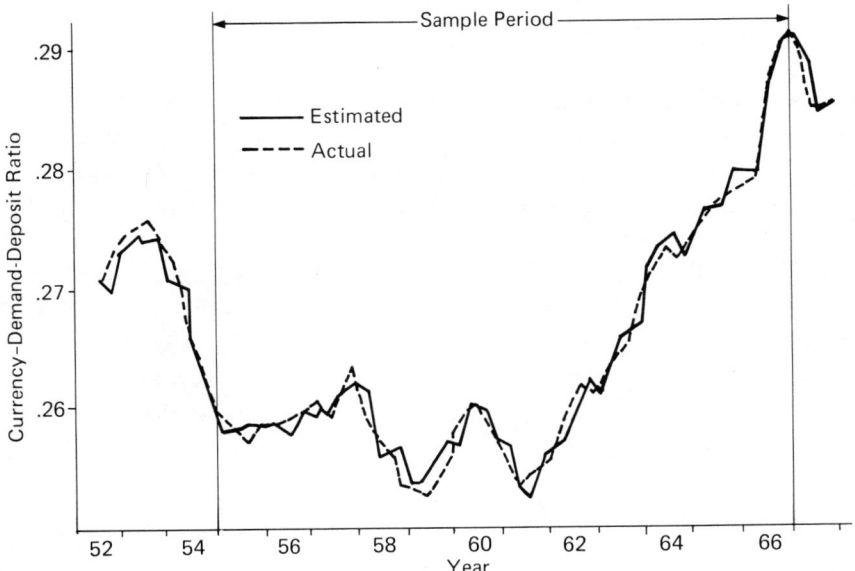

Effects of the Spread of Credit Cards. We hypothesize that credit cards are at least in part a currency-saving device, and hence that an increase in credit-card credit outstanding relative to consumption would reduce *Mc/C*. Furthermore, we expected that the ratio of credit outstanding to consumption would show a very marked rising trend over the post-war period. Unfortunately, there is no entirely satisfactory measure of credit-card credit outstanding by itself. The closest approximation we could secure is represented by the series "charge accounts plus service credit."

To our surprise this series rose appreciably faster than consumption up to the mid-fifties, but has had amazingly little trend since. It is therefore not surprising that when this variable was added, it had a totally insignificant coefficient. We interpret this result not as a rejection of the hypothesis that credit cards are a currency-saving device, but rather as an indication that this effect cannot be measured with these data.

1.4 System Estimation: The Joint Determination of the Rate of Interest and the Stock of Money

The Closed System

In this section we consider a complete submodel of interest rate and money supply determination which encompasses the theory and empirical results presented in the preceding pages. For reference we have reproduced in Table 1–5, lines 1 and 2, the empirically

TABLE 1–5   Equations of the Monetary Sector

1. $Md = -.0021iY - .0043 r_s Y + .0542 Y + .0046(N \cdot P) + .833 Md_{-1}$
2. $FR = (.001 - .00204 S_2 - .00237 S_3 - .00223 S_4)\bar{D}_{-1} - .00122 i \bar{D}_{-1}$
   $\quad + .00144 d\bar{D}_{-1} + .646(1 - \delta) \Delta RU - .502 \delta \Delta CL + .394 RL$
   $\quad + .705 FR_{-1}$
3. $D = \dfrac{RU - \tau T - FR}{\delta}$
4. $Md^{ns} = \lambda D - Mg$
5. $Md = JsMd^{ns}$

estimated equations reported in row 3 of Table 1–3 and row 2 of Table 1–2. Line 3 of Table 1–5 shows the reserve identity (1.19). If D, the stock of member bank demand deposits could be identified with Md, the stock of demand deposits held by the public, then the above three equations could be regarded as a closed system of simultaneous equations in the three variables: free reserves, the treasury bill rate, and the stock of demand deposits, with all other variables exogenous. In fact, Md and D differ in a number of respects. First, not all demand deposits, relevant to the determination of the legal reserve requirements of member banks, reflect the public's demand for money balances. Sizable deposits are held by the U.S. Treasury in tax and loan accounts at commercial banks. Such deposits clearly do not reflect the public's demand for transactions balances and are excluded from the demand deposit adjusted concept which we have used in the empirical results presented in section 1.3. Second, not all banks are members of the Federal Reserve System, and therefore there is a discrepancy between privately held demand balances subject to reserve requirements and total privately held deposits. Finally, we have used a seasonally adjusted series for the demand deposit adjusted concept, while our deposits subject to reserve requirement are not seasonally adjusted.[29] These three problems have been subsumed in the identities presented in lines 4 and 5 of Table 1–5. Identity 4 is derived from the definition of the ratio, λ, of total demand deposits at all commercial banks to total member bank deposits, D, both seasonally unadjusted

$$\lambda \equiv \frac{Md^{ns} + Mg}{D} \qquad (1.43)$$

where Md^{ns} is private deposits not seasonally adjusted and Mg is U.S. Treasury deposits at all commercial banks. Once we have calculated λ for all time periods from (1.43) we treat it as an exogenous variable to our subsystem.[30] Identity 5 reflects the seasonal adjustments which have been made in the official series. The seasonal factor, Js, which varies slightly from year to year, is also treated as an exogenous variable in our system.

The system 1 to 5 is represented in a flow chart in Figure 1–6, with arrows indicating the causal flow among the endogenous variables. This diagram clearly indicates the major sources of exogenous influences upon the sector: (i) gross national product through the demand side of the market; (ii) the instruments of monetary policy,

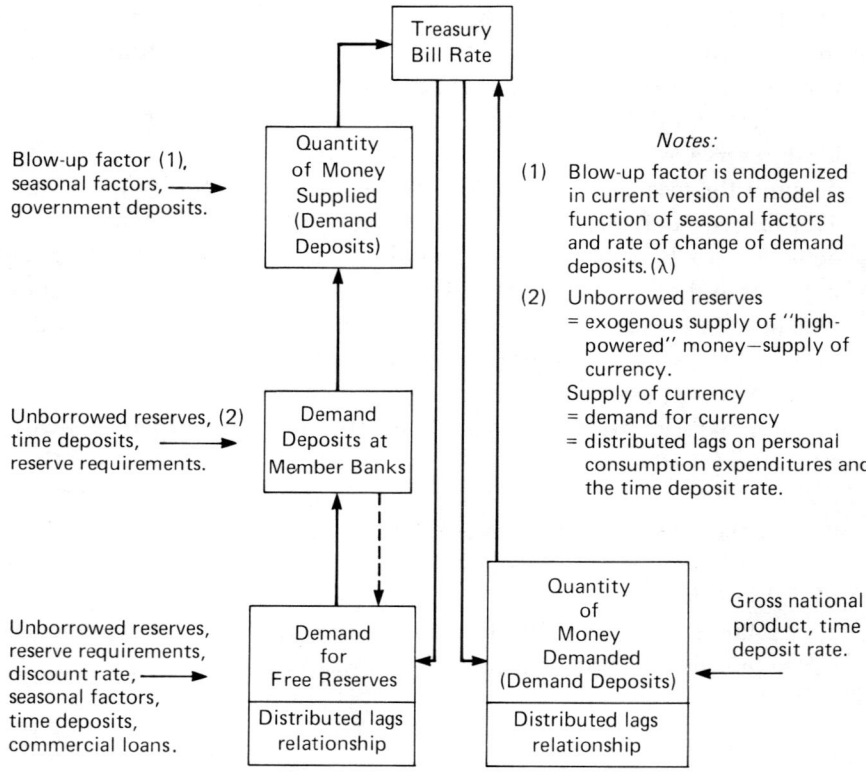

Figure 1-6. Flow Chart for Demand-Deposit Component of Money Supply.

unborrowed reserves, the discount rate, and reserve requirements through the supply side; and (iii) time deposits and commercial loans which are exogenous to our submodel.

Simulation of the Least Squares Estimates

In preceding sections, we have reported on the properties, statistical and economic, of the component equations of our system. We now wish to examine the behavior of the equations considered as a system with the aid of the closing identities given in Table 1–5. We are particularly interested in establishing how well our model can account for the observed behavior of the stock of demand deposits and the treasury bill rate, both within the period of observation and in extrapolation.

Our vehicle for this investigation is dynamic simulation. In this procedure a set of initial conditions, including lagged dependent variables and the contemporaneous exogenous variables, are supplied to the model. Solution values are determined for the first-period endogenous variables. The initial conditions are then updated in time, using the contemporaneous exogenous variables and the first-period solution values for the lagged endogenous variables, and a second-period solution is generated. This procedure is repeated for subsequent periods.[31]

With this procedure the simulated errors will differ from the single equation estimation errors for two reasons. First, in the simulation procedure, the equations are evaluated as a system, so that endogenous variables which appear on the right-hand side of structural specifications assume their simulated, not historical values. Second, the procedure of using the *lagged simulated* values, rather than the *lagged historical* values of the endogenous variables implies that the simulation errors are generated in part as weighted sums of the past errors.

The period chosen for the simulation analysis was 1955: I–1968: I which includes the entire sample period for the estimation plus *five* post-sample quarters. The results are presented graphically in Figures 1–7, 1–8, and 1–9 which compare actual and simulated values. Table 1–6 presents some summary statistics.

From Figure 1–7 it can be seen that the computed value of demand deposits tracks the long-run behavior of the series well, at least within the period of observation ending in 1966: IV. The root-mean-

TABLE 1-6 Root Mean Square Errors of Single Equations and Dynamic Simulation

	Single Equation		Dynamic Simulation	
	Sample	Sample and Extrapolation	Sample	Sample and Extrapolation
A. LEAST SQUARES ESTIMATES				
Md	.49	.506	.888	1.048
FR	.072	.092	.117	0.135
i	—	—	.331	0.347
B. TWO-STAGE ESTIMATES				
Md	.734	.757	1.014	1.066
FR	.072	.091	0.135	0.139
i	—	—	0.287	0.285

square error, is 0.89 billion, well below 1 percent. There are clearly some periods in which the errors are consistently sizable, most notably in 1959. However, because the errors are highly serially correlated the computed values tend to grow and decline with the actual, even in this period. In the remaining periods in which the money supply declined mildly (1957: IV, 1962: I to 1962: III, and 1966: I to 1966: IV) the computed value either declined or at least levelled off. Unfortunately the results of the extrapolation are not too encouraging since in the last three quarters the computed value completely misses the sharp rise of the actual series.

Figure 1-8 shows the results for free reserves, a variable that, in contrast to demand deposits, exhibits little long-run trend, but has sharp cyclical fluctuations. Our simulation again tracks these fluctuations rather well. However, the simulation errors of Figure 1-8 provide little new information since it can be verified that the errors of Figure 1-8 are roughly proportional to those of 1-7, with the proportionality factor averaging around −7.5.[32] Nevertheless, Figure 1-8 is useful to bring into perspective the complexity of the task of tracing short-run fluctuations in free reserves which constitute the endogenous component of the stock of deposits.

Table 1-6 reports the standard deviations of the simulation errors for both Md and FR, and compares them with the single-equation

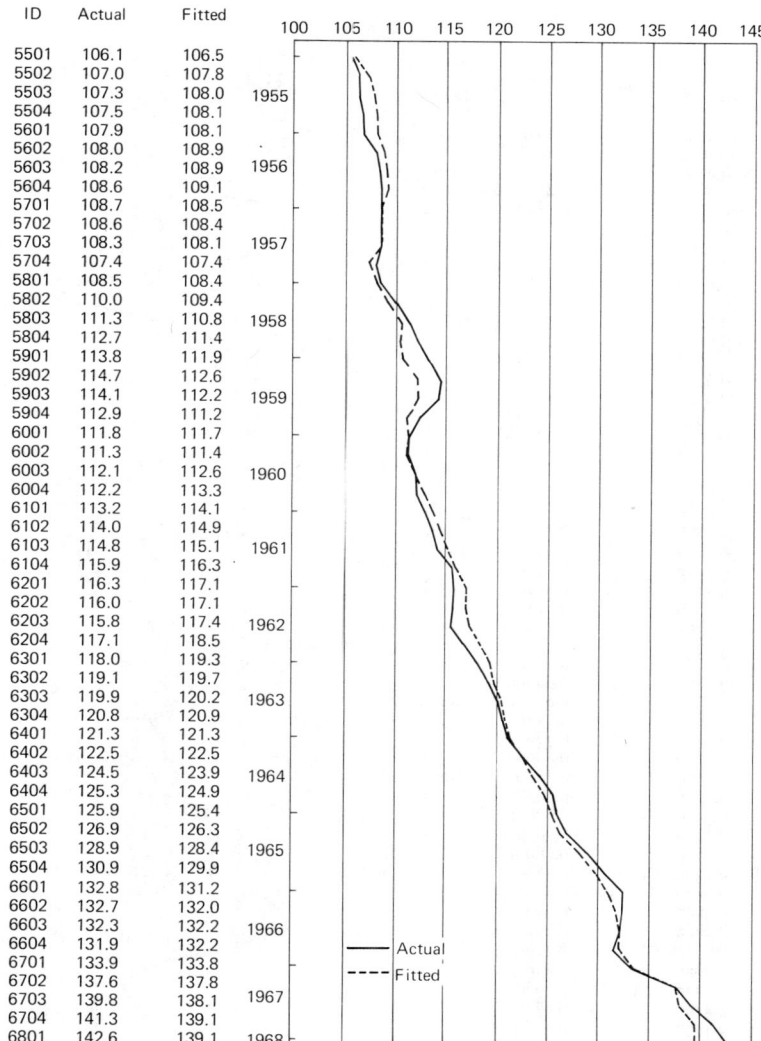

ID	Actual	Fitted	
5501	106.1	106.5	
5502	107.0	107.8	
5503	107.3	108.0	1955
5504	107.5	108.1	
5601	107.9	108.1	
5602	108.0	108.9	
5603	108.2	108.9	1956
5604	108.6	109.1	
5701	108.7	108.5	
5702	108.6	108.4	
5703	108.3	108.1	1957
5704	107.4	107.4	
5801	108.5	108.4	
5802	110.0	109.4	
5803	111.3	110.8	1958
5804	112.7	111.4	
5901	113.8	111.9	
5902	114.7	112.6	
5903	114.1	112.2	1959
5904	112.9	111.2	
6001	111.8	111.7	
6002	111.3	111.4	
6003	112.1	112.6	1960
6004	112.2	113.3	
6101	113.2	114.1	
6102	114.0	114.9	
6103	114.8	115.1	1961
6104	115.9	116.3	
6201	116.3	117.1	
6202	116.0	117.1	
6203	115.8	117.4	1962
6204	117.1	118.5	
6301	118.0	119.3	
6302	119.1	119.7	
6303	119.9	120.2	1963
6304	120.8	120.9	
6401	121.3	121.3	
6402	122.5	122.5	
6403	124.5	123.9	1964
6404	125.3	124.9	
6501	125.9	125.4	
6502	126.9	126.3	
6503	128.9	128.4	1965
6504	130.9	129.9	
6601	132.8	131.2	
6602	132.7	132.0	
6603	132.3	132.2	1966
6604	131.9	132.2	
6701	133.9	133.8	
6702	137.6	137.8	
6703	139.8	138.1	1967
6704	141.3	139.1	
6801	142.6	139.1	1968

Figure 1-7. Dynamic Simulation of Demand Deposits: Least Squares Coefficients (Plot of Actual and Fitted Values).

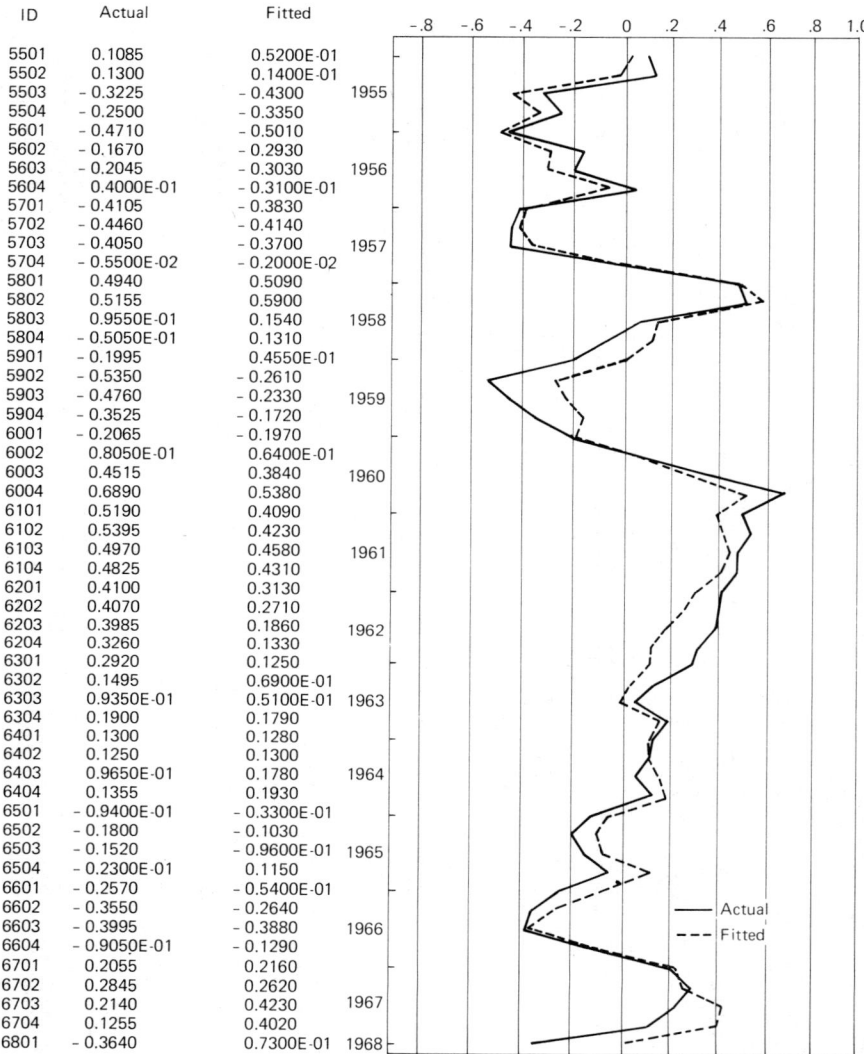

ID	Actual	Fitted	
5501	0.1085	0.5200E-01	
5502	0.1300	0.1400E-01	
5503	-0.3225	-0.4300	1955
5504	-0.2500	-0.3350	
5601	-0.4710	-0.5010	
5602	-0.1670	-0.2930	
5603	-0.2045	-0.3030	1956
5604	0.4000E-01	-0.3100E-01	
5701	-0.4105	-0.3830	
5702	-0.4460	-0.4140	
5703	-0.4050	-0.3700	1957
5704	-0.5500E-02	-0.2000E-02	
5801	0.4940	0.5090	
5802	0.5155	0.5900	
5803	0.9550E-01	0.1540	1958
5804	-0.5050E-01	0.1310	
5901	-0.1995	0.4550E-01	
5902	-0.5350	-0.2610	
5903	-0.4760	-0.2330	1959
5904	-0.3525	-0.1720	
6001	-0.2065	-0.1970	
6002	0.8050E-01	0.6400E-01	
6003	0.4515	0.3840	1960
6004	0.6890	0.5380	
6101	0.5190	0.4090	
6102	0.5395	0.4230	
6103	0.4970	0.4580	1961
6104	0.4825	0.4310	
6201	0.4100	0.3130	
6202	0.4070	0.2710	
6203	0.3985	0.1860	1962
6204	0.3260	0.1330	
6301	0.2920	0.1250	
6302	0.1495	0.6900E-01	
6303	0.9350E-01	0.5100E-01	1963
6304	0.1900	0.1790	
6401	0.1300	0.1280	
6402	0.1250	0.1300	
6403	0.9650E-01	0.1780	1964
6404	0.1355	0.1930	
6501	-0.9400E-01	-0.3300E-01	
6502	-0.1800	-0.1030	
6503	-0.1520	-0.9600E-01	1965
6504	-0.2300E-01	0.1150	
6601	-0.2570	-0.5400E-01	
6602	-0.3550	-0.2640	
6603	-0.3995	-0.3880	1966
6604	-0.9050E-01	-0.1290	
6701	0.2055	0.2160	
6702	0.2845	0.2620	
6703	0.2140	0.4230	1967
6704	0.1255	0.4020	
6801	-0.3640	0.7300E-01	1968

Figure 1-8. Dynamic Simulation of Free Reserves: Least Squares Coefficients (Plot of Actual and Fitted Values).

errors of the money supply (or free reserve) equation. It appears that within the period of observation the simulation error is some 80 percent larger than the money demand error and some 60 percent larger than the supply equation error. The amplification is thus substantial but not altogether surprising. The simulation error reflects not only the interaction of the single-equation errors but also the substitution of the lagged dependent variable with the simulated value. This substitution is likely to be the primary contributor to the substantial serial correlation of the simulation errors which is apparent in Figure 1–7.

The table also confirms the sizeable deterioration of the fit in the extrapolation. This appears to be related to the poor performance of the supply function. The single equation error of this equation rises by nearly 30 percent while the fit of the money demand equation does not worsen appreciably.

Turning to Figure 1–9, we see that the model also succeeds in accounting for the broad features of behavior of the treasury bill rate. The root-mean-squared error is 33 basis points. The peaks of 1957, 1959–1960 and 1966, and the sharp troughs of 1958 and 1967 are predicted with approximately correct amplitude and timing. The most disturbing feature of this simulation is the intracycle behavior of the simulation errors. These can be roughly characterized as cyclical with high frequency and low amplitude—a "spiking" effect. It is apparent from the graph that this feature can be largely traced to the "spiking" of the simulated series which exhibits sharp short-run fluctuations that find no counterpart in the actual series. One might conjecture that this failure reflects an underestimation of the short-run elasticity of both demand and supply with respect to the treasury bill rate, resulting from simultaneous equation bias. By underestimating these elasticities we would be led to overestimate the variation in the treasury bill rate necessary to accommodate short-run shifts of the demand or supply schedule (arising for example from movements of Y or RU or from the error component).

Below, we report the results obtained by an alternative estimating procedure designed to lessen the simultaneous equation bias.

An Alternative Estimation Technique

The object of our alternative estimation procedure was to replace the endogenous variables, current and lagged, on the right-hand

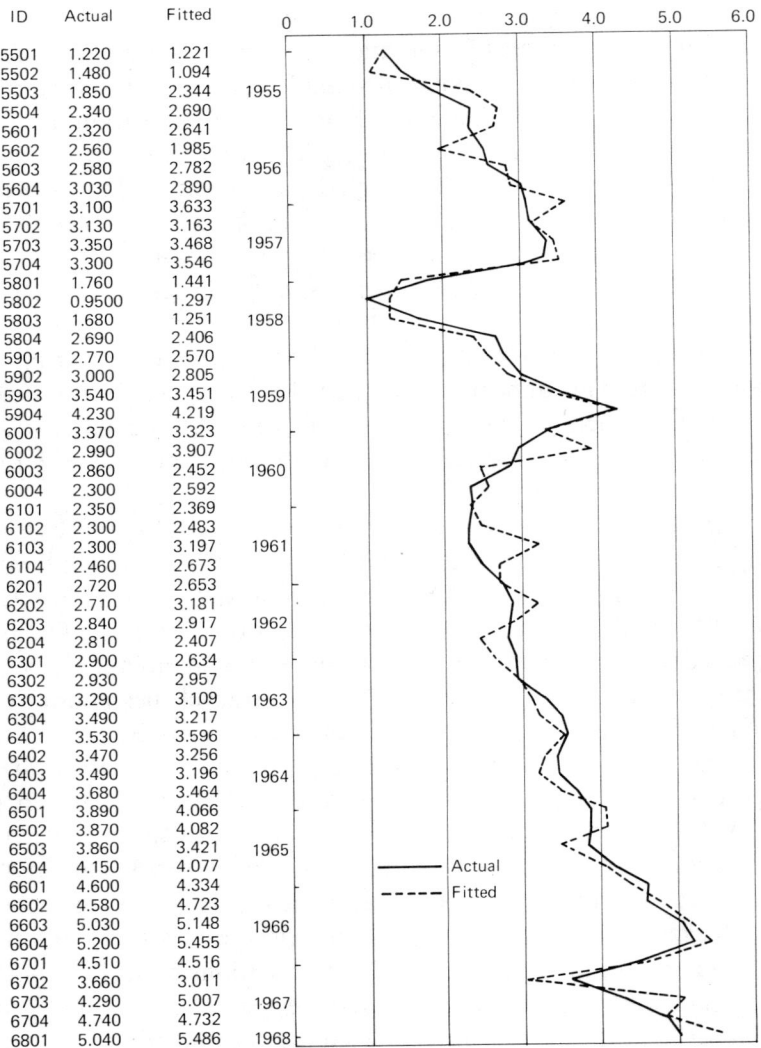

ID	Actual	Fitted	
5501	1.220	1.221	
5502	1.480	1.094	
5503	1.850	2.344	1955
5504	2.340	2.690	
5601	2.320	2.641	
5602	2.560	1.985	
5603	2.580	2.782	1956
5604	3.030	2.890	
5701	3.100	3.633	
5702	3.130	3.163	
5703	3.350	3.468	1957
5704	3.300	3.546	
5801	1.760	1.441	
5802	0.9500	1.297	
5803	1.680	1.251	1958
5804	2.690	2.406	
5901	2.770	2.570	
5902	3.000	2.805	
5903	3.540	3.451	1959
5904	4.230	4.219	
6001	3.370	3.323	
6002	2.990	3.907	
6003	2.860	2.452	1960
6004	2.300	2.592	
6101	2.350	2.369	
6102	2.300	2.483	
6103	2.300	3.197	1961
6104	2.460	2.673	
6201	2.720	2.653	
6202	2.710	3.181	
6203	2.840	2.917	1962
6204	2.810	2.407	
6301	2.900	2.634	
6302	2.930	2.957	
6303	3.290	3.109	1963
6304	3.490	3.217	
6401	3.530	3.596	
6402	3.470	3.256	
6403	3.490	3.196	1964
6404	3.680	3.464	
6501	3.890	4.066	
6502	3.870	4.082	
6503	3.860	3.421	1965
6504	4.150	4.077	
6601	4.600	4.334	
6602	4.580	4.723	
6603	5.030	5.148	1966
6604	5.200	5.455	
6701	4.510	4.516	
6702	3.660	3.011	
6703	4.290	5.007	1967
6704	4.740	4.732	
6801	5.040	5.486	1968

Figure 1-9. Dynamic Simulation of Treasury Bill Rate: Least Squares Coefficients (Plot of Actual and Fitted Values).

side of our specifications with instrumental variables which are functions of only exogenous variables.[33] Our instrumental variables were obtained from the dynamic simulations described above. The solution values, generated by this simulation procedure, are functions of the ordinary least squares parameter estimates, the exogenous variables, and the (presample-period) initial conditions of the endogenous variables. Both the demand and supply equation were reestimated with a correction for serial correlation, using the instruments for the current and lagged endogenous variables on the right-hand side. This procedure is not consistent[34] but it may reduce some of the biases of the ordinary least squares coefficient estimates.

The results of this estimation technique applied to the money-demand equation (1.42a) and the free-reserve equation (1.24) are reported in the last row of Tables 1–3 and 1–2, respectively.[35] In both cases the standard deviation of the residual error increases, but this is as expected since, if there is least squares bias, then that method will underestimate the variance of the true structural error. It is significant, however, that for both equations the estimates of the coefficients of the endogenous variable have moved in the direction we anticipated.

In the first equation, the coefficient of i, and thus the short-run elasticity of the bill rate, has more than doubled in absolute value. Similarly, the speed of adjustment of actual demand deposits to target levels has doubled as the coefficient of the lagged variable Md_{-1}/Y falls; yet the relationship between the coefficients of i and r_s has been maintained as the coefficient of r_s also increased considerably in absolute value. The long-run elasticities do not change appreciably because of the offsetting effects of the preceding two changes.

Turning to the second equation, we note again, that the estimated coefficient of the treasury bill rate has increased by nearly one-third and now, as suggested by our model, exceeds that of the discount rate. Similarly, the coefficient of lagged free reserves falls somewhat, implying a faster speed of adjustment.

Simulation Results with the Alternative Estimates

The results obtained in a dynamic simulation test based on the alternative coefficient estimates are reported in Figures 1–10 and 1–11 and in the last three rows of Table 1–6. The results for the money

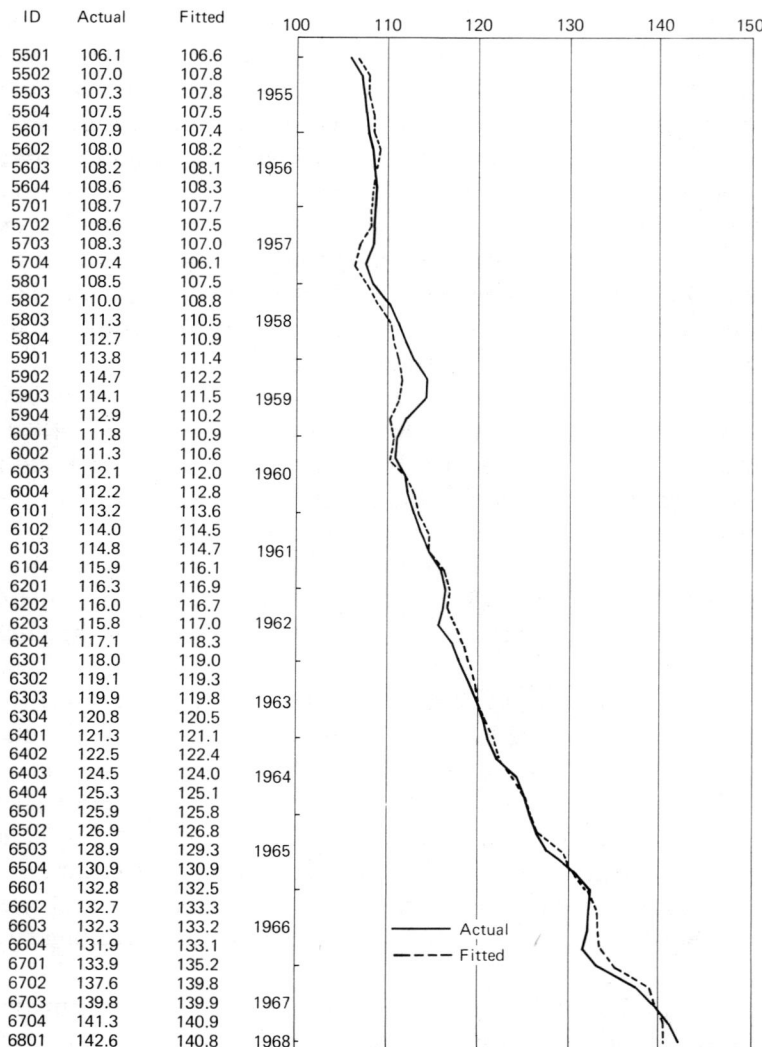

Figure 1-10. Dynamic Simulation of Demand Deposits: Two-Stage Coefficients (Plot of Actual and Fitted Values).

ID	Actual	Fitted
5501	1.220	1.449
5502	1.480	1.654
5503	1.850	2.439
5504	2.340	2.766
5601	2.320	2.716
5602	2.560	2.428
5603	2.580	2.823
5604	3.030	2.983
5701	3.100	3.309
5702	3.130	3.079
5703	3.350	3.273
5704	3.300	3.177
5801	1.760	1.746
5802	0.9500	1.595
5803	1.680	1.742
5804	2.690	2.528
5901	2.770	2.677
5902	3.000	2.929
5903	3.540	3.205
5904	4.230	3.676
6001	3.870	3.336
6002	2.990	3.606
6003	2.360	2.736
6004	2.300	2.676
6101	2.350	2.439
6102	2.300	2.604
6103	2.300	3.037
6104	2.460	2.887
6201	2.720	2.725
6202	2.710	2.983
6203	2.840	2.865
6204	2.810	2.557
6301	2.900	2.725
6032	2.930	2.924
6303	3.290	3.105
6304	3.490	3.237
6401	3.530	3.501
6402	3.470	3.406
6403	3.490	3.430
6404	3.680	3.554
6501	3.890	3.973
6502	3.870	4.090
6503	3.860	3.862
6504	4.150	4.276
6601	4.600	4.452
6602	4.580	4.696
6603	5.030	5.042
6604	5.200	5.229
6701	4.510	4.614
6702	3.660	3.806
6703	4.290	4.823
6704	4.740	4.747
6801	5.040	5.205

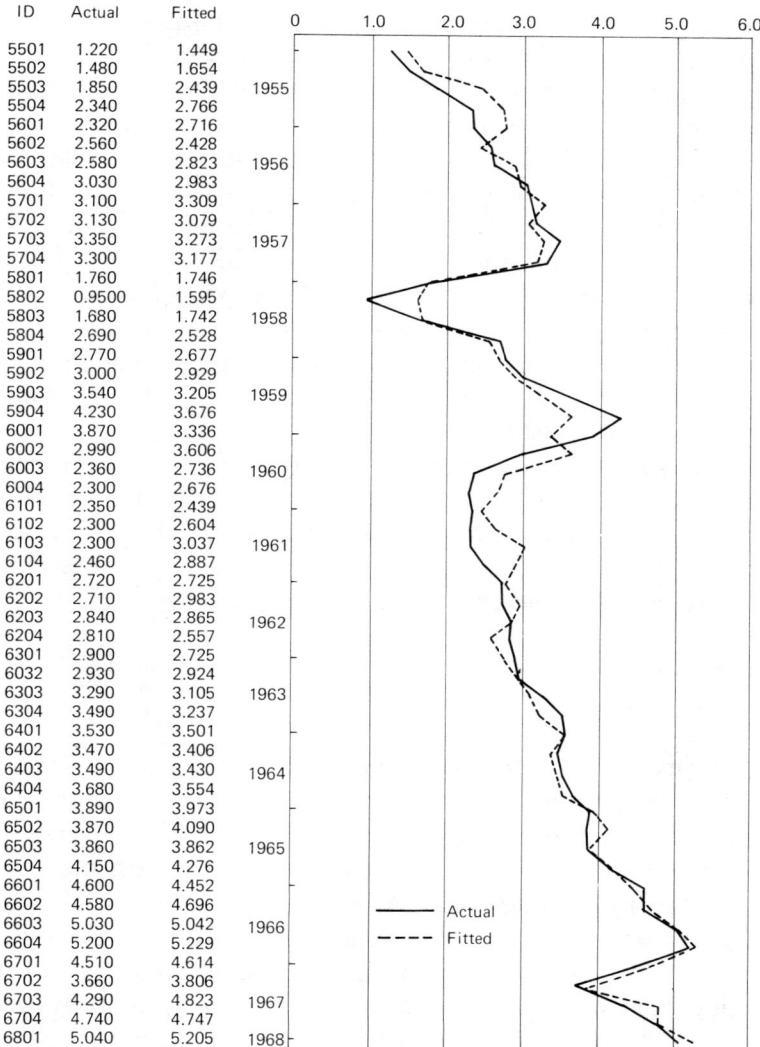

Figure 1-11. Dynamic Simulation of Treasury Bill Rate: Two-Stage Coefficients (Plot of Actual and Fitted Values).

supply are rather disappointing, since the root-mean-square error, instead of improving, grows from 0.89 to 1.01 billion. However, a comparison of Figures 1–7 and 1–10 reveals that the entire deterioration can be traced to an even larger underestimation in the troublesome period, 1958–1959. From the middle of 1960, and including the extrapolation period, the new simulation tracks better, though not by a large margin. In the case of the bill rate the improvement is more clear-cut and uniform. For the period of fit the root-mean-square error improves from 33 to 29 basis points. The spiking phenomenon is generally reduced, though this improvement seems to have been achieved at the cost of missing the extreme fluctuations registered by the actual series in 1958: II and 1959: IV. Finally, the two-stage estimate performs distinctly better in the extrapolation test. In contrast to the experience with the least square estimates the performance of every one of our variables in the extrapolation period is not appreciably different from that in the period of observation. This supports the view that the two-stage procedure provides more reliable estimates of the underlying structure.

Some Remarks on the Problem of Specifying the Exogenous Policy Variables

In our estimation, as well as in the simulation tests, we have relied on the assumption that unborrowed reserves, reserve requirements, and the discount rate can be regarded as policy variables exogenously set by the Federal Reserve and hence uncorrelated with the error terms of the structural equations. As is well known, this specification is subject to serious questions. In setting these variables the Fed can be expected to be influenced by the behavior of other variables including the money supply and the bill rate, which by our hypothesis are affected by the error term. In particular, in certain periods the Fed could have set an interest target and used open-market operations (and possibly other tools) to keep the bill rate pegged at the desired level. In this case the bill rate should be taken as exogenous for estimation purposes and unborrowed reserves (or other policy variables) as endogenous. Similarly, in such periods simulation tests treating the bill rate as endogenous lose their value.

There are grounds for holding that such a situation may have prevailed during the early 1960s when, because of balance of payment considerations, the Fed seems to have been concerned primarily with maintaining in the short run a stable or slowly rising treasury bill rate. This may explain why in this period, in Figure 1–11 as well as in Figure 1–9, the movements of the simulated value of the bill rate seem to bear little relation to the relatively minor movements that actually occurred in this variable.

Since at present we cannot tell with confidence which variables should be treated as endogenous at different times, nor do we have powerful techniques for estimating parameters when certain variables are endogenous at one time and exogenous at others, there is little we can do at the moment except be aware of possible biases, test what difference alternative specifications would make, and make proper allowances in assessing the result of simulation tests of goodness-of-fit. For purposes of policy simulation, given estimates of the coefficients, one can readily treat as exogenous the bill rate or the money supply as long as some policy variable is correspondingly endogenized.

Conclusion

In this chapter we have formulated, estimated, and tested a structural model of the money supply and short-term interest rates in the present U.S. economy. These variables are seen as resulting from the interaction of the demand for money by the public and the supply of money which reflects the behavior of the Federal Reserve setting certain policy variables, the behavior of the commercial banks in managing their assets and liabilities in response to fluctuations in their reserves and the demand for commercial loans, and the behavior of the U.S. Treasury cash balance reflecting fiscal and debt management operations. The coefficients have been estimated both by least squares and by an alternative two-stage procedure. The results provide support for our model in that the estimated coefficients, especially those derived from the two-stage experiment, are in agreement with the a priori specifications and the model accounts rather well for the behavior of the variables it purports to explain.

Needless to say, both the model and the methods of estimation and testing need refinement and improvement. Furthermore, the specifications may need to be modified in the light of institutional changes and emerging financial innovations.[36] Nonetheless, we feel that the results presented in this study are sufficiently encouraging to have justified their use in the present form as a component of the FMP model.[37]

Appendix 1A Comments on the Orr and Mellon Model

The Orr and Mellon model[38] derives the optimal credit expansion for a profit-maximizing bank facing random cash flows and a legal reserve requirement. Comparisons are drawn between the bank's response to an injection of excess reserves under conditions of uncertainty and the action indicated by traditional deposit-creation analysis. The purpose of this note is to point out three major errors in the presentation of this model—misspecification of the bank's expected profit function, consideration of only local optima, and a misleading parametric tabulation of the optimal solution.[39] No attempt is made here to update the model to hold under current reserve requirement regulations.

The reader is referred to the original article for a full discussion of the model and assumptions. For convenience, the variables are defined below:

R = the volume of excess reserves at the beginning of the evaluation period
D = the volume of new deposit liabilities created during the period via the granting of loans
L = the loss of reserves during the period
ρ = the legal reserve ratio ($0 < \rho < 1$)
i = rate of interest earned on loans
M = lump-sum penalty for violation of reserve requirements
r = penalty for each dollar of reserves which the bank is short
P = expected profit over the evaluation period
$\Phi(L)$ = probability density function of L (assumed normal with mean proportional to the level of new deposits created during the period but variance *independent* of deposit liabilities).
k = ratio of mean reserve loss to level of new deposits created.

The model is summarized as follows:

Reserve Loss

$$L = kD + \varepsilon \quad \text{with} \quad \varepsilon \sim N(0, 1) \qquad (1.44)$$

Probability
Density Function

$$\therefore \Phi(L) = N(kD, 1)$$
$$= \frac{1}{\sqrt{2\pi}} e^{-(L-kD)^2/2} \qquad (1.45)$$

Reserve
Condition

$$\text{Deficiency} = \text{reserves required} - \text{reserves held}$$
$$= \rho(D-L) - (R-L)$$
$$= (1-\rho)L - (R-\rho D)$$
$$= (1-\rho)\left(L - \frac{R-\rho D}{1-\rho}\right)$$
$$= (1-\rho)(L-v)$$

where
$$v \equiv \frac{R-\rho D}{1-\rho} \qquad (1.46)$$

v is the critical value of realized reserve losses above which a deficiency will be realized. Note that each dollar of reserve loss in excess of this critical value leads to a deficiency of only $(1-\rho)$ dollars (because of the reserves "freed up" when deposits are withdrawn).

Expected Profit Function

$$P(D) = iD - M \int_v^\infty \Phi(L)dL - r \int_v^\infty (1-\rho)(L-v)\Phi(L)dL \qquad (1.47)$$

The first term represents the interest earned on loans granted during the period; the second term is the lump-sum penalty times the probability of reserve deficiency; and the third term is variable penalty cost times the expected deficiency.

At this point, the first shortcoming of the Orr and Mellon model has been encountered. Equation (1.47) was derived logically from the assumptions of the model and is in complete agreement with the Orr and Mellon text. Their own mathematical specification of the expected profit function [eqs. 2 and 4, p. 617] differs, however, in that each dollar of reserve loss, rather than reserve deficiency, is penalized.

Expected Profit Maximization

A necessary condition for the optimality of a lending policy is that

$$\frac{\partial P}{\partial D} = 0 \tag{1.48}$$

Rewrite (1.47) as

$$P = iD - [M - rv(1-\rho)]\int_v^\infty \Phi(L)dL - r(1-\rho)\int_v^\infty L\Phi(L)dL \tag{1.49}$$

Thus

$$\frac{\partial P}{\partial D} = i - [M - rv(1-\rho)]\,\Phi(v)\left[\frac{\rho}{1-\rho} + k\right] - [1 - F(v)](r\rho)$$

$$- r(1-\rho)v\Phi(v)\left(\frac{\rho}{1-\rho}\right) - r(1-\rho)\int_v^\infty L\frac{\partial \Phi(L)}{\partial D}dL \tag{1.50}$$

where

$$F(x) \equiv \int_{-\infty}^{x} \Phi(L)\,dL \tag{1.51}$$

Integrate by parts, as follows:

$$\int_v^\infty L\frac{\partial \Phi(L)}{\partial D}dL = \int_v^\infty L\Phi(L)(L - kD)k\,dL$$

$$= k\left[-L\Phi(L)\right]_v^\infty - k\int_v^\infty -\Phi(L)\,dL$$

$$= k\{v\Phi(v) + [1 - F(v)]\} \tag{1.52}$$

and substitute in equation (1.50).

$$\therefore \frac{\partial P}{\partial D} = i - \Phi(v)\left(\frac{\rho}{1-\rho} + k\right)\{[M - rv(1-\rho)] + r(1-\rho)v\}$$

$$- [1 - F(v)][r(1-\rho)]\left(\frac{\rho}{1-\rho} + k\right) \tag{1.53}$$

$$0 = i - \left(\frac{\rho}{1-\rho} + k\right)\{M\Phi(v) + r(1-\rho)[1 - F(v)]\}$$

Equation (1.53) can be solved by numerical methods for the value of D, say $\hat{D}$. This solution is a local maximum only if

$$\frac{\partial^2 P}{\partial D^2} = -\left(\frac{\rho}{1-\rho}+k\right)^2 \Phi(\hat{v})[M(\hat{v}-k\hat{D})+r(1-\rho)] < 0 \quad (1.54)$$

where $\hat{v}$ is the value of v for $D = \hat{D}$.

The slope of the expected profit function given by (1.53) approaches a limit asymptotically for indefinitely large values of D.

$$\lim_{D\to\infty}\left(\frac{\partial P}{\partial D}\right) = i - \left(\frac{\rho}{1-\rho}+k\right)[r(1-\rho)]$$
$$= i - [\rho + k(1-\rho)]r$$

Asymptotically, \$1 in credit expansions earns i. It will also increase the already certain deficiency by requiring \$$\rho$ more in reserves and by producing additional reserve losses of \$$k$ or an extra reserve shortage of \$$(1-\rho)k$; this deficiency of \$$[(1-\rho)k+\rho]$ incurs a penalty of r. If

$$\lim_{D\to\infty}\left(\frac{\partial P}{\partial D}\right) > 0$$

then one should recognize that, even if the solution of (1.53) is a local maximum, it will not be the global maximum.[40]

While the infinite solution may not be realistic, the model must be modified to preclude it, say by maximizing expected profits subject to an upper-bound constraint on the probability of deficiency. If we define the probability of deficiency,

$$\alpha \equiv \int_v^\infty \Phi(L)\, dL = 1 - F(v) \quad (1.56)$$

we can see that

$$\frac{\partial \alpha}{\partial D} = \Phi(v)\left(\frac{\rho}{1-\rho}+k\right) > 0 \quad (1.57)$$

(1.57) implies that we can find P as a function of α because of the strictly monotonic relationship between α and D. Figure 1–12 indicates what this function may look like for the case of $i > [\rho + k(1-\rho)]r$. $P(\alpha)$ and $P(D)$ will have the same basic shape except for the change in scale of the abscissa. The heavier shaded portions of $P(\alpha)$ represent an opportunity locus of combinations of risk (probability of deficiency) and expected profit from which a rational bank would choose.[41] $\alpha(\hat{D})$ is the risk level associated with the local profit-maximizing level of D. The right-hand segment of this profit-risk locus generally occurred only for very high values of D and α in the many cases tabulated in preparing this Appendix; since, at this point, many of the assumptions of the model become especially strained (e.g. r, i, and variance of L all independent of D) this variation will not be pressed further except to note that any upper bound on α falling between the two segments of the profit-risk opportunity locus is sufficient to re-establish $\hat{D}$ as a valid optimal solution.

The derivation of the value $\alpha(\hat{D})$ in the context of the Orr and Mellon model is extremely useful from another point of view. In particular, it sheds light on whether or not the authors' tabulation of optimal values of D has any validity. Table 1-7 is an expansion of

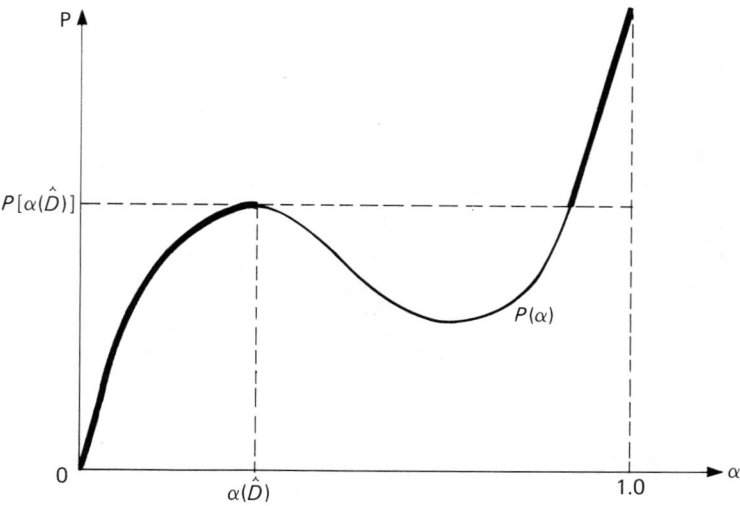

Figure 1-12. Profit-Risk Opportunity Locus.

TABLE 1–7 Optimal Values of D under Uncertainty Compared with Traditional Values

Case	M	r	i	k	R	D_{err}	D_{cor}	α	D^*	D_{mod}	α
1	20	.01	.0025	.7	10	8.9	8.9	.0000	13.2	8.9	.0000
2	20	.01	.0025	.7	1000	1311.	1311.	.0000	1316.	1312.[a]	.0000
3	0	.01	.0025	.7	10	10.5	10.7	.0097	13.2	12.7	.3289
4	20	.01	.0025	.3	10	15.7	15.7	.0001	22.8	15.7	.0001
5	20	.5	.0025	.7	10	8.9	8.9	.0000	13.2	8.9	.0000
7	20	.01	.0025	0	10	35.4	∞	1.0000	50.0	∞	1.0000

[a] In case 2, $D_{mod} - D_{cor} = 0.1$ which produces a change in the fourth significant digit.

its counterpart in the original article [p. 619]. The case numbers and parameter values are theirs;[42] case 6 is irrelevant because of the differentiation error noted earlier (see note 39); ρ equals 0.2 for all cases.

Proceeding, from left to right in Table 1–7, the following additional definitions are necessary:

D_{err} = original Orr and Mellon solution
D_{cor} = solution to Orr and Mellon objective function, differentiation corrected[43]
D^* = deterministic solution[44]
D_{mod} = solution to objective function of equation (1.47), i.e., $\hat{D}$.

The value of D^* is calculated by suppressing the stochastic disturbance ε in (1.44), that is, by assuming

$$L = kD \tag{1.44a}$$

and by finding the value of L that would just exhaust the initial excess reserves, R; that is,

$$L = v \tag{1.58}$$

(1.58) and (1.44a) together give

$$D^* = \frac{\dfrac{R}{1-\rho}}{\left(\dfrac{\rho}{1-\rho}+k\right)} \qquad (1.59)$$

The following points are noteworthy. First, with the exception of the infinite solution in case 7, $D_{err} \approx D_{cor}$. Second, the values of α, not calculated by Orr and Mellon, are all ridiculously low for the finite solutions. Third, even with the objective function presented here, D_{mod} differs significantly from D_{cor} in only one case, the third. Not coincidentally, this is the only finite solution to exhibit a nontrivial probability of ever being deficient. The specific characteristic of this case is the zero lump-sum penalty cost.

The problem here, the third of the major errors, is that the value chosen for one of the parameters is inappropriate for the assumptions of the model. When the variance of reserve losses is set at unity, the system is no longer scale free. Taking M to have a value of 20 turns out to be equivalent to imposing an indefinitely large lump-sum penalty on the realization of a deficiency. One ramification of this large fine was the surprising result that neither mathematical error nor misspecification produced any change in the finite optimal solutions. Table 1–8 is presented to show the sensitivity of $\hat{D}$ and α to M.

It can be observed that if we begin with the Orr and Mellon case 3, and increase M from 0.0 to 0.1 to 1.0, the value of $\hat{D}$ drops from 12.7 to 10.7 to 9.8, and the probability of deficiency from 0.33 to 0.01 to 0.001. A second point is that the sensitivity of $\hat{D}$ to other parameters falls quickly, the larger is M. Finally, the Orr and Mellon conclusion that uncertainty must lower the expansion multiplier is shown to be wrong by the marked (a) counter examples. With the aid of the second-order conditions for a local maximum, it is easy to see analytically why one may be led numerically to this false conclusion. Rewrite (1.54) as

$$\hat{D} < \frac{\dfrac{R}{1-\rho}+\dfrac{r(1-\rho)}{M}}{\left(\dfrac{\rho}{1-\rho}+k\right)} \quad \text{or} \quad \hat{D} < D^* + \frac{r(1-\rho)}{M\left(\dfrac{\rho}{1-\rho}+k\right)} \qquad (1.60)$$

TABLE 1-8 Sensitivity of $\hat{D}$ and α to Changes in M and Other Parameters

r	M	ρ	$\hat{D}$	α	P
.01	0.0	.1	13.20	.342	.0309
		.2	12.69	.329	.0300
	0.1	.1	10.89	.011	.0261
		.2	10.69	.010	.0257
	1.0	.1	9.85	.001	.0237
		.2	9.82	.001	.0238
005	0.0	.1	14.29 [a]	.685	.0326
		.2	13.59 [a]	.658	.0314
	0.1	.1	10.90	.012	.0261
		.2	10.70	.010	.0258

[a] Expansion here is greater than under certainty.
$i = 0.0025$, $k = 0.7$, and $R = 10$.

If M is so large that it dominates the values of other parameters, then we have approximately

$$\hat{D} < D^* \tag{1.61}$$

If on the other hand small values of M are considered, it is apparent that $\hat{D}$ can exceed D^*.[45]

Orr and Mellon were misled by a poor experimental design. It is obvious that one cannot examine a grid of all combinations of possible levels of parameters; nevertheless, it is imperative that key factors be isolated and examined. To demonstrate that the solution for $\hat{D}$ is still inadequately explored, Table 1–9 is presented. Here the initial excess reserves, R, are set at 1.0 (the variability of reserve losses). Not surprisingly, there are many cases which require a cutback, rather than expansion, to maximize expected profits.

TABLE 1-9 Sensitivity of $\hat{D}$ to Parameters when $R = 1.0$

r	M	ρ	$\hat{D}$	α	P
.01	0.0	.1	0.869	.342	.0001
		.2	0.850	.329	.0004
	0.1	.1	−1.433	.011	−.0048
		.2	−1.152	.010	−.0039
	1.0	.1	−2.48	.001	−.0071
		.2	−2.02	.001	−.0058
.005	0.0	.1	1.964	.685	.0018
		.2	1.744	.658	.0018
	0.1	.1	−1.429	.012	−.0048
		.2	−1.145	.010	−.0039

$i = 0.0025$, $k = 0.7$, and $R = 1.0$.

Appendix 1B Gauss-Seidel Solution Method: Convergence and Damping Factors

The Gauss-Seidel method is frequently used to solve a set of simultaneous equations. Assume, for example, the linear model:

$$Y = BY + CX + U \quad (1.62)$$

where

B = the $m \times m$ matrix of endogenous variable right-hand-side coefficients
C = the $m \times l$ matrix of predetermined variable coefficients
Y = the $m \times T$ matrix of m endogenous variables
X = the $l \times T$ matrix of l predetermined variables
U = the $m \times T$ matrix of stochastic disturbances
T = the number of observations

The form in which the model is written implies that each of the m equations can be normalized on a different endogenous variable;

that is, that the principal diagonal of B is zero. The Gauss-Seidel method attempts to find a solution, for *each* time period, to the system:

$$y_t = By_t + z_t \qquad (1.63)$$

where
y_t = one column of Y
z_t = one column of $(CX + U)$

In doing so, it takes (1.63), which is a relationship among contemporaneous endogenous variables and a predetermined set of numbers (the z vector), and transforms the system into a set of first-order simultaneous difference equations in applying its iterative method of solution.

This note examines that feature of the method and describes when, if ever, the selection and implementation of a damping factor will lead to convergence even when a solution does in fact exist.

Since we are talking about the solution in a particular time period, it will be convenient to drop the *time* subscript; the system then becomes:

$$y = By + z \qquad (1.64)$$

Henceforth, subscript notation will be used to represent instead the value of an endogenous variable at a particular *iteration*. The Gauss-Seidel method assumes an initial guess at the solution to (1.64), say y_0. This guess is plugged into the right-hand side of (1.64) to evaluate the next iteration value of y, or y_1; y_1 is then used to calculate y_2, etc. The distinguishing characteristic of the Gauss-Seidel method is that, in moving through the system of equations (1.64), the new elements of y that are calculated on the left-hand side replace past iteration values in the y vector on the right-hand side of all equations "lower" in the set. The iteration values of y are, thus, updated one element at a time, not as a complete vector. This can be formally stated in the following system, which defines the $(i+1)$th iteration values in terms of the ith:

$$\begin{aligned}
y_{1,i+1} &= 0 + b_{12}y_{2,i} + b_{13}y_{3,i} + \cdots + b_{1m}y_{m,i} + z_1 \\
y_{2,i+1} &= b_{21}y_{1,i+1} + 0 + b_{23}y_{3,i} + \cdots + b_{2m}y_{m,i} + z_2 \\
&\vdots \\
y_{m,i+1} &= b_{m1}y_{1,i+1} + b_{m2}y_{2,i+1} + b_{m3}y_{3,i+1} + \cdots + 0 + z_m
\end{aligned} \qquad (1.65)$$

The b_{jk} represents the (j,k)th element of B. Note that the most recently evaluated value of each element of y is used in calculating the new iteration values.

It is convenient to rewrite (1.65) as a standard first-order simultaneous difference equation system. Substitute for the $(i+1)$th iteration values wherever possible on the right-hand side of (1.65). We then arrive at:

$$y_{1,i+1} = 0 + a_{12}y_{2,i} + a_{13}y_{3,i} + \cdots + a_{1m}y_{m,i} + z_1^*$$
$$y_{2,i+1} = 0 + a_{22}y_{2,i} + a_{23}y_{3,i} + \cdots + a_{2m}y_{m,i} + z_2^*$$
$$\vdots \qquad \vdots \qquad \vdots \qquad \vdots \qquad (1.66)$$
$$y_{m,i+1} = 0 + a_{m2}y_{2,i} + a_{m3}y_{3,i} + \cdots + a_{mm}y_{m,i} + z_m^*$$

where the a_{kj} are easily derived from the b_{kj}.
For example,

$$a_{12} = b_{12}, \quad a_{13} = b_{13}, \quad a_{1m} = b_{1m},$$
$$a_{22} = b_{21}b_{12},$$
$$a_{23} = b_{21}b_{13} + b_{23}, \quad \text{etc.}$$

Similarly, z_k^* can be derived from the z_k and b_{kj}.

Letting A represent the matrix $\{a_{kj}\}$, (1.66) can be summarized as

$$y_{i+1} = Ay_i + z^* \qquad (1.67)$$

Iteration continues in the Gauss-Seidel method until y_{i+1} differs, element by element, from y_i by less in absolute value than some specified (small) amount. The search for a solution, then, involves not only finding the ultimate solution to the difference-equation system (1.67) but also determining whether or not the method leads us to it; that is, we want the "particular solution" to (1.67) but must also investigate the "stability" of this system. It is most important to note that this latter question has nothing to do with the dynamic properties of the original system (1.62).

The characteristic equation of the homogeneous part of (1.67) is

$$|A - sI| = 0 \tag{1.68}$$

where s is a characteristic root of the matrix A. If the largest of the moduli of the m roots is less than unity, the iterative method converges to the particular solution:

$$\bar{y} = (I - A)^{-1} z^* \tag{1.69}$$

Should any of the moduli of the roots exceed unity, then there will be divergence.

Consider now the entrance of a damping factor, λ, into the system where $0 < \lambda < 1$. The process is now defined as follows: feed y_i into system at iteration $(i+1)$ and output a set of values y_{i+1}; if convergence tests are not passed, replace y_{i+1} with a weighted average of current and last iteration values, i.e., $\lambda y_{i+1} + (1-\lambda) y_i$; repeat for iteration $(i+2)$. Algebraically, this can be represented as:

$$y_{i+1} = (\lambda)[A y_i + z^*] + (1 - \lambda)[y_i]$$

or

$$y_{i+1} = [(\lambda)A + (1-\lambda)I] y_i + \lambda z^* \tag{1.70}$$

The particular solution to this new system is

$$\bar{y} = [I - (\lambda)A - (1-\lambda)I]^{-1} \lambda z^*$$
$$= (I - A)^{-1} z^*$$

as before, in (1.69). The characteristic equation of the new system is

$$|[(\lambda)A + (1-\lambda)I] - rI| = 0 \tag{1.71}$$

or

$$\left| A - \frac{(r + \lambda - 1)}{\lambda} I = 0 \right| \tag{1.72}$$

where r is a characteristic root of the damped system. Comparing

(1.72) with (1.68),

$$s = \frac{r+\lambda-1}{\lambda}$$

or

$$r = \lambda s + (1-\lambda) \tag{1.73}$$

Consider here only one of the unstable cases, the one in which the dominant root, s, with the largest modulus, is real, negative, and greater than unity in absolute value. This corresponds to what seems the most troublesome and most frequently encountered of the cases in which divergence occurs. In a two-variable model, representing a normal supply and demand relationship, this is the case of the explosive oscillatory cobweb model.

To find the solution with the iterative method, we require that:

$$r > -1 \tag{1.74}$$

Combining (1.74) and (1.73) to find the maximum damping factor λ permissible,

$$\lambda < \frac{2}{1-s} < 1 \tag{1.75}$$

A minimum acceptable damping factor is the one which sets the new characteristic root to zero, or

$$\lambda > \frac{1}{1-s} \tag{1.76}$$

Combining (1.75) and (1.76), reasonable limits on λ are:

$$0 < \frac{1}{1-s} < \lambda < \frac{2}{1-s} < 1 \tag{1.77}$$

Within this range, there is an optimal damping factor which minimizes the modulus of the dominant root; this is the value of λ at which the modified s ceases to be dominant or, in some cases, where the modulus of a dominant complex root has a minimum with respect to λ.

Figure 1–13 demonstrates the effect of damping on real roots.

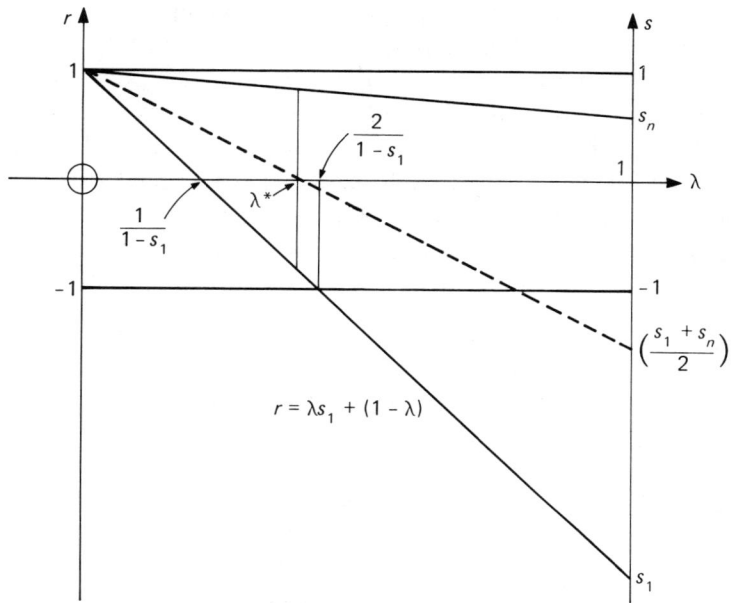

Figure 1-13. Effect of Damping on Real Roots.

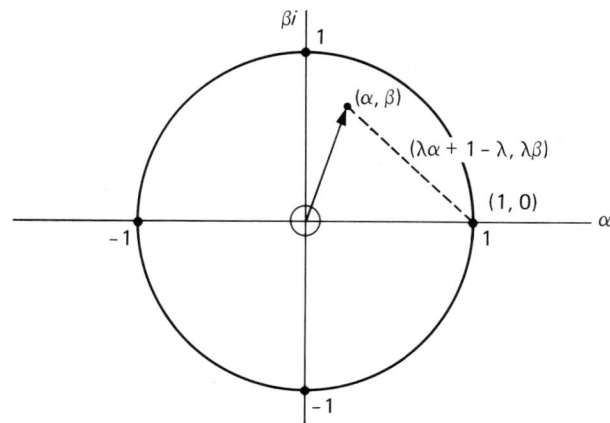

Figure 1-14. Effect of Damping on Complex Roots.

85

The root s_1 on the right-hand vertical line is mapped by damping into the root r according to the value of λ measured horizontally. The diagonal line joining s_1 on the s axis to the point equalling unity on the r axis is the graph of equation (1.73). Assume the real roots are numbered from 1 to n in ascending order of algebraic magnitude. Figure 1–13, therefore, depicts a special case of the earlier example: the dominant root is less than -1, but in addition, there are no positive roots greater than $+1$. The special values of λ, i.e.,

$$\frac{2}{1-s_1} \quad \text{and} \quad \frac{1}{1-s_1}$$

discussed earlier are marked. The optimal value of λ is

$$\lambda^* = \frac{1}{1-\left(\dfrac{s_1+s_n}{2}\right)}$$

where any change in λ leads to a switch in the root that is dominant after damping.

Figure 1–14 illustrates in the complex plane what would happen to a nondominant complex root $\alpha+\beta i$. It is evident that again the modulus of the original root is mapped by damping into unity as λ approaches zero. Note that, here, the modulus may decrease in size before increasing to unity.

Of course, if there are other roots whose moduli exceed unity, then a satisfactory damping factor may not exist. If, for example, a real root greater than one also existed, a negative λ would be required which would be unacceptable in damping the effects of the (first) negative root. That such another root should not exist may be too much to hope for.

Consider the following simple example:

Supply $p_t = a_t + bq_t$ $b > 0$
Demand $q_t = c_t + dp_t$ $d < 0$

The Gauss-Seidel interpretation is:

$$p_{i+1} = a + bq_i$$
$$q_{i+1} = c + dp_{i+1} = (c+da) + (db)q_i$$

This system converges if $|db|<1$; note also that $db<0$. The characteristic roots of the Gauss-Seidel system are 0 and db.

Reservering the order of the equations changes none of the above results,[46] since.

Demand $\qquad q_t = c_t + dp_t \qquad d < 0$

Supply $\qquad p_t = a_t + bq_t \qquad b > 0$

leading to:

$$q_{i+1} = c + dp_i$$
$$p_{i+1} = a + bq_{i+1} = (a+bc) + (bd)p_i$$

If, on the other hand, we renormalize the system, then

Supply $\qquad q_t = -\frac{1}{b} a_t + \frac{1}{b} p_t \qquad b > 0$

Demand $\qquad p_t = -\frac{1}{d} c_t + \frac{1}{d} q_t \qquad d < 0$

leading to:

$$q_{i+1} = -\frac{a}{b} + \frac{1}{b} p_i$$

$$p_{i+1} = -\frac{c}{d} + \frac{1}{d} q_{i+1} = \left(-\frac{c}{d} - \frac{a}{bd}\right) + \left(\frac{1}{db}\right) p_i$$

Now, for convergence we require

$$\left|\frac{1}{db}\right| < 1 \quad \text{or} \quad |db| > 1,$$

the opposite of the previous conditions. If this were the divergent normalization, we could simply apply a damping factor of λ where

$$\frac{1}{1-\frac{1}{db}} < \lambda < \frac{2}{1-\frac{1}{db}}$$

The possibility of a rather narrow range for λ suggests starting with a high value and lowering it until convergence is obtained.

We conclude, however, that the use of damping to produce convergence in the Gauss-Seidel method is not guaranteed, although usually useful.[47] This latter conclusion might only apply to simpler and smaller models in a supply-demand format; in a larger linear model, with both negative and positive real roots exceeding unity in absolute value (or perhaps a "divergent" negative root combined with a "divergent" complex pair), a simple damping scheme will not produce convergence. Experimentation by the author with various second-order damping schemes (where y_{i+1} is replaced by a weighted average of current, last, and second-last iteration values) has not yet proven useful. It is most difficult to generalize about large nonlinear models, where the system (1.63) is only a local linear approximation, which changes from one iteration to the next; here, it becomes computationally very difficult to say anything about characteristic roots. Nevertheless, the rapidly expanding successful usage of this method on such models seems to suggest that we have, at least until something better comes along, a valuable tool for working with econometric models.

Notes

[1] For example, see Meigs [53], Orr and Mellon [64], Goldfeld [38], Goldfeld and Kane [39], Hester and Pierce [41], and DeLeeuw [25].
[2] A comment on the Orr and Mellon model is contained in Appendix 1A of this chapter.
[3] The changes (September 1968) in the method of calculating required reserves alter the form of this decision problem somewhat. More important, though, the method of arriving at an aggregate money supply requires some modification to accommodate the new system.
[4] The validity of this conclusion depends on the tacit assumption that the bank we are dealing with is but a small component of the banking system, and that therefore it will not anticipate that the acquisition or sale of assets will significantly affect its own deposits. It might not be a good approximation for a heavily concentrated banking system such as exists in other countries. And even in the U.S., it may not hold in special cases, such as certain acquisitions of newly issued government securities.

⁵ For expository convenience, we assume that i is independent of the size of portfolio I, i.e., that the average and marginal rate of return coincide. Dropping this assumption would not affect any conclusion, except that in (1.8) and later equations i should be interpreted as the marginal rate of return of funds allocated to I.

⁶ An anonymous econometrician suggested that the term "sector exogenous" be coined for use in such a situation—meaning, exogenous to the sector. He then went on the lobby for the obvious abbreviation "sexogenous."

⁷ This conclusion is at first sight surprising, for given RU and bank assets, an increase in T can only come from a shift from demand deposits into time deposits and such a shift releases reserves by an amount $(\delta - \tau) \Delta T$. But this inference is valid only if the shift is totally unanticipated and there is no response to forecast errors, i.e., if $n_D = n_T = 0$. Indeed, it can be verified that under these conditions the coefficient of ΔT in (1.18) is precisely $(\delta - \tau)$. When the shift is at least partially anticipated and/or errors corrected, the situation is more complex because assets do respond to the shift. The outcome depends then on the comparative responsiveness of I to changes in T and D. Specifically, from the definition of n_T^*, we can infer that

$$n_T^* \gtreqless 0 \quad \text{as} \quad \frac{1-n_T}{1-n_D} \gtreqless \frac{\tau(1-\delta)}{\delta(1-\tau)} \approx \frac{\tau}{\delta}$$

⁸ The main difficulty is that $\widehat{FR}$ and r are not directly observable. The first problem can be easily handled by substituting for $\widehat{FR}$ in (1.18) from equation (1.11a). The variable r poses a more serious difficulty; for the more recent years, it could be measured by the observed Federal Funds rate, but even this approach breaks down for earlier years when prevailing conventions prevented banks from ever bidding the Federal Funds rate above the discount rate. We instead will use (1.17) to "solve r out."

⁹ The system (1.11a), (1.17), and (1.18) can be reduced by substitution to

$$FR - \mu F(i, R[d, FR]) - Q = 0$$

By implicit differentiation, we find:

$$a_3 \approx \frac{\partial FR}{\partial Q} = \frac{1}{1 - \mu F_r R_{FR}}$$

$$a_1 \approx \frac{\partial FR}{\partial i} = \mu F_i \left(\frac{\partial FR}{\partial Q}\right) = \mu F_i a_3$$

$$a_2 \approx \frac{\partial FR}{\partial d} = \mu F_r R_d \left(\frac{\partial FR}{\partial Q}\right) = \mu F_r R_d a_3$$

Therefore

$$0 < \frac{\partial FR}{\partial Q} < 1, \quad \frac{\partial FR}{\partial i} < 0, \quad \frac{\partial FR}{\partial d} > 0, \quad \text{and} \quad \left|\frac{\partial FR}{\partial i}\right| > \left|\frac{\partial FR}{\partial d}\right|$$

It is sufficient for the last inequality that $-F_r \approx F_i \approx f'$ and that R_d does not exceed unity, a condition which seems likely to hold, as shown in section 1.2.

10 This reference seems reasonable, at least in the case of a positive spread; it is conceivable, however, that on the negative side, the nonlinearity may become pronounced well before a spread of 100 points is reached. However, since there have been very few occasions in which d has persistently exceeded i by more than 50 basis points, it is very hard to detect the nonlinearity empirically.

11 Using the results of note 9, we deduce

$$A_1' = \frac{a_1}{1 - a_3(1-\mu)} \approx \frac{F_i}{1 - F_r R_{FR}}$$

$$A_2' = \frac{a_2}{1 - a_3(1-\mu)} \approx \frac{F_r R_d}{1 - F_r R_{FR}}$$

It can be verified that these two expressions in turn are the partial derivatives of $\partial \widehat{FR}/\partial i$ and $\partial \widehat{FR}/\partial d$ obtained by total differentiation of the system (1.11a), (1.17), and (1.18) for the case where $FR = FR_{-1}$ and all components of Q other than FR_{-1} are zero, so that (1.18) reduces to $FR = \widehat{FR}$.

12 One might also be inclined to think that C should be smaller than B_1 on the ground that there should be a larger response to an initial condition such as $FR(t-1)$ than to a variable changing within the period, such as RU. This relation, however, need not hold if n_D were sufficiently larger than n_F. This can be verified by considering the limiting case $n_D = 1$, $0 < n_F < 1$. We then find $B_1 = 0 < C = [\mu_3(1 - n_F)]^m$.

[13] Note that dependence of B_j on δ is entirely due to the factor C'/δ since the remaining factor

$$\frac{\mu a_3}{n_F m[1 - a_3(1-\mu)]}$$

can be shown to be independent of μ (and hence of δ) along the lines of note 11. Now both numerator and denominator of the former factor increase with δ and therefore B_j should be relatively insensitive to variations in δ. Since the coefficients A_1 and A_2 are also functions of C' but do not contain the δ in the denominator, we might have scaled $i(t)$ and $d(t)$ in (1.23) by δ. This has indeed been tested in our attempt to find the most stable form of the coefficients, but it made very little empirical difference.

[14] The current time index, t, is now understood.

[15] One can establish that, given the prevailing values of δ and τ over the period of observation, our model would be consistent with a coefficient of the time deposit variable at least as low as -0.3, as compared with the estimated value of 0.03.

[16] The Durbin-Watson statistic in this situation is, of course, little help in detecting the presence of serial correlation. We report it in Table 1–2 for the sake of completeness; although a value close to 2 would not indicate the absence of serial correlation, an extremely low value would have provided affirmative evidence of the existence of positive serial correlation in the residuals.

[17] See Friedman [31].

[18] See Latane [49, 50].

[19] Another study which distinguished short-run and long-run demand for money is Chow [16]. This study, however, involves quite different assumptions about the origin of the demand for money.

[20] See also Laidler [48] for evidence on the effect of interest rates within the framework of the Friedman model.

[21] See Modigliani and Sutch [58].

[22] The difference in specifications would seem to become important only when rates of change of income are subject to wide fluctuations in time, i.e., essentially in the case of hyperinflation. In such situations, the more complex specification of Allais has obvious merits while his neglect of interest rates on money fixed assets becomes totally unimportant.

[23] In order to allow a larger range of variation for the variable and

thus increase the efficiency of the test, the period of fit was extended back to the beginning of 1950. The remaining coefficients are affected only moderately, tending to closer agreement with those of row 2 (Table 1–3).

24 Rewrite (1.37) as (1.37a),

$$M^* = K(i)(aY + bW) = K(i)\left(a + b\frac{W}{Y}\right)Y \qquad (1.37a)$$

If W/Y is a constant, (1.37a) is indistinguishable from (1.37).

25 This series was obtained from SEC data.

26 Before 1962 this variable was assigned a value of zero.

27 The gradual adjustment model has the somewhat uncomfortable implication that a one-time change in the money supply, with income constant, would initially be accommodated by an overshooting of the short-term rate to a level below the long-run equilibrium value (1.37). This feature would be attenuated if the initial fall in the rate induces a temporary increase in money holdings, as implied by a negative coefficient for the rate of change of i.

28 We have added to (1.42a) the real-income variable despite its negligible contribution, because this variable appears elsewhere in the complete model and because we wished to retest its significance using the statistical methods of Section 1.4.

29 In addition, the current definition of demand deposits adjusted includes foreign bank balances held at Federal Reserve banks. The behavior of these balances, as well as foreign-owned balances at commercial banks, is presumably sensitive to developments in both foreign and U.S. capital markets. Unfortunately, this introduces a measurement error into the concept for balances demanded. It also adds another residual factor in the demand-supply identity.

30 In the context of the larger FMP model we have endogenized this variable. Its behavior over the sample period can be accurately replicated by seasonal variables and a secular trend.

31 It should be noted that these are exact or deterministic simulations. The stochastic disturbance terms of the estimated specifications have been set identically equal to zero. A description of the solution technique is presented in Appendix 1B.

32 Indeed, if we denote by $U(Md)$ and $U(FR)$ the simulation error in Md and in FR, respectively, in a given quarter, then from Table 1–5 one can infer that:

$$U(Md) \equiv -\left(\frac{Js\lambda}{\delta}\right) \cdot U(FR);$$

also the quantity $Js\lambda/\delta$ has tended to remain reasonably stable in the short run, averaging around 7.5, though exhibiting a mildly rising trend.

[33] The standard two-stage least squares technique (TSLS) uses a first-stage estimation of the reduced form to obtain instrumental variables. This procedure breaks down in our case since (i) a large number of variables are required in the first-stage estimation when the errors of the structural equations are serially correlated and (ii) we expect substantial variation of the reduced-form coefficients over time arising from the nonlinearities in the structural specifications. Our procedure here is really not an application of instrumental variable estimation per se, but an ad hoc two-stage estimator in the spirit of TSLS.

[34] This method is similar to the class of estimators discussed by Klein [46, pp. 66–70]. It differs in that Klein assumes that the simulation is performed using structural coefficients which were obtained from a consistent estimation procedure such as TSLS. In this nonlinear case, our procedure is subject to the same uncertainties regarding consistency as the methods which Klein discusses. In addition, the method is unlikely to be consistent because there is a high probability that the simulation errors (the actual value of the endogenous variable—solution value) will be correlated with the exogenous variables. This latter problem arises only since we are using a two-stage least squares computational design rather than the more general instrumental variable framework.

As this manuscript was undergoing a final draft, the author became aware of the recent work by Brundy and Jorgenson [14] and Dutta and Lyttkens [29] on estimators of this type, but having superior asymptotic properties.

[35] Equation (1.42a) was estimated normalized on the bill rate, i. Errors in variables considerations led to making the variable with the larger relative error variance the dependent variable.

[36] In particular, work will continue on further tests for the effects on both the demand and supply specifications of the emergence of the CD market and of changes in the method of computing required reserves. Eventually, we shall have to consider what effects the activity in the Eurodollar market in 1969 had on our structure.

37 That is, version 4.1.

38 Orr and Mellon [64].

39 The original article also contained a differentiation error, subsequently corrected by the authors in "Errata," *American Economic Review*, September 1963. Because of the last two shortcomings mentioned in the text, the authors were unable to see any significant change in the corrected optimal solutions.

40 The corresponding limit in the original article was $i-r$; with the differentiation corrected, the limit was $i-kr$. The contradiction raised between these mathematical results and intuition led to this comment. Note also that

$$\lim_{D \to -\infty} \frac{\partial P}{\partial D} = i > 0$$

Infinite contraction is never profitable.

41 We could also constrain the expected reserve deficiency. In this simple model, the two constraints have a one-to-one correspondence. The one in the text can be represented as

$$\alpha = 1 - \Psi(v - kD) < \beta$$

where Ψ is the distribution function of a standard normal deviate and β is the maximum acceptable risk of deficiency. The alternative can be represented as:

$$\text{expected deficiency} = (1 - \rho)(kD - v) < \gamma$$

where γ is the maximum acceptable deficiency in dollars. Both imply constraints on $(v - kD)$ which is monotonic in D.

43 The relationship of r to i is puzzling; Orr and Mellon offer no explanation.

43 The authors did not recognize the impact of their correction on the solution for case 7.

44 In case 7, D^* was incorrectly calculated at 40. in the original article. This number was also used in their text [p. 621]. The "Errata," ibid., noted this error.

45 It can be shown further that $\hat{D} < D^*$ if, and only if, $\alpha < 0.5$. This conclusion is independent of R essentially because α is not a function of R, but of the parameters i, ρ, k, M, and r only. For

example, the α columns in Tables 1–8 and 1–9 in the text are identical, although R changes from 10.0 to 1.0.

[46] This is the true only for the two variable model. Cf. Fromm and Klein [35, pp. 380–382]. This appendix was prepared independently of the discussion just cited. The similarity is only in the example used and not in content.

[47] When a model's specification is basically nailed down, very few insoluble problems of convergence are encountered. In particular, damping solved all simulation difficulties for the studies of Chapters 2–4. In the model of section 1.4, we occasionally had to renormalize an equation.

2 Ex Post and Ex Ante Predictive Performance

2.1 One-Quarter-Ahead Sample-Period Predictive Performance and Comparison with Time Series Models

In this chapter, we evaluate the predictive performance of the FMP model; we confine our investigation to one-quarter-ahead extrapolations. Some of the forecasts are ex post or conditioned upon the actual historical values of exogenous variables. The others are ex ante, in that we have provided a mechanism for generating forecasts of key exogenous variables and then conditioning our endogenous-variable forecasts upon these, rather than on historical values.[1] The performance of the FMP model is measured both over the estimation sample period of the model, taken as 1956: I through 1966: IV, and also over a post-sample period, 1967: I through 1968: IV.

Some discussion is in order of our usage of the phrase "ex ante." In particular, this usage is not to be confused with another connotation which implies the making of subjective judgments about exogenous variables or even particular parameters and then solving the model given these judgments. This, too, is ex ante forecasting, but it is not what we have done. We wished to avoid this interaction between the forecaster and his model, the subjective setting of "fudge factors." There is no doubt that there are economists who are very adept at this; however, we are never sure that their forecasts of exogenous variables are good for their own sake or because "they make the model come out right." We have set out to measure a characteristic of the model and not of the human who uses it.

Given that an objective, accurate standard for extrapolating exogenous variables can be found—we present our candidate below—ex ante forecasting of the type we propose provides useful infor-

---

This Chapter is based on joint work with Charles R. Nelson: see Cooper and Nelson [23].

mation. It is widely agreed that the prediction performance of a model conditioned on historical values of exogenous variables is one important indicator of the validity of the model. It must also be the case that the type of exogenous variables in the model, our ability to extrapolate them, and the sensitivity of the endogenous variables of the model to them must be another indicator. If the secret of the universe were discovered and we were given the true structural model of the economy complete with five-digit parameter values, and this model contained only one exogenous variable, the change in the New York Stock Exchange stock price average, how much further would forecasters be ahead?

One sensible procedure for projection of exogenous variables would be the exploitation of information contained in the past history of each exogenous variable for extrapolation into the future. The method of extracting such information used in this chapter is the modeling of the exogenous variables as discrete, linear stochastic processes taking advantage of the characteristic autocorrelation properties of economic time series. The implied extrapolative predictions are free of the ambiguities that would result from judgmental procedures; though naive from an economic standpoint, these models are statistically sophisticated. The predictions of the same class of time-series models for the endogenous variables also serve as rather high standards of accuracy for comparison with our econometric model forecasts. These time-series models dominate simpler standards that are commonly used including "no change," "equal change," first-order autoregressive, etc. The time series models then provide a relatively objective basis both for computing ex ante predictions and also for evaluating ex post and ex ante predictions of the FMP model.

Examination of the correlation between errors made by the FMP and time-series model predictions indicates overlap in the information which they contain. In order to evaluate the marginal contribution of each predictor we combine them, in section 2.2, into linear composites choosing weights to minimize squared error. Some implications of this procedure for optimal control settings of policy variables are explored in section 2.3. Finally, post-sample predictions are evaluated in section 2.4. The remainder of this section introduces the time series models and presents various statistical tests of the FMP and time series predictions over the FMP model's sample period.

The time-series models were selected from the general class of discrete, linear stochastic processes of integrated autoregressive moving average (ARIMA) form, made popular among economists by Box and Jenkins. Thus if z_t denotes the observation on series z in time t, and B denotes the backshift operator (i.e., $B^k z_t = z_{t-k}$) then the processes belonging to this class may be expressed by

$$\phi_p(B)(1-B)^d z_t = \theta_q(B) u_t + \theta_0 \qquad (2.1)$$

where $\phi_p(B)$ and $\theta_q(B)$ are polynomials in B of degrees p and q, respectively, having zeros outside the unit circle; θ_0 is a constant; and the u_t's are a sequence of independently and identically distributed random disturbances which drive the process. Thus the dth difference of the series is by hypothesis a stationary autoregression with a moving average disturbance. Empirical implementation of the models focuses on use of the sample correlogram as an aid in specification of p, d, and q. Parameters of the model are fitted by iterative minimization of the sum of squared residuals, $\sum \hat{u}_t^2$, which leads to maximum likelihood estimates if the u_t's are normal.[2] The general methodology is developed in detail by Box and Jenkins [10] and outlined by Nelson [62]. Given the fitted model, predictions are computed by evaluation of the expectation of a future observation conditional on past observations. The predictions furnished by the time-series models utilize, then, only information from the past history of the series.

The seventeen ARIMA models presented in Table 2–1 are fitted over a sample period of 1947: I through 1968: IV. Estimates of the standard deviations of the disturbances appearing in the table are also those of one-quarter-ahead prediction errors since these residuals are the prediction errors during the sample period. These models are quite similar to those described by Nelson [63], to whom the reader is referred for comments on the particular issues which arise in building ARIMA models using quarterly macroeconomic data. Note that most of the models involve only a few parameters and few lagged values.[3]

The variables displayed in Table 2–1 fall into three categories: the first six are key endogenous variables of interest, to which all tests are applied;[4] the second eight are another eight endogenous variables that are looked at in some tests; and, the last are three exogenous variables which are extrapolated by ARIMA models.

TABLE 2–1 ARIMA Models for FMP Variables,
Fitted Through 1966: IV

Variable Name	ARIMA Model
Nominal GNP ($ billion)	$(1-.615B)(1-B)z_t = u_t + 2.75$ $\hat{\sigma}_u = 4.76$
GNP deflator (%)	$(1-.522B)(1-B)z_t = u_t + .259$ $\hat{\sigma}_u = .460$
Real GNP ($ [1958] billion)	$(1-.414B)(1-B)z_t =$ $(1+.301B^2-.366B^4)u_t + 2.68$ $\hat{\sigma}_u = 4.61$
Unemployment rate (%)	$(1-1.45B+.609B^2)z_t$ $= (1+.291B)u_t + .713$ $\hat{\sigma}_u = .323$
Long-term interest rate (%)	$(1-.487B+.172B^2)(1-B)z_t = u_t$ $\hat{\sigma}_u = .110$
Short-term interest rate (%)	$(1-.727B+.428B^2)(1-B)z_t = u_t$ $\hat{\sigma}_u = .264$
Consumers' expenditures on nondurables ($ billion)	$(1-.435B-.551B^2)(1-B)z_t$ $= (1-.223B-.583B^4)u_t + .0546$ $\hat{\sigma}_u = 1.54$
Consumers' expenditures on durables ($ billion)	$(1-B)z_t = u_t + .656$ $\hat{\sigma}_u = 1.95$
Nonfarm inventory investment ($ billion)	$(1-.865B)(1-B)z_t$ $= (1+.264B^2-.577B^4)u_t + .594$ $\hat{\sigma}_u = 2.86$
Expenditures on producers' durables ($ billion)	$(1-B)z_t = (1+.348B)u_t + .517$ $\hat{\sigma}_u = 1.06$
Expenditures on producers' structures ($ billion)	$(1-.874B)(1-B)z_t$ $= (1-.546B-.518B^4)u_t + .0335$ $\hat{\sigma}_u = .435$
State and local government expenditures ($ billion)	$(1-B)^2 z_t = (1-.695B)u_t$ $\hat{\sigma}_u = .521$

Table 2-1 (continued)

Variable Name	ARIMA Model
Consumer goods price index (%)	$(1-.418B)(1-B)z_t = u_t + .250$ $\hat{\sigma}_u = .474$
Yield on U.S. treasury bills (%)	$(1-.608B+.425B^2)(1-B)z_t = u_t$ $\hat{\sigma}_u = .290$
Deflated government expenditures ($[1958] billion)	$(1-.431B)(1-B)z_t = u_t$ $\hat{\sigma}_u = 3.81$
Deflated exports ($[1958] billion)	$(1-B)z_t = u_t$ $\hat{\sigma}_u = 1.28$
Unborrowed reserves at member banks plus currency ($ billion)	$(1-B^4)(1-B)z_t = (1+.252B-.503B^4)u_t$ $\hat{\sigma}_u = .308$

The very large number of exogenous variables and so-called "variable coefficients"[5] in the FMP model requires that, for ex ante prediction, a subset of these—presumably particularly important ones—be selected for projection and the rest be set at their historical values. The variables selected were deflated federal government expenditures, deflated exports, and unborrowed reserves at member banks plus currency outside banks.

Of particular note is the model for real GNP. While a number of seasonally adjusted quarterly series exhibit a degree of "negative seasonality" or over-adjustment, usually most evident in the residuals produced by ARIMA estimation, this characteristic is strong enough in the case of real GNP to warrant inclusion of a moving average term at the seasonal lag, that is, the term $(-\theta_4 u_{t-4})$. It is probably because of the original seasonal adjustment procedures (extensions of the ratio to moving average method) that this negative seasonality is of a moving average rather than autoregressive nature. Thus the correlation at seasonal lags is essentially restricted to adjacent years rather than being repeated at integer multiples of the seasonal lag.

Several criteria are used for evaluating prediction performance. We rely primarily on root mean square error (RMSE) to measure inaccuracy. Additional information on the nature of the error is provided by the mean and standard deviation; the latter would coincide with RMSE when the former is zero, if identical degrees of freedom were used as denominator. Theil's Inequality Coefficient represents an attempt at normalizing the RMSE to convey some absolute standard of performance, regardless of the series being forecasted. Other measures are reported later such as correlations across variables and time to indicate where there might be room for improvement in accuracy.

Most of our comments will be directed toward the ex ante results although we do occasionally refer to the ex post results whenever there is some marked difference from ex ante results or the ex ante results need some standard of comparison. Tables show both ex post and ex ante results. Summary statistics for sample-period errors are presented in Table 2–2. While one might expect ex ante errors to be larger, in general, than ex post errors, this is apparently not the case for this model, notable examples being FMP predictions of several GNP components and the consumer goods price index. Since we use ARIMA predictions of the exogenous variables in the *current period only* in carrying out ex ante simulations, one should not expect those variables with distributed lag responses and small (in absolute value) lag coefficients for the zero lag—i.e., the current period—to differ greatly between ex post and ex ante simulations. Thus, the extent of change reflects how close in the model's causal structure to exogenous influence some variables are. In the FMP model, for example, the bill rate, a key variable in a central sector of the model, changes substantially; however, the price indices are much more sluggish in their reactions to stimuli and show little change.

The mean errors reported in Table 2–2 are generally small suggesting that the predictors may be characterized as unbiased. In addition the fraction of Theil's inequality coefficients (U) due to bias (not shown here) is generally on the order of .01 or smaller. Regression of actuals on predictions yielded few significant deviations (at the 5 percent level) of the constant from zero or the slope from unity. Those results, then, generally support the characterization of the predictors as unbiased.

In comparing FMP predictions with ARIMA predictions we note that, of the first six variables, FMP (ex ante) is more accurate on four; in the remaining eight, it is more accurate in six. In particular, the FMP model has larger error for the GNP deflator,

TABLE 2-2 Summary Statistics for Ex Post and Ex Ante Sample-Period Errors of the FMP Model: 1956: I Through 1966: IV

Endogenous Variables	FMP Ex Post				FMP Ex Ante				ARIMA			
	RMSE	Mean	Std. Dev.	Theil U	RMSE	Mean	Std. Dev.	Theil U	RMSE	Mean	Std. Dev.	Theil U
Nominal GNP	3.22	.907	3.06	.00289	3.84	1.79	3.44	.00345	5.01	.579	5.00	.00449
GNP deflator	0.220	−.001	0.227	.00105	0.226	−0.012	0.228	.00108	0.223	.002	0.227	.00107
Real GNP	3.47	.893	3.36	.00330	4.06	1.73	3.69	.00386	4.87	.290	4.89	.00462
Unemployment rate	0.386	−.119	0.371	.0372	0.406	−0.151	0.381	.0391	0.297	.046	0.297	.0291
Long-term interest rate	0.099	.021	0.097	.0116	0.112	0.008	0.112	.0130	0.124	.035	0.120	.0145
Short-term interest rate	0.220	.049	0.217	.0290	0.297	0.006	0.300	.0388	0.314	.048	0.314	.0413
Consumers' expenditure on nondurables	1.34	.002	1.36	.00221	1.33	0.013	1.34	.00220	1.55	.368	1.51	.00255
Consumer's expenditure on durables	1.18	.025	1.19	.0115	1.20	0.113	1.21	.0117	1.83	.049	1.85	.0179
Nonfarm inventory investment	2.59	.896	2.45	.203	2.59	0.877	2.46	.203	3.00	.318	3.02	.227
Expenditures on producers' durables	0.815	−.192	0.801	.0116	0.749	−0.106	0.749	.0107	1.013	.115	1.018	.0145
Expenditure on producers' structures	0.492	.059	0.494	.0122	0.490	0.057	0.493	.0122	0.535	.033	0.540	.0132
State and local government expenditures	0.695	.087	0.697	.00644	0.668	0.135	0.662	.00619	0.538	.137	0.525	.00500
Consumer goods price index	0.238	.016	0.241	.00115	0.238	0.010	0.244	.00115	0.241	.017	0.242	.00116
Yield on U.S. treasury bills	0.250	.019	0.252	.0385	0.388	−0.041	0.390	.0592	0.352	.051	0.352	.0545

the unemployment rate, state and local government expenditures, and the yield on 3-month treasury bills. Had we made our comparison only with ex post predictions, the FMP model would have appeared more accurate than ARIMA on two of these four variables—the GNP deflator and the bill rate.

We offer a conjecture to explain the degree to which the ARIMA prediction of the unemployment rate outperforms the FMP predictions. The FMP model attempts to explain explicitly the demand for and supply of labor; the unemployment rate is calculated from an identity as a percentage residual. The ARIMA model, on the other hand, focuses on the unemployment rate itself. In other words, the estimation methodologies—the choice of alternative models—differ as to what errors are being minimized. This is not so much the question of an economic model versus a statistical model. The St. Louis FRB Econometric Model of Anderson and Carlson [4], for example, has a single "Okun's law" type of equation for the unemployment rate which exhibits a one-quarter-ahead RMSE only slightly greater than its ARIMA counterpart.[6] It does seem to be a problem of the structural approach to model building, however.

Two other comments on the results in Table 2–2 are in order. First, the FMP mechanism for explaining state and local government expenditures is a recognized weakness of version 4.1. Substantial corrections are incorporated in more recent versions. Second, one problem in our method of ex ante forecasting is that, in some cases, the prediction error of an exogenous variable can be directly responsible for an observed deterioration in an endogenous variable between ex post and ex ante situations. Real government expenditures, for example, is one of our forecasted exogenous variables; but it is also an important component of the endogenous total, real GNP. Since this exogenous variable exhibited a rather large $\hat{\sigma}$ (in Table 2–1), it is, in fact, surprising that the RMSE for real GNP rose only from an ex post 3.47 to an ex ante 4.06. That this difference is largely due to the direct effect of real government expenditures on the total may be seen by examining the record of other components of GNP, most of which do better ex ante than ex post. For this exogenous variable, in particular, it might be better to use some other objective forecast, such as the published official estimates.

Correlations between ex post and ex ante errors, and between FMP model errors and ARIMA errors appear in Table 2–3. These are generally indicative of the fact that the FMP model and the

TABLE 2-3 Correlations Between Ex Post, Ex Ante and ARIMA Sample-Period Errors: 1956: I Through 1966: IV

Endogenous Variables	Ex Post and Ex Ante	FMP and ARIMA Ex Post	FMP and ARIMA Ex Ante
Nominal GNP	.790	.454	.384
GNP deflator	.992	.240	.269
Real GNP	.816	.457	.519
Unemployment rate	.976	.418	.438
Long-term interest rate	.877	.577	.554
Short-term interest rate	.816	.320	.405
Consumers' expenditures on nondurables	.998	.632	.622
Consumers' expenditures on durables	.978	.592	.555
Nonfarm inventory investment	.999+	.526	.524
Expenditure on producers' durables	.960	.235	.254
Expenditure on producers' structures	.999+	.703	.703
State and local government expenditures	.989	.174	.182
Consumer goods price index	.979	.274	.295
Yield on U.S. treasury bills	.791	.152	.267

ARIMA models tend to make somewhat similar errors. It is particularly interesting that, for variables in which the ARIMA and FMP predictions have quite similar RMSE, the corresponding error correlations are not as strong as one might expect. This suggests, as we shall see, that each model contains an independent component of information. Results for the GNP deflator suggest, for example, that FMP errors are quite different from those of ARIMA.

TABLE 2-4 Serial Correlation Coefficients for Sample Period FMP Ex Post, Ex Ante, and ARIMA Prediction Errors: 1956: I Through 1966: IV

Endogenous Variables	FMP Ex Post				FMP Ex Ante				ARIMA			
	$\hat{p}_1$	$\hat{p}_2$	$\hat{p}_3$	$\hat{p}_4$	$\hat{p}_1$	$\hat{p}_2$	$\hat{p}_3$	$\hat{p}_4$	$\hat{p}_1$	$\hat{p}_2$	$\hat{p}_3$	$\hat{p}_4$
Nominal GNP	−.054	−.141	−.024	.081	.070	−.122	.103	−.117	−.047	−.053	.065	−.144
GNP deflator	.271	.110	.277	.326	.280	.178	.279	.323	−.162	.227	−.037	.404
Real GNP	−.004	−.137	.110	.189	.098	.031	.209	−.046	.063	−.202	.107	.172
Unemployment rate	.041	.111	−.125	−.143	.060	.150	−.054	−.148	−.006	−.015	−.091	−.178
Long-term interest rate	.101	−.203	.193	.090	.063	−.161	.266	−.118	−.022	−.227	.026	.188
Short-term interest rate	.035	−.265	.060	.185	−.039	−.270	.172	−.053	.055	−.249	−.088	.281
Consumers' expenditures on nondurables	−.223	.108	−.098	−.082	−.224	.118	−.090	−.089	−.129	−.125	.061	.211
Consumers' expenditures on durables	−.272	.218	−.148	−.006	−.281	.256	−.088	−.088	−.132	.126	−.074	.085
Nonfarm inventory investment	.196	−.007	−.111	−.139	.184	−.011	−.108	−.137	−.049	−.067	.048	.150
Expenditure on producers' durables	.361	.123	−.072	.145	.388	.135	.037	.089	.220	.280	−.098	.098
Expenditure on producers' structures	.206	.273	.271	−.196	.206	.270	.275	−.194	−.239	−.017	.214	−.013
State and local government expenditures	.364	.405	.429	.359	.405	.439	.436	.401	−.093	−.109	.056	.081
Consumer goods price index	.111	.068	.226	.348	.093	.137	.212	.283	−.137	.233	−.011	.271
Yield on U.S. treasury bills	−.191	−.214	.101	.150	−.124	−.255	.192	−.148	.044	−.173	−.161	.248

When serial correlation is present in prediction errors, then forecast accuracy can be improved by using past errors to predict future errors. Table 2–4 presents serial correlation coefficients for lags of one through four quarters (denoted $\hat{\rho}_1,\ldots,\hat{\rho}_4$). Most $\hat{\rho}_i$ are small relative to a standard error of 0.23 (appropriate under the hypothesis that the errors are uncorrelated)[7], an exception being FMP errors for state and local government expenditures. This latter variable was particularly poorly predicted by the FMP model relative to the ARIMA model, as noted earlier. As an indication of relative serial correlation, the number of coefficients exceeding 0.23 in absolute value is 13 for FMP ex post, 17 for FMP ex ante, and 8 for ARIMA.[8]

2.2 Composite Predictions: Single Equation and Joint Estimates

One way of assessing the relative information content of alternative predictions is to combine them into a linear composite of the form

$$A = \beta_1(FMP) + \beta_2(ARIMA) + \varepsilon \qquad (2.2)$$

where A denotes actual values, choosing weights β_1 and β_2 to minimize squared error. Since $\beta_1 + \beta_2$ will be approximately unity for unbiased predictors, equation (2.2) may alternatively be written in terms of a single parameter β as follows:

$$A = \beta(FMP) + (1-\beta)(ARIMA) + \varepsilon \qquad (2.3)$$

In general, the least squares estimate of β is given by

$$\hat{\beta} = \frac{\hat{\sigma}_2^2 - \hat{\sigma}_1\hat{\sigma}_2\hat{\rho}}{\hat{\sigma}_1^2 + \hat{\sigma}_2^2 - 2\hat{\sigma}_1\hat{\sigma}_2\hat{\rho}} \qquad (2.4)$$

where $\hat{\sigma}_1$ and $\hat{\sigma}_2$ are the estimated standard deviations of FMP and ARIMA errors respectively and $\hat{\rho}$ is the estimated correlation between errors.[9] These results are completely analogous to selection of a minimum variance portfolio of two risky securities. Note that $\hat{\beta}$ would be negative if it were the case that

$$\hat{\rho} > \frac{\hat{\sigma}_2}{\hat{\sigma}_1} \qquad (2.5)$$

or $(1-\hat{\beta})$ would be negative if

$$\hat{\rho} > \frac{\hat{\sigma}_1}{\hat{\sigma}_2} \qquad (2.6)$$

that is, the minimum squared error composite might require "short selling" of one predictor if the correlation between errors is large relative to the appropriate ratio of standard deviations. In other words, one never "short sells" the more accurate model.

When composites of FMP and ARIMA predictions are formed by least squares estimation of (2.2), tests (again, at the 5 percent level) of the hypothesis $\beta_1 + \beta_2 = 1$ could be rejected only for nominal GNP and nonfarm inventory investment. Since the deviation from unity is very small and results are little affected in those cases if the sum is in fact constrained to unity, only constrained estimates, with weights $\hat{\beta}$ and $(1-\hat{\beta})$ for FMP and ARIMA, respectively, are reported in Table 2–5. The weight $\hat{\beta}$ is significant in all cases. The weight $(1-\hat{\beta})$ is significant when the ARIMA prediction is combined with ex post FMP predictions of consumers' expenditures on nondurables, nonfarm inventory investment, expenditures on producers' durables, state and local government expenditures, the unemployment rate, the GNP deflator, the consumer price index, the treasury bill rate, and the short-term rate, and, when combined with ex ante FMP predictions, all of the above plus nominal GNP, the long-term rate, and real GNP. It is apparent that the ARIMA models are able to extract from the past histories of the endogenous variables information that is being omitted by the econometric models. An indication of the gain in forecast accuracy from formation of the composite is given by comparison of standard errors of regression reported in Table 2–5 with RMSE of errors in Table 2–2.

Diagrams indicating contributions of individual regressors—often called Tinbergen diagrams—provide an especially useful technique here. It becomes possible to represent visually the individual contributions made by the components of a composite prediction. An example in Figure 2–1 illustrates the FMP (ex ante) and ARIMA composite for the short-term interest rate. The magnitude of the contribution made by each prediction is shown as the weight given to that prediction times its value and may be compared with the total prediction (composite) as well as with the actual. The role played by each prediction during particular episodes is therefore readily discerned. To some extent, by inspecting the errors in the

TABLE 2–5   Estimated Weights for the Composite Predictions
$\beta \cdot FMP + (1-\beta) \cdot ARIMA$: 1956: I Through 1966: IV

Endogenous Variables	FMP Model									
	Ex Post					Ex Ante				
	β	$(1-\beta)$	t on $(1-\beta)$	SER	DW	β	$(1-\beta)$	t on $(1-\beta)$	SER	DW
Nominal GNP	.864	.136	1.28	3.16	1.91	.704	.296	2.70	3.59	1.54
GNP deflator	.500	.500	5.14	0.179	2.06	.498	.502	5.01	0.181	2.09
Real GNP	.790	.210	1.87	3.34	1.88	.676	.324	2.56	3.80	1.64
Unemployment rate	.309	.691	6.66	0.274	1.89	.275	.725	7.14	0.278	1.88
Long-term interest rate	.772	.228	1.59	0.097	1.74	.617	.383	2.74	0.104	1.98
Short-term interest rate	.752	.248	2.50	0.208	1.74	.548	.452	3.87	0.258	2.08
Consumers' expenditures on nondurables	.669	.331	2.17	1.30	2.45	.684	.316	2.11	1.28	2.45
Consumers' expenditures on durables	.949	.051	0.42	1.19	2.53	.906	.094	0.79	1.20	2.55
Nonfarm inventory investment	.654	.346	2.58	2.43	1.32	.653	.347	2.59	2.43	1.33
Expenditure on producers' durables	.633	.367	4.05	0.701	1.66	.689	.311	3.41	0.672	1.53
Expenditures on producers' structures	.640	.360	1.99	0.476	2.00	.645	.355	1.96	0.475	2.00
State and local government expenditures	.344	.656	7.32	0.468	2.19	.362	.638	6.87	0.467	2.10
Consumer goods price index	.501	.499	4.92	0.193	2.09	.493	.507	4.90	0.196	2.16
Yield on U.S. treasury bills	.694	.306	3.65	0.221	2.08	.435	.565	5.79	0.294	2.14

composites, one can often associate large errors with failure of one of the components.

As indicated before,[10] the forecaster is interested in the accuracy of more than one variable at a time. Equation (2.3), estimated for the various variables as in Table 2–5, will not provide optimal composites if we are, in some sense, interested in the whole set. Zellner [84] has suggested a technique for applying Aitken's generalized least squares jointly to a set of seemingly unrelated regression equations; in our case, we would then get the set of best, linear, unbiased weights for our composite equations.

Again, we stress that if the objective of the forecaster is to minimize some utility function in prediction error, he will not, in general, select predictors solely on the basis of minimizing individual mean square error, but will instead utilize any alternative which offers additional information such that, with its cost considered, total utility will rise. The indication from Table 2–5 was that, at

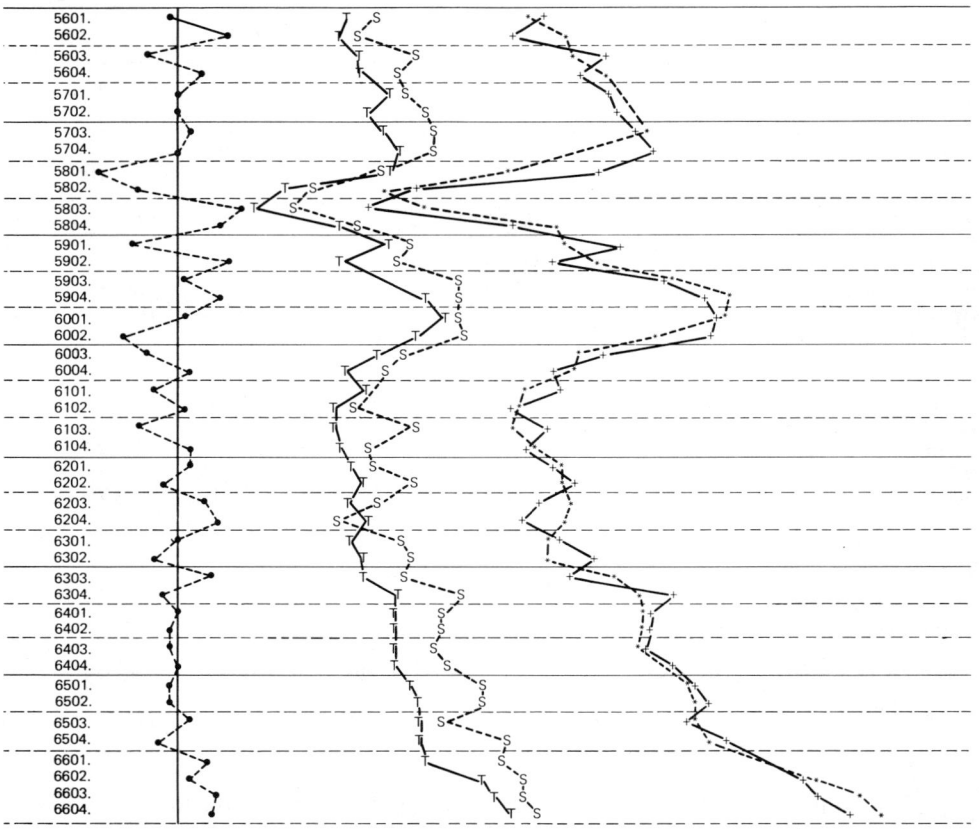

Figure 2-1. Visual Display of Composite Regression: FMP and ARIMA (1956:I Through 1966:IV) Short-Term Interest Rate

Characters	Variables
| ———	= $0 \cdot 0$
* ------	= Actual
+ ———	= Composite prediction: $\beta \cdot FMP + (1 - \beta) \cdot ARIMA$
● ------	= Error
S ------	= $\beta \cdot FMP$
T ———	= $(1 - \beta) \cdot ARIMA$

least on an equation-by-equation basis, ARIMA models made statistically significant contributions to the composites (i.e., to lowering mean square error, even given the FMP ex ante prediction). This point is strengthened by the jointly estimated composites provided in Table 2-6 (for the first six endogenous variables only).

Although the coefficients of ARIMA predictions in general fall when the ex ante composites are jointly estimated (5 out of 6 variables), their t statistics generally rise (5 out of 6 variables). The joint estimation was carried out constraining the coefficients to sum to unity (to be comparable with Table 2-5); The *joint* test for composites' weights summing to unity led to a calculated F ratio, with 6 and 252 degrees of freedom, of 1.3 for the ex post case and 3.3 for the ex ante case. Comparing these with a 5 percent

TABLE 2-6 Jointly Estimated Weights for the Composite Predictions $\beta \cdot FMP + (1-\beta) \cdot ARIMA$: 1956: I Through 1966: IV

Endogenous Variables	Ex Post			Ex Ante		
	β	$(1-\beta)$	SER[a]	β	$(1-\beta)$	SER
Nominal GNP	.93 (27.0)	.07 (1.9)	3.13	.84 (21.6)	.16 (4.0)	3.52
GNP deflator	.73 (12.4)	.27 (4.6)	0.187	.67 (9.6)	.33 (4.8)	0.185
Real GNP	.91 (25.0)	.09 (2.4)	3.35	.83 (18.5)	.17 (3.9)	3.82
Unemployment rate	.36 (4.3)	.64 (7.7)	0.271	.35 (4.6)	.65 (8.5)	0.276
Long-term interest rate	.81 (7.7)	.19 (1.9)	0.096	.67 (6.9)	.33 (3.5)	0.103
Short-term interest rate	.69 (9.1)	.31 (4.0)	0.206	.49 (5.7)	.51 (6.0)	0.256
Equality constraint imposed on β ($\&\therefore[1-\beta]$) across variables	.90 (35.5)	.10 (3.9)	—	.75 (22.5)	.25 (7.5)	—

Note: Only minor quantitative differences in estimates are obtained if the sum-to-unity constraint is *not* imposed; there are *no* qualitative differences and the maximum change in a β is on the order of 0.06, with the great majority of changes being very much smaller in absolute value.

[a] SER and t statistics are based on 44 observations, without adjustment for number of regressors.

critical value of 2.1, we see that the deviation of the weights from unity for the ex ante composites is significant; however, relaxation of the constraint produces only minor numerical differences and no qualitative differences.

In section 2.3, we raise the question as to whether or not the weights on different predictors in composite equations should be interpreted as subjective probabilities that their respective model is the true one. We do not answer this complex question here but do offer some evidence leaning toward a negative reply. It seems to us that if the weights are indeed probabilities of a model's being true, then the same weight should apply to all variables predicted by the model. If the FMP model is thought to be the true one with $100\beta_0$ percent probability and the ARIMA model with $100(1-\beta_0)$ percent then the composite equation for *each* variable predicted by both models should attach weight β_0 to the FMP predictor and $(1-\beta_0)$ to the ARIMA predictor. We note emphatically that our approach to these composite equations differs radically from the Bayesian one, say, as described by Zellner [87] or Geisel [36]. We are not aiming here for a discovery of which is the "true model"; rather, as stated earlier, we simply wish to improve forecasting performance by pooling available information. The Bayesian method of estimating coefficients of the composite equation, for example, does not utilize the observed correlations between errors made by different predictors. The question as to whether or not the weights can be conceived of as applying to the models as a whole rather than to individual economic variables is still very important, even in a general framework. Accordingly, we tested the linear hypothesis of equality in corresponding weights across equations for the two sets of composites of Table 2–6. In both cases, the null hypothesis (equality) could easily be rejected at even the 1 percent level of significance. As an example, we found the F ratio with 10 and 252 degrees of freedom for the equality of weights across the ARIMA and FMP ex ante composites to be 7.6 as compared with a critical value of 1.9. A test for not only equality but also the extra restriction of the weights summing to unity produced an F ratio of 6.9 to be compared with a rejection value of 1.8. For curiosity only, we include in Table 2–6 one extra row to represent the imposition of the constraint of equality of corresponding weights across equations (as well as the unity restriction already in effect). The implication —appropriately qualified—is that, although both predictors are highly significant, the ARIMA contribution is much more important in ex ante forecasting than it is in ex post forecasting. This, of course, reinforces previous observations.

The reader is referred to the previously cited paper by Cooper and Nelson [23] for an application of the composite technique to three predictors: the FMP model, time-series models, and the St. Louis FRB Econometric Model. In the three-way composite equations, we found that the contributions of the time-series models were no longer significant at all for nominal and real GNP and the deflator, even ex ante. The other two cases of clear nonsignificance were the FMP model for the unemployment rate and the St. Louis model for the long-term interest rate. These results were obtained when the composite equations were estimated both individually and jointly.

2.3 Policy Implications of Composite Predictions

It is intriguing to consider the possibility that composite predictions may have implications for the determination of optimal settings of policy instruments. Consider first the problem in the context of a single model of the economy of the form

$$Y = f(M, X) + \varepsilon \qquad (2.7)$$

where Y is income, M a policy instrument, X a vector of other variables which enter into the model, and ε is a disturbance term. Now if the target or desired value of Y is Y^* then the optimal choice of M for minimum squared error loss[11] is that which equates the conditional expectation of Y with Y^*, that is, the M which satisfies

$$Y^* = f(M, X) \qquad (2.8)$$

Taking a linear approximation to $f(\ )$ in the neighborhood of Y^*, then

$$Y^* \approx kM + \tilde{f}(X) \qquad (2.9)$$

and the optimal setting M^* is given by

$$M^* \approx \frac{Y^* - \tilde{f}(X)}{k} \quad \text{for} \quad k \neq 0 \tag{2.10}$$

Now suppose that the policy maker has at hand two alternative models of the economy, $f_1(\ )$ and $f_2(\ )$, neither of which is he willing to accept to the exclusion of the other.[12] Given this element of uncertainty—that is, uncertainty about the validity of the models—how should the policy maker use the information he does have to set M? Under these circumstances the least squares composite provides the minimum loss prediction. Thus it would appear that the optimal setting of M is the one which satisfies the equation

$$Y^* \approx \beta[k_1 M + \tilde{f}_1(X_1)] + (1 - \beta)[k_2 M + \tilde{f}_2(X_2)] \tag{2.11}$$

where the subscripts 1 and 2 refer to the two models.

There are at least two interpretations of the meaning of the weights β and $(1-\beta)$. One is that the policy maker assumes that one of the two models is the "true" model and β and $(1-\beta)$ are (subjective) probabilities on the veracity of the respective models. Another interpretation, and the one implied here, is that there is no presumption that either model is correct, rather both are subject to errors of specification as representations of the true economic system. Further, as alternative approximations to the economic system each contains information about Y, some of which is common to the other model and some of which is unique. Under this interpretation the composite prediction is simply the optimal linear extraction of information from the two models.

Solving (2.11) for the optimal setting M^{**} we have

$$M^{**} \approx \beta\left(\frac{Y^* - \tilde{f}_1(X_1)}{\beta k_1 + (1-\beta)k_2}\right) + (1-\beta)\left(\frac{Y^* - \tilde{f}_2(X_2)}{\beta k_1 + (1-\beta)k_2}\right) \tag{2.12}$$

Note that M^{**} is not the simple, β and $(1-\beta)$ weighted average of individually optimal settings for M;[13] rather it is the weighted average of two values of M each constructed using a weighted average of the respective policy multipliers. A particularly interesting special case is the one for $k_2 = 0$, that is, when the policy variable does not appear at all in the second model. This would occur if, say, the first model was the quantity theory and the second the Keynesian expenditure model and M the money supply, or if the first model was the FMP model and the second an ARIMA model. The value of M^{**} would then be given by

$$M^{**} \approx M_1^* + \frac{1-\beta}{\beta}\left(\frac{Y^* - \tilde{f}_2(X_2)}{k_1}\right) \tag{2.13}$$

where M_1^* is the optimal setting implied by model 1 when considered alone. The second term in (2.13) can be regarded as an adjustment to M_1^*. That term is, of course, inversely related in magnitude to the weight placed on the first model. The portion within the parentheses depends on the discrepancy between the target Y^* and the prediction of Y, namely $\tilde{f}_2(X_2)$, made by the second model. The rule described by (2.13) amounts then to saying that, although the second model itself attributes no effect to M, the policy maker should note the deviation from target predicted by the *second* model and adjust the setting of M by an amount determined by k_1, the multiplier for M from the *first* model.

To clarify the policy mechanism further, consider the result obtained if β is small. In that case adjustments in M^{**} will generally be quite large because the coefficient $(1-\beta)/\beta$ is large. At first blush it may seem odd that large adjustments are made in the policy instrument associated with the model that receives smaller weight. The rationale for this, however, is apparent from the fact that only deviations in Y from target enter into the loss function.[14] Since in effect the composite attributes little efficacy to M if β is small it makes sense intuitively, and is in fact analytically optimal, to make large costless adjustments in this policy instrument.

A number of interesting issues are raised by this analysis; for example, is the optimality of the procedure affected by changes in the behavior of the economic system under the new policy regime? How should the effect of the setting of M on the information gleaned from further observation of the system be incorporated into the policy decision? Should the same weights be applied to a vector of variables being forecast if the weights are to be interpreted as subjective probabilities? Such questions go outside the scope of this book.[15]

2.4 Post-Sample Predictive Performance

A more stringent test of an econometric model is its ability to predict

TABLE 2–7 Summary Statistics for Post-Sample Errors: 1967: I Through 1968: IV

Endogenous Variables	FMP						ARIMA		
	Ex Post			Ex Ante					
	RMSE	Mean	Theil U	RMSE	Mean	Theil U	RMSE	Mean	Theil U
Nominal GNP	5.27	3.26	.00319	7.14	5.01	.00434	5.67	3.20	.00344
GNP deflator	0.265	0.045	.00111	0.265	0.027	.00111	0.306	0.250	.00128
Real GNP	3.98	2.33	.00289	5.93	3.91	.00431	3.12	0.99	.00226
Unemployment rate	0.720	−0.613	.0930	0.769	−0.663	.0988	0.285	−0.142	.0392
Long-term interest rate	0.207	0.122	.0179	0.193	0.103	.0166	0.200	0.086	.0172
Short-term interest rate	0.462	0.232	.0427	0.427	0.172	.0393	0.372	0.015	.0337
Consumers' expenditures on nondurables	4.91	−3.86	.00561	4.86	−3.82	.00555	3.62	0.92	.00416
Consumers' expenditures on durables	3.22	2.14	.0210	3.33	2.32	.0217	2.37	1.09	.0153
Nonfarm inventory investment	3.13	1.22	.240	3.16	1.18	.241	6.27	0.21	.416
Expenditures on producers' durables	3.35	2.42	.0294	3.40	2.58	.0298	1.68	0.43	.0145
Expenditures on producers' structures	0.88	0.13	.0155	0.88	0.12	.0154	1.64	0.19	.0288
State and local government expenditures	2.64	2.16	.0144	2.75	2.27	.0152	0.87	0.04	.00467
Consumer price index	0.342	−0.132	.00147	0.364	−0.144	.00156	0.433	0.314	.00186
Treasury bill rate	0.641	0.102	.0668	0.624	0.018	.0644	0.551	0.084	.0572

post-sample data. Post-sample prediction performance is also of considerable interest to the operational forecaster who never has the luxury of making within-sample period predictions.

The post-sample period here for the FMP model consists of the eight quarters, 1967: I through 1968: IV. RMSE, mean error, and the inequality coefficient over the post-sample period for the FMP model, ex post and ex ante, as well as for the ARIMA model, appear in Table 2–7. A considerable deterioration in accuracy is evident relative to sample-period results for most variables and predictors, although for real GNP and the unemployment rate, ARIMA predictions have smaller RMSE. It is also apparent that the deterioration is generally more severe for the FMP model than for the ARIMA models. Generally, the differences between ex post and ex ante results are surprisingly small; nominal and real GNP are important exceptions. When we compare ex ante predictions with ARIMA predictions over the first six endogenous variables, the ARIMA predictions have smaller RMSE and U for four of them; the FMP predictor of the long-term interest rate remains (in the post-sample period) better than the ARIMA predictor and the FMP predictor of the GNP deflator is now *more* accurate than its ARIMA counterpart. Among the remaining eight endogenous variables, ARIMA predictors have the smaller RMSE and U for five relative to both ex post and ex ante FMP predictors.

The post-sample deterioration of the FMP model does not seem to be confined to any particular subgroup of variables, but is fairly much across the board. The fact that all GNP components suffer implies that we cannot place any direct blame on key components like the forecasted exogenous variable (real government expenditures) or state and local government expenditures, as we have done earlier in section 2.1.[16]

Finally, it is interesting to extend the post-sample comparison to composites for the respective models. This is done for the first six variables in Table 2–8.[17] On the question of accuracy of the composites relative to individual predictor accuracy, FMP composites ex ante are more accurate than the model's ex ante predictions for all six variables although less accurate than ARIMA predictions of nominal GNP, real GNP, and the unemployment rate. Thus, it is apparent that the pooling of information in the form of linear composites remains useful in the post-sample period in spite of relative deterioration of the accuracy of both the predictors. Except for the unemployment rate, a strategy of choosing a single predictor on the basis of lower RMSE in the

TABLE 2–8 Summary Statistics for Post-Sample Errors from the Composite Regressions: 1967: I Through 1968: IV

Endogenous Variables	$\beta \cdot FMP + (1-\beta) ARIMA$					
	Ex Post			Ex Ante		
	RMSE	Mean	Theil U	RMSE	Mean	Theil U
Nominal GNP	4.95	3.26	.00300	5.84	4.47	.00355
GNP deflator	0.265	0.148	.00111	0.250	0.139	.00105
Real GNP	3.35	2.05	.00243	4.17	2.97	.00303
Unemployment rate	0.335	−0.287	.0452	0.336	−0.285	.0454
Long-term interest rate	0.198	0.113	.0171	0.186	0.096	.0160
Short-term interest rate	0.394	0.178	.0363	0.330	0.101	.0302

sample period would have been inferior to a strategy of using the composites, on the basis of post-sample results.

The conclusion suggested by examination of post-sample prediction clearly reinforces that suggested by the sample period results. Namely, no single predictor can be said to dominate the others in the sense of subsuming their information content; rather each contains a marginal increment of information which may be usefully exploited.

Notes

[1] See Nelson [63] for an evaluation of ex post prediction performance of the FMP model. Ex post predictions are also included here essentially because they are a most appropriate benchmark for the ex ante predictions. Enzler and Stekler [30] also discuss the forecasting performance of the FMP model, concentrating on a period in which operational forecasters with the FMP model conditioned their predictions upon particularly poor extrapolations of key exogenous variables.

[2] It should be stressed that the objective in specification and estimation of the ARIMA models was not minimization of squared errors per se. Rather it was to arrive at the simplest model consistent with the stochastic structure of the series. Thus parameters are included only if they are statistically significant or if their omission results in autocorrelated residuals.

[3] Differences between models used here for FMP variables and corresponding models used by Nelson [63] are due to slight revisions in data decks and implementation of a program for ARIMA model estimation which permits zero restrictions on coefficients, useful when p or q is large.

[4] These six, in particular, correspond to variables predicted by the St. Louis FRB model, which was also studied by Cooper and Nelson [23]. The long-term interest rate is Moody's AAA corporate bond rate and the short rate is the rate on 4–6 months prime commercial paper.

[5] The "variable coefficients" of the FMP model are exogenous variables generally of a policy-related nature and often entering into the model in a multiplicative way, a typical example being the reserve requirement ratios.

[6] See Cooper and Nelson [23, Table 8].

[7] See Anderson [5].

[8] The degree of correlation between errors *across* variables should be indicative of common effects from shocks to the economy. Such correlations are also of interest to the operational forecaster who may be concerned about the relationships between errors for different variables. In general, the forecaster's loss function will depend upon such interactions as well as on single variable accuracy. To economize on the number of tables and to avoid exhausting the reader's patience we have omitted presenting these calculations here. They are, of course, available from the author.

Correlations of FMP sample-period ex post errors and ARIMA errors across variables are very close to those reported by Nelson [63] (whose results omit real GNP) and differ little from corresponding correlations of ex ante errors.

[9] To derive (2.4) note that the composite error is given by

$$\varepsilon = \beta(A - FMP) + (1 - \beta)(A - ARIMA)$$

The least squares estimate of β is given then by the solution of

$$\frac{\partial \sum \varepsilon^2}{\partial \beta} = 0$$

which implies (2.4).

[10] See note 8.

[11] The loss function is assumed to include only the loss arising from deviation of the target from its desired value. We do not include any loss associated with the setting of the policy instrument; see Holt [42]. The form and parameters of $f(\ )$ are taken as given, since this section is largely illustrative. The certainty equivalence results following in the text do *not* take into account the estimation process.

[12] The following discussion may be more relevant when we are talking about two *econometric* models. It is equally valid, however, for the case of one econometric model and an ARIMA model; see Cooper and Nelson [23].

[13] It *is*, however, a weighted average of the individually optimal settings for M. Rewrite (2.12) as

$$M^{**} \approx \frac{\beta k_1}{\beta k_1 + (1-\beta)k_2}\left(\frac{Y^* - \tilde{f}_1(X_1)}{k_1}\right) + \frac{(1-\beta)k_2}{\beta k_1 + (1-\beta)k_2}\left(\frac{Y^* - \tilde{f}_2(X_2)}{k_2}\right)$$
$$\approx wM_1^* + (1-w)M_2^* \qquad (2.12a)$$

where M_i^* is the individually optimal setting for M in model i ($i = 1, 2$), and w is the weight applied to the setting of model 1. We are indebted to Carl Christ for this observation.

We find the particular form used in the text more useful, though, since we would have trouble with (2.12a) if $k_2 = 0$ (which is our next step). The weight $(1-w)$ becomes zero, but M_2^* becomes indefinitely large (∞).

[14] See the first two sentences of note 11.

[15] Chapter 4 is one example of the application of the FMP model to policy decision making.

[16] A newer version of the FMP model (about the first labelled the MPS model) was obtained in the spring of 1971 with data through 1970: II. While some equations were estimated on data beyond the end of 1968, it is generally fair to say 1969: I on represents a post-sample period. RMSE calculated over the six quarters indicate that this newer version exhibited less ex post predicton deterioration than did the version in the text over its own post-sample period. Improvement in extrapolative ability relative to the earlier version was most notable for the unemployment rate and the two short-term interest rates. Surprisingly, though, the relative deterioration of nominal GNP was even greater than that for the model reported in the text.

[17] These are the single-equation estimated composites, not the jointly optimal ones. Nelson [63] used the latter composites in ex post prediction tests.

3 Stochastic Simulation

3.1 Reasons for and Descriptions of Stochastic Simulation Techniques

Most simulation studies of econometric model properties are *deterministic*. Additive disturbances in the model's stochastic equations are set at their mean value, zero. The term "*stochastic* simulation run" is used in this volume to represent a simulation run in which these disturbances are set, rather, equal to pseudorandom numbers with "appropriate" properties. Each drawing of a set of disturbances for a simulation run leads to different results; when we replicate a stochastic simulation run, we generate one realization of a vector of random variables representing the outputs of the simulation experiment. Only occasionally, however, will one realization be useful to us.[1] More often we need many replications—i.e., many stochastic simulation runs—in order to have meaningful results. (There is little we can learn from a sample of 1.) Since a stochastic simulation experiment will, thus, be many times more costly than a deterministic simulation, we must begin by discussing the reasons for stochastic simulation.

First, Slutzky [72] has asserted that the incorporation of random disturbances into a stable, economic model could reproduce cyclical behavior in the endogenous variables of the model; and Adelman and Adelman [1] have demonstrated this effect in simulation of the Klein-Goldberger model. Second, since the formulation of the model and the methods underlying the estimation of its parameters include stochastic components, abandoning this specification for simulation experiments is certainly a methodological inconsistency. Third, Howrey and Kelejian [43] have demonstrated that deterministic simulations of nonlinear models can lead to results systematically different from the real properties of the model. Their point is that we are usually concerned with the characteristics of the reduced form of the model, which, for nonlinear models, will include

---

The Morgan Guaranty Trust Company of New York and the NBER Computer Research Center in Cambridge, Massachusetts generously supported the computational expenses incurred for this chapter.

nonlinear functions of the structural disturbances. The expectation of the solution of the model will not be identical to the result obtained by setting structural disturbances at their expectation and then solving the model. The expectation of a nonlinear function does not equal the function of the expectation—and the FMP model is certainly nonlinear. Fourth, the solution values of endogenous variables from multiple replications exhibit empirical distributions, the study of which allows the drawing of statistical inferences and the testing of hypotheses. In ordinary deterministic simulation, we have no way of judging the significance of a particular result, such as the difference in root-mean-square error of two alternative experiments or the multiplier effect of a change in a particular exogenous variable. Fifth, in studying economic policy, it is necessary to permit deviations from expected values of time paths—i.e., shocks to the system—and to investigate the properties of the induced oscillation under the various policy regimes. This is of particular importance, for example, in the study of automatic stabilization rules. Use of the deterministic forms of models when exogenous variables follow steady time paths would be likely to lead to the recommendation of some sort of constant growth-rate rules for policy instruments in order to keep target variables constant or growing at constant rates, since econometric models are usually systems of difference equations. In practice, economic relations do not hold exactly and it is not possible to keep variables precisely at their target levels. There will be discrepancies between target and actual values of variables whatever policies are used. The use of stochastic simulation explicitly insures the existence of differences between actual and target variables under all policy regimes. The second half of Chapter 4 illustrates this particular motivation.[2]

We now discuss the simulation technique. An econometric model can usually be represented in the form

$$y_{i,t} = f_i(y_{j,t-\delta}, x_{k,t}) + h_{i,t} u_{i,t} \qquad \begin{aligned} i,j &= 1,\ldots,m \\ k &= 1,\ldots,n \\ \delta &= 0,1,\ldots,\Delta \end{aligned} \qquad (3.1)$$

$$\frac{\partial f_i}{\partial y_{j,t}} = 0 \qquad j = i$$

where $y_{i,t}$ are the current endogenous variables, $y_{j,t-\delta}$ are current and lagged values of endogenous variables, $x_{k,t}$ are the exogenous variables, and $h_{i,t}$ are multiplicative factors to the random disturbances $u_{i,t}$. The form of (3.1) implies that each equation can be "normalized" on a different endogenous variable. In each period, lagged values of endogenous variables and current and lagged values of the exogenous variables are given so that (3.1) becomes a system of m equations to be solved for the m unknowns $y_{i,t}$. In the case of the FMP model these equations are not generally linear; nonetheless, the normalization, together with the fact that most of the partial derivatives of each f_i with respect to its arguments are zero, permits very rapid solution of the model with a modified Gauss-Seidel iterative method as described in Appendix 1B.

The disturbances $h_{i,t} u_{i,t}$ are assumed to be additive; the $u_{i,t}$ are further assumed to have a multivariate normal distribution with mean zero and to be serially uncorrelated. The variance-covariance matrix is estimated from the other parameters of the model. The $h_{i,t}$ are scaling factors which take into account the fact that equations may not be scaled or normalized for simulation exactly as they were during the estimation of the model. The $u_{i,t}$ are to be generated by the same stationary process that, in estimation, was assumed to be generating the regression residuals; this requires the $h_{i,t}$ to be the ratio of the simulation dependent (left-hand-side) variable to the regression dependent variable when the scaling is changed and the negative reciprocal of the variable's regression coefficient when the normalization is changed.

The generation of the $u_{i,t}$ requires three distinct steps. First a pseudorandom number generator produces numbers which behave as if they were independent, uniformly distributed, random variables. The generating mechanism used in this chapter and the next follows Payne, Rabung, and Bogyo [65] and has desirable properties for a thirty-two-bit word-size computer such as the IBM 360.[3]

Second, a logarithmic-trigonometric transformation is used to produce independently distributed standard normal deviates.[4] In particular, if x_1 and x_2 are independently and uniformly distributed on the interval [0, 1], then the pair, y_1 and y_2, where

$$y_1 \equiv \sqrt{-2 \log x_1} \cos(2\pi x_2)$$
$$y_2 \equiv \sqrt{-2 \log x_1} \sin(2\pi x_2)$$
(3.2)

will be independently and normally distributed with mean 0 and variance 1. If $g(y_1, y_2)$ is the joint probability density function of y_1 and y_2, and J is the Jacobian of the transformation of x_1 and x_2 into y_1 and y_2, then

$$g(y_1, y_2) = 1 \cdot \|J^{-1}\|$$

$$= \frac{x_1}{2\pi} \tag{3.3}$$

But,

$$y_1^2 + y_2^2 = -2\log x_1 \tag{3.4}$$

so that

$$x_1 = e^{-(y_1^2/2 + y_2^2/2)} \tag{3.5}$$

and therefore

$$g(y_1, y_2) = \frac{1}{2\pi} e^{-(y_1^2/2 + y_2^2/2)}$$

$$= \left[\frac{1}{\sqrt{2\pi}} e^{-y_1^2/2}\right]\left[\frac{1}{\sqrt{2\pi}} e^{-y_2^2/2}\right] \tag{3.6}$$

The second equality of (3.6) demonstrates that $g(y_1, y_2)$ is simply the product of two univariate normal probability density functions in y_1 and y_2.[5]

Third, applying a technique developed by McCarthy [52], the $u_{i,t}$ are generated from the output of step two, constraining their covariance matrix to equal the sample covariance matrix estimated from regression residuals. McCarthy's technique is still applicable when this latter matrix is singular, as is the case in the FMP model.[6] Let R be a $T \times 1$ vector of independently distributed standard normal deviates and U be a $T \times m$ matrix of true structural disturbances (independent of elements of R). Then the generated pseudostructural disturbances, S, where

$$S \equiv \frac{1}{\sqrt{T}} U'R \tag{3.7}$$

are normally distributed with mean and covariance matrix given by

$$E(S) = 0 \tag{3.8}$$

$$E(SS') = \frac{1}{T} E(U'U) \tag{3.9}$$

Equation (3.9) follows from writing the ijth element of the left-hand-side matrix as

$$\left(\frac{1}{T}\right) E \left[\sum_{b=1}^{T} \sum_{a=1}^{T} (r_a r_b)(u_{ai} u_{bj}) \right]$$

where the r_i are elements of R and the u_{ij} the elements of U; the independence of the r_i with each other and with the u_{ij} leads to (3.9) directly. With a consistently estimated model we can produce a calculated matrix $\hat{U}$ whose elements converge in distribution to those of U.[7] Using $\hat{U}$ in place of U in (3.7) leads to pseudostructural disturbances with the appropriate properties asymptotically.

In the experiments that follow, most of the sixty-six stochastic equations were shocked; a few were not because they fell in sectors of the model that were exogenized. For the purpose of the runs in this chapter, areas of the model determining part of the employment sector; the flows of funds from savings and loans companies, etc.; and the demand for currency were omitted. Subsequent developments in the specification of the first and third of these areas allowed us to introduce them for the stochastic simulation experiments of Chapter 4 (where they were essential to the experiments performed).

Sections 3.2 and 3.3 report results of dynamic and one-period stochastic simulations, respectively, over the period 1956: I to 1968: IV. The one-period simulations are analogous to the one-quarter-ahead extrapolations of the previous chapter; lagged endogenous variables are set at their historical values so that simulation errors are not cumulative through time. In both sections, all exogenous variables take on historical values.[8] Twenty-five replications were run in addition to a deterministic simulation for comparative purposes. The means and variances of generated $u_{i,t}$ across both observations and replications were calculated and checked roughly with the means and variances of the regression disturbances over the simulation period. The variances of the generated disturbances corresponded quite closely to those observed for the regression errors, and means were closer to zero than their regression counterparts with only two minor exceptions (out of a total of 59 cases).[9]

One caveat is in order. The coefficients of estimated equations are treated as constants. It might be argued that the coefficients should themselves be regarded as random. However, randomizing these coefficients would have required a large amount of information (on the covariance matrix of the estimated parameters) not readily available and would have substantially increased the cost of the simulations.

3.2 Dynamic Simulation Results

Since almost a quarter of a million values of endogenous variables were generated (and stored) during the simulation runs for this section, it is essential to do a lot of summarizing and pruning in order to convey any feeling at all about the nature of the results. Since there is still at this time little accumulated experience with stochastic simulation of economic models, our purpose throughout these next two sections will be descriptive, but concentrating more on the technique than the substance of the model.

One important dimension of the results will be the effect of the nonlinearity of the FMP model. It is generally believed that we can learn nothing new about the validity of a linear model by stochastic simulation; we can calculate analytically all we need to know about its behavior as a dynamic, simultaneous system by examining the reduced form and characteristic equation, etc. Since simulation is, nevertheless, still a very easy tool of analysis to use, we might carry out deterministic simulation, but a stochastic simulation involving a large number of replications would not be justified by its cost. If we have a statistical hypothesis on a policy multiplier to test, for example, we need not generate an empirical distribution for it when we can use known results to perform the test.[10] We examine a few different aspects of the nonlinearity of the FMP model, since, if we find that this nonlinearity can essentially be ignored, the cheaper deterministic simulation might be indicated. The main aspects investigated are the relationship between the mean of stochastic solutions and a deterministic solution and the distribution of the time paths of stochastic solutions about the stochastic mean. Section 3.4 also provides information on this question.

In addition to the significance of nonlinearity, we look at the properties through time of the stochastic solutions. In particular, we discuss both plots and tables of the important time paths and various summary measures. We also examine the relationship between various summary measures averaged over the stochastic solutions and the same measures calculated on the stochastic mean.

No formal statistical testing is conducted here; we leave this to the stochastic simulation policy experiments in the second half of Chapter 4. In this section and the next, we simply probe the nature of stochastic simulation.

Five variables have been selected for the reporting purposes in the figures and tables following; they are: nominal GNP, GNP deflator, real GNP, a long-term interest rate, and a short-term interest rate.[11] Figures 3–1 to 3–5 are time series' plots for the five variables. The "a" part of each figure has five time paths: the mean of stochastic solutions in each period; the stochastic mean plus and minus the standard deviation of stochastic solutions in each period; the minimum of the stochastic solutions in each period; and the maximum, similarly defined. The "b" part of each figure has three time paths: the actual or historical value; the stochastic mean (again); and the deterministic solution. In the "a" parts, each time path is plotted with a solid line since there is no problem of interpretation—the center path is the stochastic mean, the next two outward represent plus and minus a standard deviation, and the outermost two are the minimum and maximum. In the "b" parts, actual values are plotted with a solid line, the deterministic solution with a dashed line, and the stochastic mean with a dotted line. Where no dotted line is shown, the stochastic mean coincides with the deterministic solution, at least within the resolution of the figure.

Following the figures are summary tables of the simulation for the five variables, Tables 3–1 to 3–5. Calculations were performed only every fourth quarter to make the tables manageable. There are five main types of information presented. (i) The actual values in the 13 quarters ($52 \div 4$) appear in the second column. (ii) The next five columns record the deterministic solution in the 13 quarters plus four measures of goodness-of-fit, each calculated from the beginning of the simulation to the current quarter: correlation coefficient (CORR.), root-mean-square error (RMSE), mean absolute error (MAE) and mean error (ME). (iii) The same statistics as in (ii) but corresponding to the mean stochastic solution appear in the next five columns. (iv) The four measures of goodness of fit were similarly calculated for each individual stochastic replication; the mean (μ) and the standard deviation (σ) of these measures across replications takes up the next eight columns. (v) Some of the data underlying the "a" parts of Figures 3–1 to 3–5—namely, in each quarter, the standard deviation (STD. DEV.), minimum (MIN.), maximum

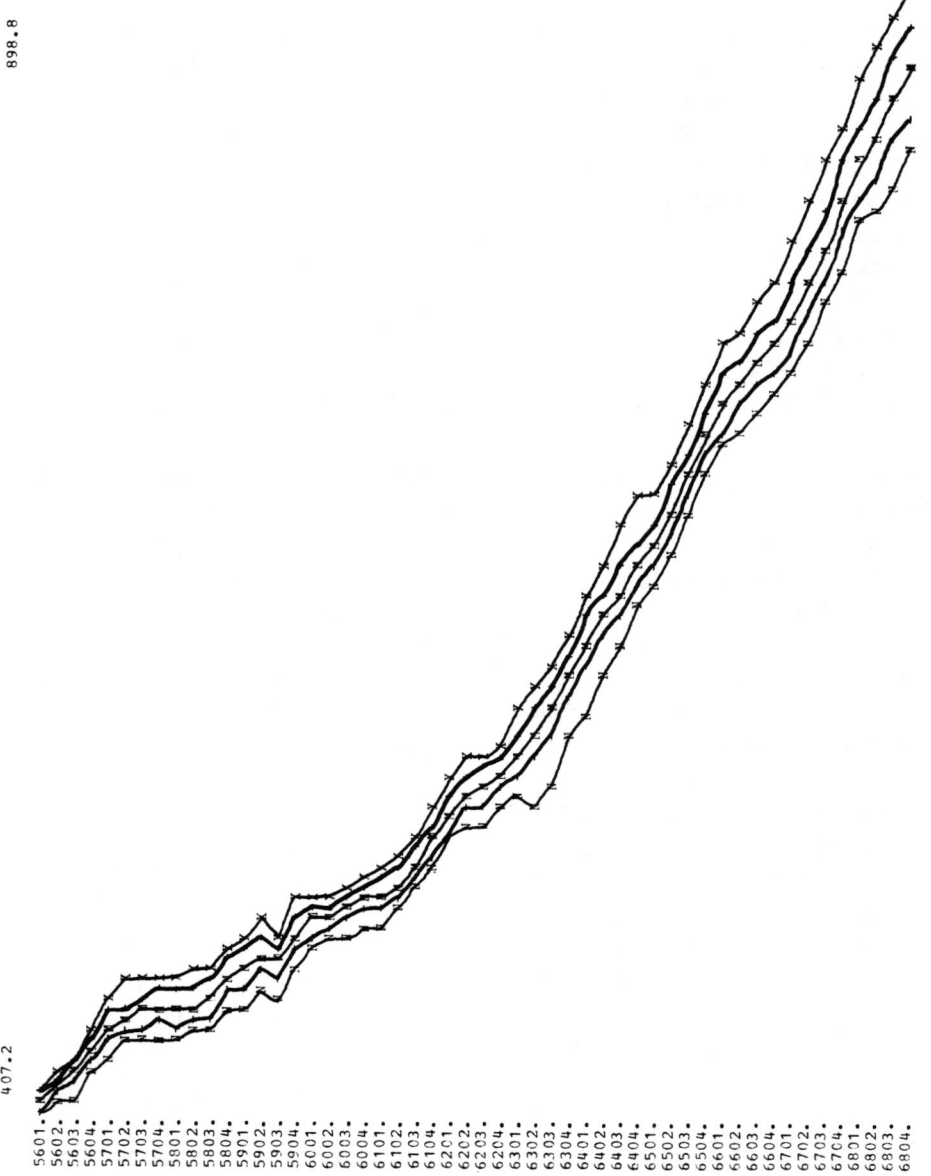

Figure 3-1a. Mean, Standard Deviation, Minimum, and Maximum of Stochastic Dynamic Solutions: Nominal GNP.

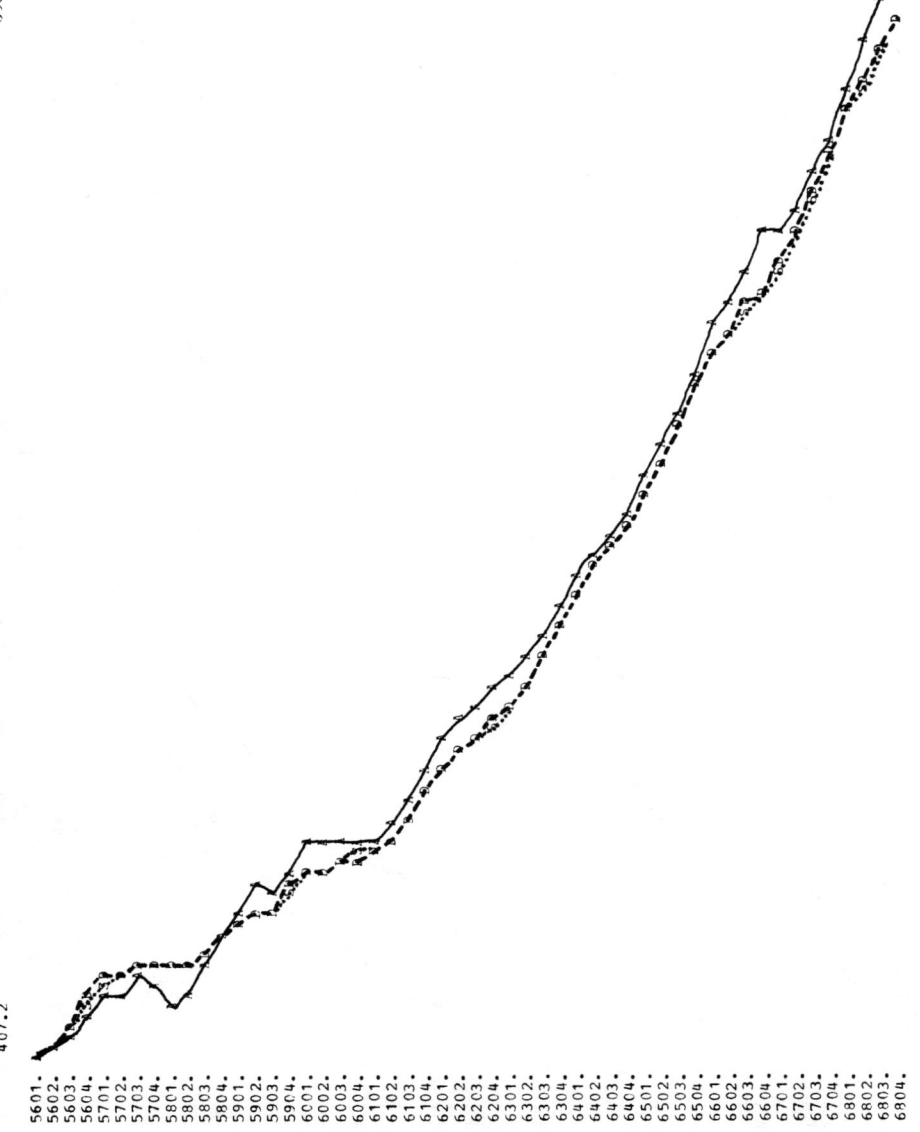

Figure 3–1b. Actual, Deterministic Dynamic Solution, and Mean Stochastic Dynamic Solution: Nominal GNP.

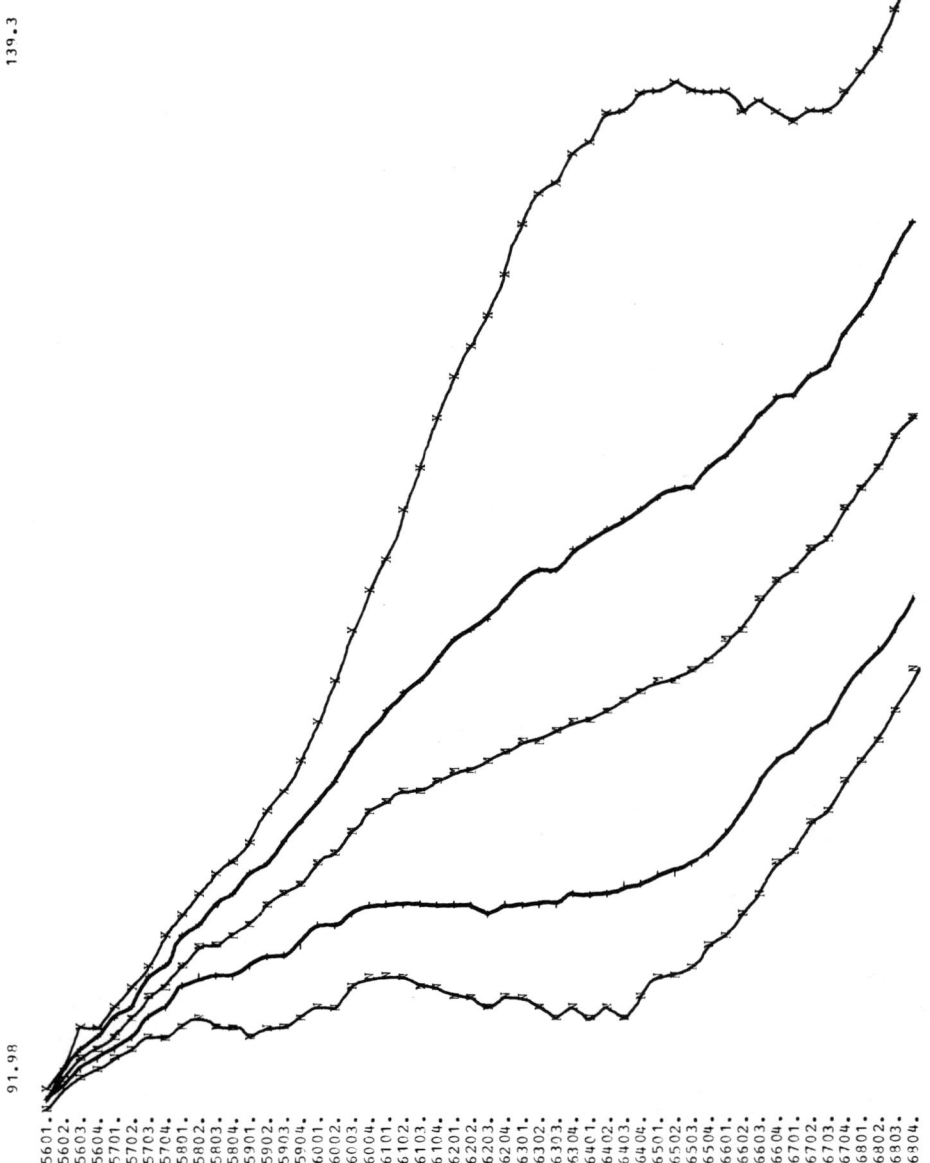

Figure 3-2a. Mean, Standard Deviation, Minimum, and Maximum of Stochastic Dynamic Solutions: GNP Deflator.

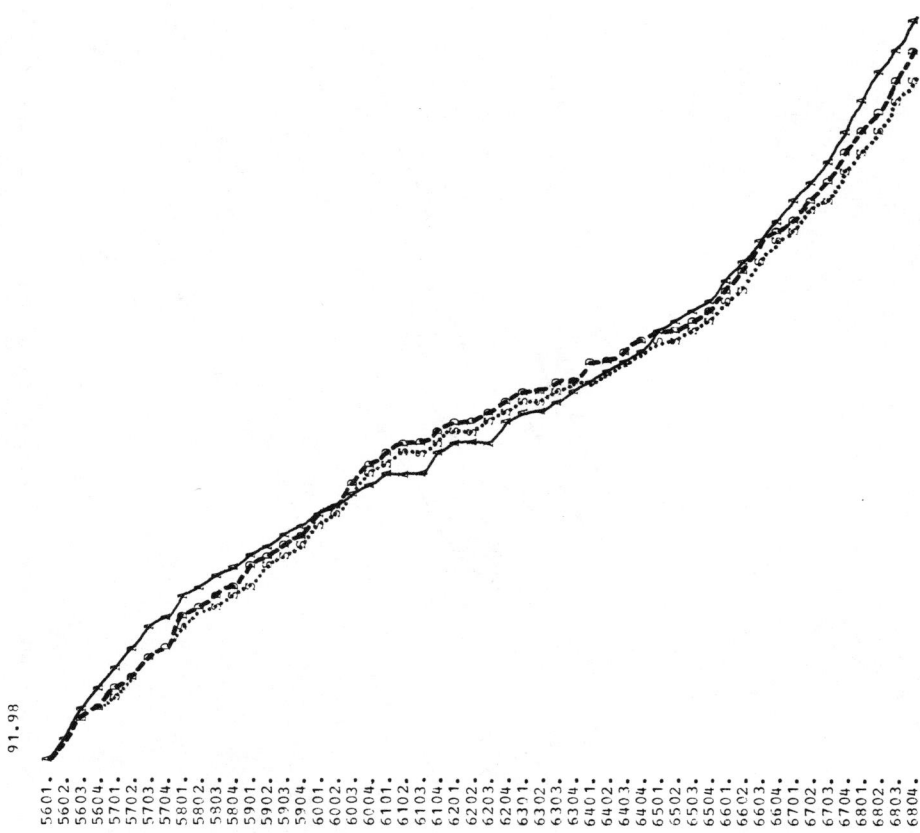

Figure 3-2b. Actual, Deterministic Dynamic Solution, and Mean Stochastic Dynamic Solution: GNP Deflator.

Figure 3-3a. Mean, Standard Deviation, Minimum, and Maximum of Stochastic Dynamic Solutions: Real GNP.

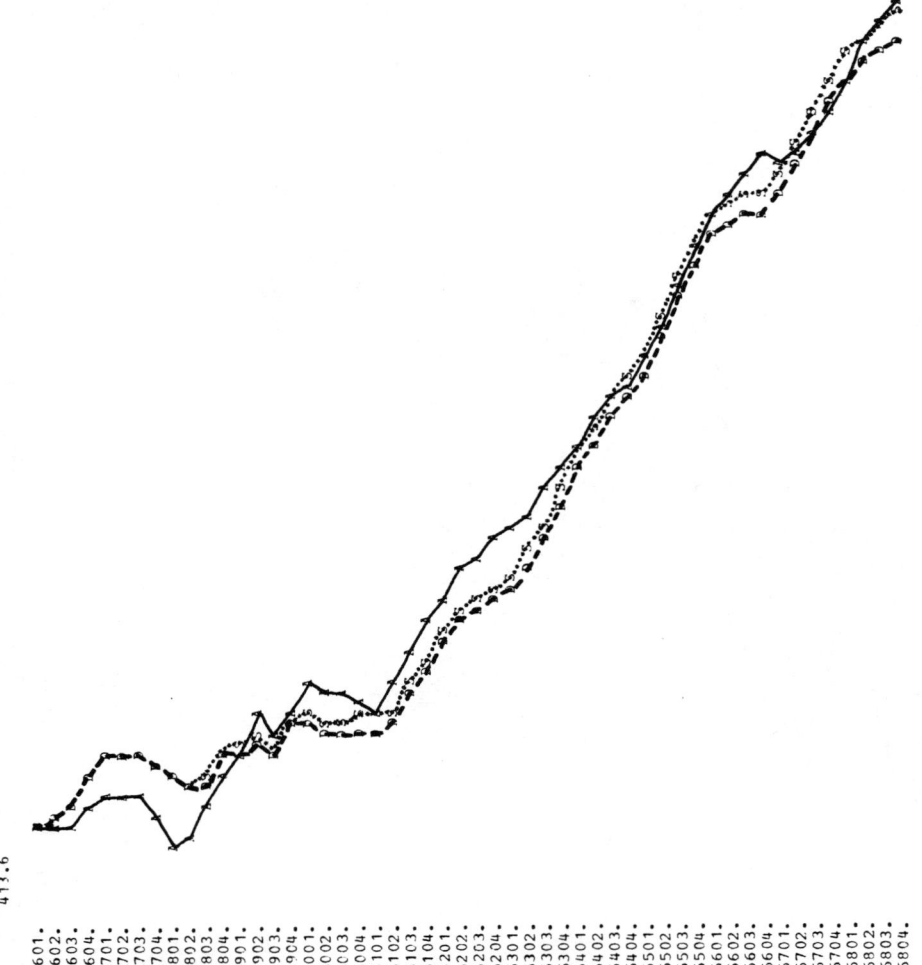

Figure 3–3b. Actual, Deterministic Dynamic Solution, and Mean Stochastic Dynamic Solution: Real GNP.

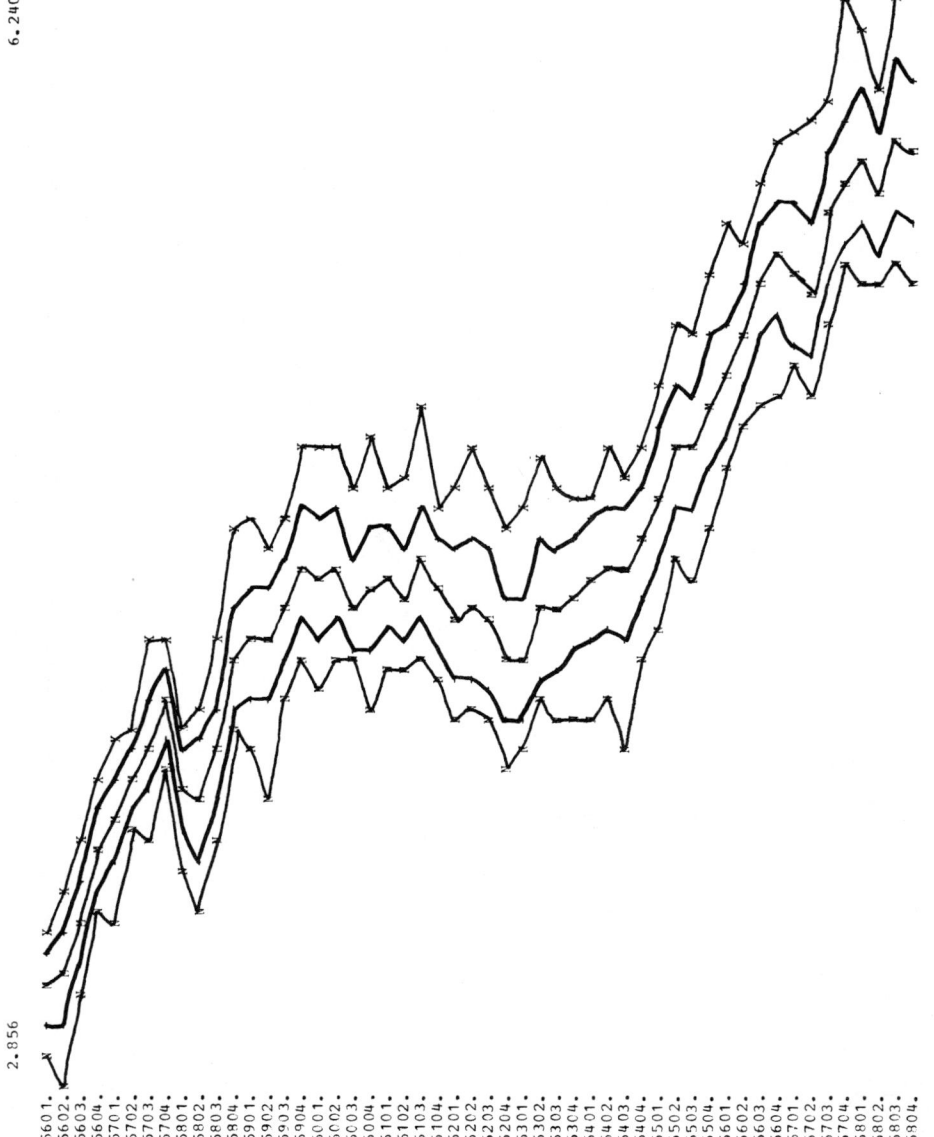

Figure 3-4a. Mean, Standard Deviation, Minimum, and Maximum of Stochastic Dynamic Solutions: Long-Term Interest Rate.

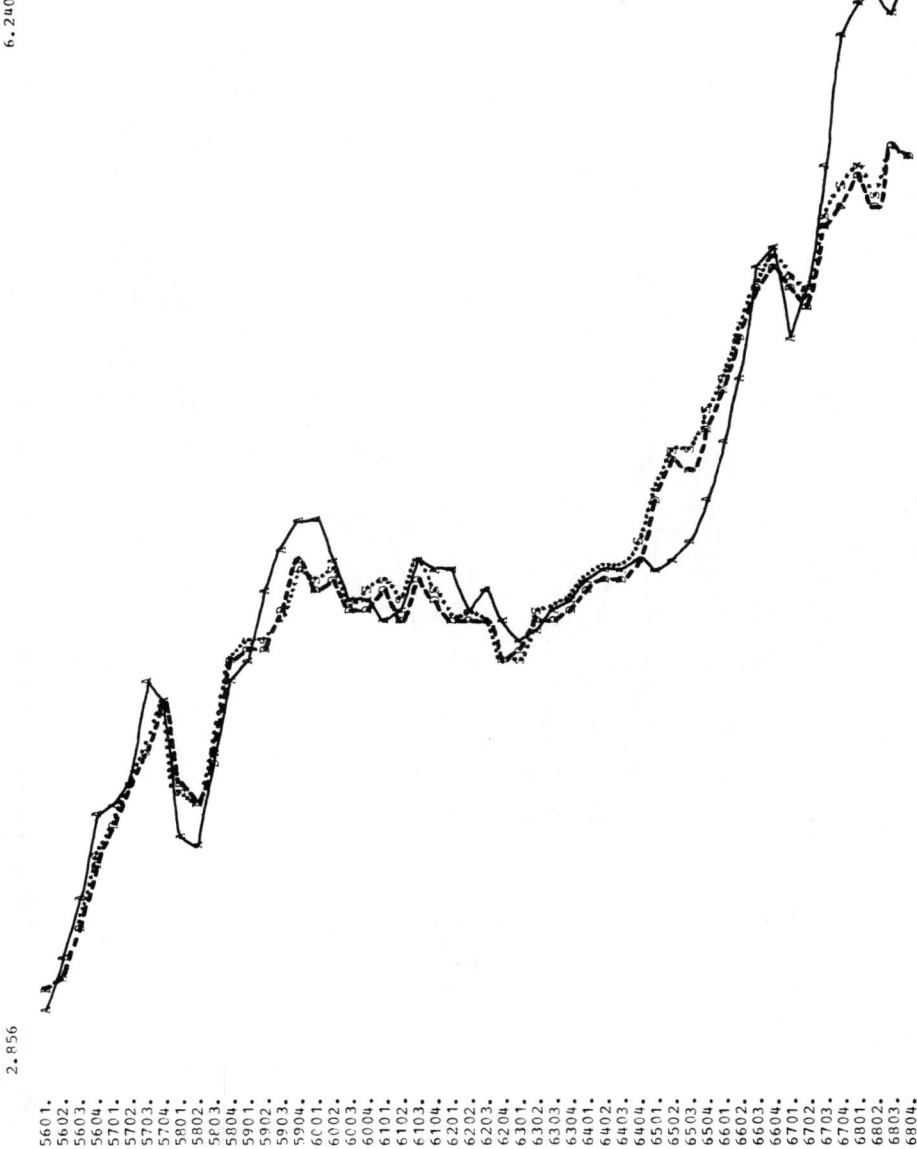

Figure 3-4b. Actual, Deterministic Dynamic Solution, and Mean Stochastic Dynamic Solution: Long-Term Interest Rate.

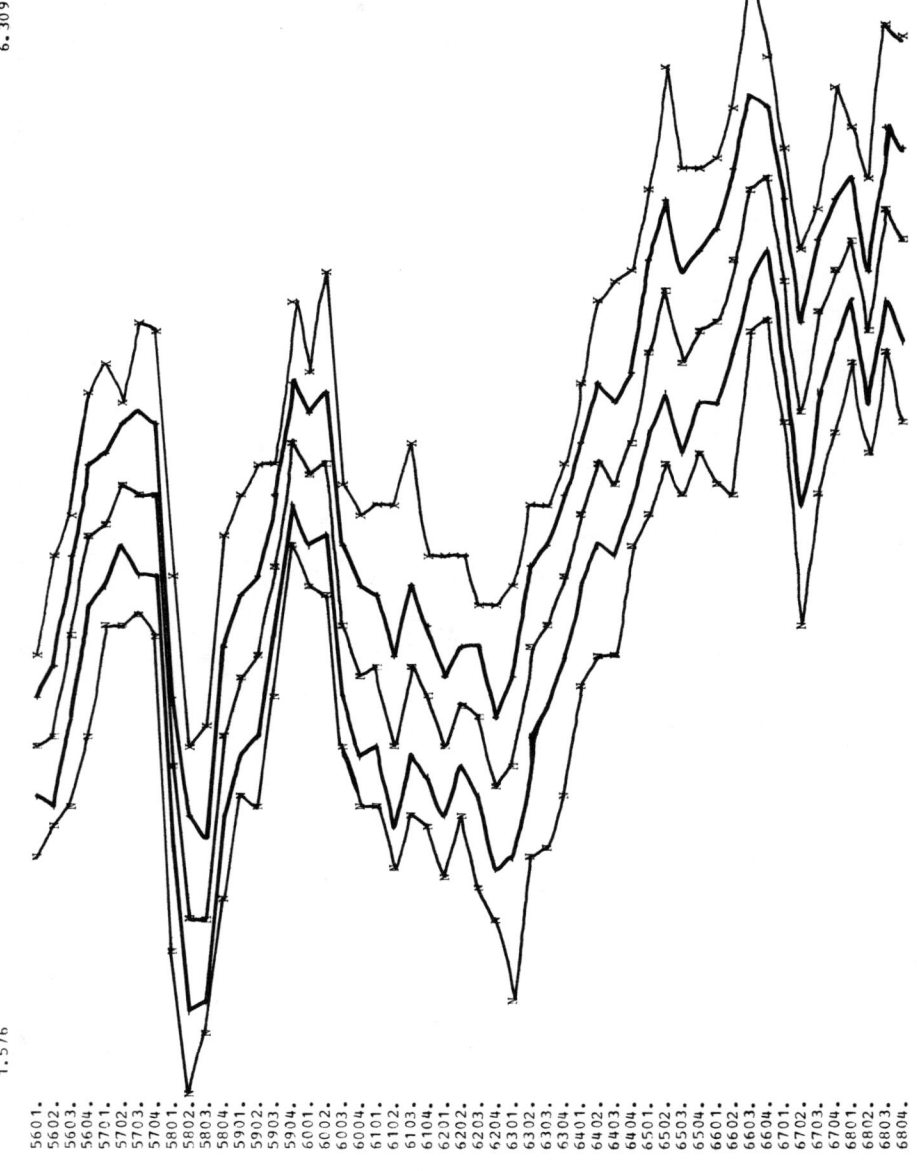

Figure 3-5a. Mean, Standard Deviation, Minimum, and Maximum of Stochastic Dynamic Solutions: Short-Term Interest Rate.

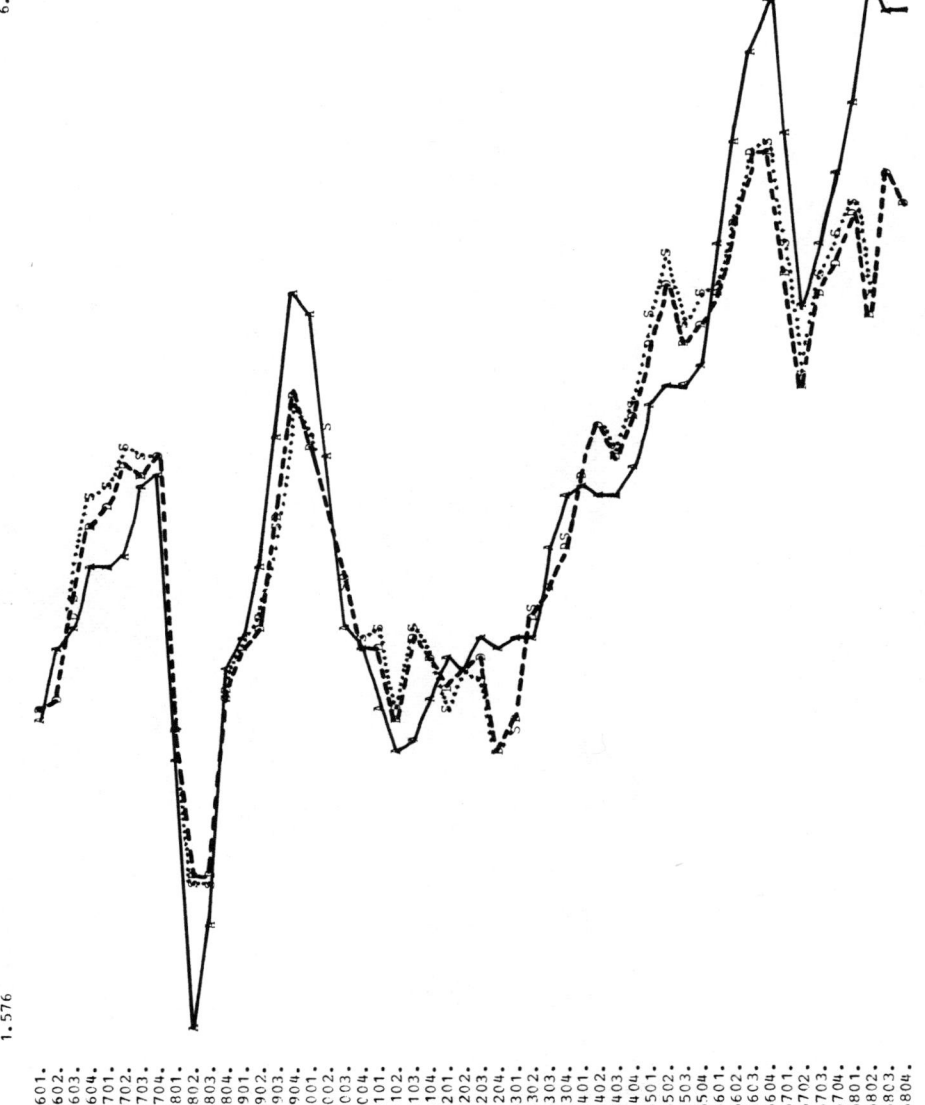

Figure 3-5b. Actual, Deterministic Dynamic Solution, and Mean Stochastic Dynamic Solution: Short-Term Interest Rate.

TABLE 3-1   Dynamic Simulation Summary: Nominal GNP

Year (4th Qtr.)	Actual	Deterministic Solution					Mean Stochastic Solution					Individual Replications: Goodness-of-Fit							Individual Replications: Distribution			
		SOLN.	CORR.	RMSE	MAE	ME	SOLN.	CORR.	RMSE	MAE	ME	CORR. μ σ		RMSE μ σ		MAE μ σ		ME μ σ		STD. DEV.	MIN.	MAX.	RANGE
1956	429.5	436.2	.99+	4.0	3.4	−3.4	435.1	.99+	3.4	2.8	−2.8	.98 .03	4.7 2.1	3.9 1.8	−2.8 2.7	5.2	424.5	444.0	19.5
1957	441.5	453.0	.99	6.8	5.9	−5.9	452.5	.99	6.0	5.2	−5.2	.98 .01	7.3 3.5	6.1 3.0	−5.2 3.7	6.9	440.0	465.5	25.5
1958	464.4	466.6	.96	8.6	7.1	−7.1	465.9	.96	7.8	6.4	−6.4	.94 .03	9.1 3.7	7.6 3.3	−6.4 4.0	7.7	452.5	479.2	26.7
1959	490.5	485.1	.95	8.7	7.4	−3.4	484.1	.96	8.3	6.9	−2.6	.94 .04	10.0 2.7	8.2 2.5	−2.6 4.1	7.0	468.7	498.1	29.4
1960	503.3	497.1	.97	9.3	8.1	−0.5	499.7	.98	8.8	7.5	−0.1	.96 .02	10.4 2.6	8.6 2.4	−0.1 3.6	5.6	488.6	509.0	20.4
1961	537.7	525.3	.98	9.3	8.2	1.0	525.1	.99	8.8	7.6	1.3	.97 .02	10.5 2.4	8.7 2.3	1.3 3.2	6.7	515.4	540.3	24.9
1962	572.0	556.1	.99	9.9	8.9	2.7	555.3	.99	9.7	8.5	3.0	.98 .01	11.4 2.7	9.5 2.4	3.0 3.1	8.5	538.5	568.2	29.7
1963	605.8	596.2	.99	10.2	9.2	3.9	597.7	.99	10.0	8.9	4.1	.99 .01	11.9 3.0	9.9 2.6	4.1 3.1	10.0	572.5	617.2	44.7
1964	645.1	643.4	.99	9.8	8.7	4.0	645.4	.99	9.5	8.3	4.0	.99 .01	11.8 3.2	9.8 2.7	4.0 3.4	9.1	630.6	675.3	44.7
1965	710.0	702.4	.99+	9.5	8.6	4.3	703.2	.99+	9.3	8.1	4.3	.99 .00	11.7 3.1	9.8 2.8	4.3 3.6	9.6	685.1	728.0	42.9
1966	768.2	743.3	.99+	10.5	9.3	5.4	742.1	.99+	10.4	8.9	5.4	.99+.00	12.8 3.1	10.5 2.8	5.4 3.9	12.5	721.9	769.0	47.1
1967	811.0	806.6	.92+	10.5	9.3	5.7	805.9	.99+	10.5	9.1	5.9	.99+.00	13.4 3.1	10.9 2.8	5.9 4.2	15.5	775.7	837.1	61.4
1968	887.4	863.2	.99+	11.4	10.0	6.7	861.9	.99+	11.5	9.8	6.9	.99+.00	14.6 3.9	11.7 3.2	6.9 4.8	20.0	827.3	898.8	71.5

TABLE 3-2 Dynamic Simulation Summary: GNP Deflator

Year (4th Qtr.)	Actual	Deterministic Solution					Mean Stochastic Solution					Individual Replication: Goodness-of-Fit								Individual Replications: Distribution			
		SOLN.	CORR.	RMSE	MAE	ME	SOLN.	CORR.	RMSE	MAE	ME	CORR. μ	CORR. σ	RMSE μ	RMSE σ	MAE μ	MAE σ	ME μ	ME σ	STD. DEV.	MIN.	MAX.	RANGE
1956	95.4	94.6	.99+	0.5	.4	.4	94.6	.99	0.5	0.4	0.4	.99	.01	0.6	0.2	0.5	0.2	0.4	0.3	0.4	93.8	95.5	1.7
1957	98.5	97.3	.99+	1.0	.8	.8	97.1	.99+	1.0	0.9	0.9	.99	.01	1.1	0.5	0.9	0.4	0.9	0.5	0.9	95.2	99.2	4.0
1958	100.6	99.7	.99	0.9	.8	.8	99.3	.99	1.1	1.0	1.0	.99	.01	1.3	0.7	1.1	0.6	1.0	0.7	1.6	95.3	102.1	6.8
1959	102.1	101.8	.99	0.9	.8	.8	101.4	.99	1.1	1.0	1.0	.98	.02	1.4	0.9	1.2	0.8	1.0	1.0	2.4	95.7	106.6	10.9
1960	104.0	104.7	.99	0.8	.7	.5	104.2	.99	1.0	0.9	0.8	.98	.02	1.7	1.1	1.5	0.9	0.8	1.3	3.6	97.6	113.5	15.9
1961	105.1	106.1	.99	0.8	.8	.3	105.7	.99	0.9	0.8	0.6	.97	.03	2.2	1.4	1.8	1.1	0.6	1.8	5.2	97.1	120.8	23.7
1962	106.3	107.3	.99	0.9	.8	.1	106.9	.99	0.9	0.8	0.4	.97	.05	2.7	1.9	2.2	1.4	0.4	2.4	6.4	96.6	126.8	30.2
1963	107.8	108.4	.99	0.9	.8	.0	108.0	.99	0.8	0.7	0.3	.96	.08	3.2	2.3	2.5	1.7	0.3	2.9	7.3	96.2	132.0	35.8
1964	109.6	109.8	.99	0.8	.8	−.1	109.4	.99	0.8	0.7	0.3	.95	.10	3.6	2.7	2.9	2.1	0.3	3.4	7.9	96.7	134.6	37.7
1965	111.5	111.2	.99	0.8	.7	.0	110.7	.99	0.8	0.7	0.3	.94	.09	3.9	2.9	3.2	2.3	0.3	3.8	8.0	98.7	134.7	36.0
1966	115.2	114.6	.99	0.8	.7	.0	114.0	.99	0.8	0.7	0.4	.95	.06	4.2	3.1	3.4	2.5	0.4	4.1	7.7	102.1	133.8	31.7
1967	118.9	117.9	.99	0.8	.7	.1	117.0	.99	0.9	0.8	0.5	.96	.04	4.5	3.1	3.7	2.6	0.5	4.3	7.5	105.6	134.6	29.0
1968	123.5	122.3	.99	0.8	.7	.2	121.2	.99	1.1	0.9	0.6	.96	.03	4.8	3.1	3.9	2.6	0.6	4.4	7.8	110.3	139.3	29.0

TABLE 3-3 Dynamic Simulation Summary: Real GNP

Year (4th Qtr.)	Actual	Deterministic Solution					Mean Stochastic Solution					Individual Replication: Goodness-of-Fit							Individual Replications: Distribution			
		SOLN.	CORR.	RMSE	MAE	ME	SOLN.	CORR.	RMSE	MAE	ME	CORR. μ σ		RMSE μ σ		MAE μ σ		ME μ σ		STD. DEV.	MIN.	MAX.	RANGE
1956	450.3	461.2	.94	6.6	5.5	−5.5	460.2	.95	5.9	5.0	−5.0	.89	.09	6.9	2.7	5.8	2.2	−5.0	3.1	5.6	450.1	471.3	21.2
1957	448.2	465.6	.91	11.5	10.1	−10.1	466.1	.90	11.0	9.6	−9.6	.84	.06	11.7	4.1	10.0	3.5	−9.6	3.7	7.2	455.7	484.4	28.7
1958	461.6	467.8	.64	12.9	11.3	−11.3	469.4	.66	12.8	11.3	−11.3	.57	.16	13.8	4.2	11.8	3.8	−11.3	4.1	9.9	449.3	489.3	40.0
1959	480.4	476.5	.74	11.6	9.9	−7.2	477.8	.79	11.4	9.6	−7.6	.62	.29	13.6	3.7	11.4	3.3	−7.6	5.0	12.7	452.3	504.9	52.6
1960	483.7	474.9	.83	11.7	10.3	−3.4	480.1	.87	10.9	9.4	−4.4	.67	.30	14.2	3.9	11.9	3.5	−4.4	6.0	16.1	441.7	513.2	71.5
1961	511.7	495.0	.90	12.1	10.8	−0.6	497.9	.93	10.8	9.4	−2.1	.72	.31	16.0	5.2	13.2	4.2	−2.1	8.0	25.7	433.9	549.7	115.8
1962	538.3	518.2	.95	13.0	11.7	1.9	521.5	.97	11.4	10.1	0.2	.83	.34	18.3	8.1	15.1	6.0	0.2	10.7	32.5	424.6	578.3	153.7
1963	562.1	550.1	.97	13.3	12.2	3.6	555.8	.98	11.4	10.1	1.5	.87	.35	20.5	10.6	16.8	7.8	1.5	13.5	38.8	433.8	615.2	181.4
1964	588.5	585.7	.97	12.8	11.6	3.9	592.6	.98	10.7	9.3	1.4	.90	.29	22.6	12.3	18.3	9.2	1.4	16.2	41.9	468.6	667.3	198.7
1965	636.6	631.7	.98	12.3	10.9	4.1	638.1	.99	10.2	8.6	1.2	.94	.15	24.1	13.7	19.7	10.6	1.2	18.5	42.7	517.2	715.9	198.7
1966	677.1	648.7	.99	12.3	11.0	4.8	653.4	.99	10.0	8.4	1.7	.97	.08	25.5	14.7	21.0	11.6	1.7	20.4	40.3	554.9	716.7	161.8
1967	681.8	684.2	.99	11.9	10.5	4.6	691.3	.99	9.8	8.1	1.3	.98	.05	26.3	15.1	21.8	12.3	1.3	21.7	42.0	585.5	768.8	183.3
1968	718.4	705.6	.99	11.6	10.2	4.9	714.1	.99	9.5	7.8	1.1	.98	.04	27.5	15.9	22.9	13.1	1.1	23.2	47.3	594.6	789.7	195.1

TABLE 3-4 Dynamic Simulation Summary: Long-Term Interest Rate

Year (4th Qtr.)	Actual	Deterministic Solution					Mean Stochastic Solution					Individual Replication: Goodness-of-Fit							Individual Replications: Distribution			
		SOLN.	CORR.	RMSE	MAE	ME	SOLN.	CORR.	RMSE	MAE	ME	CORR. μ	σ	RMSE μ	σ	MAE μ	σ	ME μ	σ	STD. DEV.	MIN.	MAX.	RANGE
1956	3.68	3.53	.98	.09	.09	.05	3.56	.98	.08	.08	.06	.93	.05	.14	.05	.11	.04	.06	.08	.12	3.36	3.76	.40
1957	4.00	4.00	.97	.10	.08	.06	4.00	.98	.09	.07	.06	.94	.02	.14	.04	.12	.03	.06	.08	.10	3.80	4.21	.41
1958	4.09	4.13	.94	.10	.08	.02	4.13	.95	.09	.08	.02	.91	.03	.15	.04	.12	.03	.02	.07	.16	3.93	4.54	.61
1959	4.57	4.44	.97	.11	.09	.04	4.42	.97	.11	.09	.04	.94	.02	.17	.04	.14	.03	.04	.08	.17	4.14	4.78	.64
1960	4.32	4.28	.97	.11	.09	.05	4.35	.97	.11	.09	.04	.94	.02	.17	.04	.14	.03	.04	.08	.18	3.97	4.80	.83
1961	4.41	4.32	.98	.11	.09	.04	4.34	.97	.10	.08	.03	.94	.02	.17	.04	.14	.03	.03	.08	.16	4.06	4.60	.54
1962	4.26	4.12	.97	.11	.09	.05	4.14	.97	.10	.08	.04	.93	.03	.18	.04	.14	.03	.04	.08	.19	3.81	4.54	.73
1963	4.33	4.29	.97	.10	.08	.05	4.33	.97	.10	.08	.04	.92	.03	.18	.04	.15	.03	.04	.08	.17	3.94	4.63	.69
1964	4.43	4.46	.97	.10	.08	.04	4.49	.97	.09	.07	.03	.92	.03	.18	.04	.15	.03	.03	.08	.18	4.13	4.79	.66
1965	4.61	4.84	.95	.12	.09	.02	4.90	.95	.13	.09	.00	.90	.03	.20	.04	.16	.04	.03	.08	.20	4.53	5.30	.77
1966	5.38	5.33	.97	.12	.09	.01	5.34	.97	.12	.09	−.01	.93	.02	.20	.04	.16	.04	−.01	.07	.18	4.94	5.70	.76
1967	6.04	5.52	.97	.14	.10	.02	5.57	.97	.14	.10	.00	.94	.02	.21	.04	.17	.03	.00	.07	.19	5.32	6.11	.79
1968	6.24	5.67	.97	.20	.14	.06	5.66	.97	.20	.13	.04	.95	.02	.26	.04	.20	.03	.04	.07	.22	5.26	6.23	.97

TABLE 3-5 Dynamic Simulation Summary: Short-Term Interest Rate

Year (4th Qtr.)	Actual	Deterministic Solution					Mean Stochastic Solution					Individual Replication: Goodness-of-Fit							Individual Replications: Distribution			
		SOLN.	CORR.	RMSE	MAE	ME	SOLN.	CORR.	RMSE	MAE	ME	CORR. μ σ		RMSE μ σ		MAE μ σ		ME μ σ		STD. DEV.	MIN.	MAX.	RANGE
1956	3.63	3.79	.92	.13	.11	−.01	3.92	.92	.19	.17	−.07	.81 .16	.33 .09	.28 .08	−.07 .18	.30	3.06	4.54	1.48
1957	3.99	4.08	.93	.19	.15	−.10	4.08	.92	.25	.21	−.16	.81 .11	.37 .11	.31 .10	−.16 .14	.33	3.51	4.76	1.25
1958	3.21	3.10	.95	.25	.19	−.13	3.07	.95	.27	.23	−.17	.88 .06	.40 .11	.32 .10	−.17 .15	.36	2.37	3.92	1.55
1959	4.76	4.36	.95	.26	.20	−.04	4.32	.93	.29	.24	−.06	.85 .07	.41 .10	.34 .09	−.06 .12	.26	3.88	4.92	1.04
1960	3.27	3.29	.94	.27	.20	−.02	3.34	.93	.29	.23	−.04	.84 .07	.41 .08	.34 .08	−.04 .10	.37	2.78	4.01	1.23
1961	3.06	3.25	.94	.27	.21	−.06	3.22	.92	.29	.24	−.08	.81 .08	.42 .09	.34 .07	−.08 .09	.33	2.68	3.86	1.18
1962	3.26	2.86	.92	.26	.20	−.03	2.84	.90	.29	.24	−.04	.79 .07	.42 .07	.34 .06	−.04 .09	.32	2.31	3.63	1.32
1963	3.91	3.71	.91	.26	.20	−.00	3.75	.89	.28	.23	−.02	.77 .08	.42 .06	.33 .06	−.02 .09	.36	2.81	4.21	1.40
1964	4.06	4.25	.91	.25	.20	−.02	4.32	.89	.27	.23	−.04	.78 .07	.41 .06	.33 .05	−.04 .09	.27	3.90	5.05	1.15
1965	4.47	4.66	.92	.26	.21	−.05	4.79	.90	.29	.25	−.07	.82 .05	.43 .07	.34 .06	−.07 .08	.33	4.26	5.44	1.18
1966	6.00	5.36	.95	.28	.23	−.01	5.42	.94	.30	.26	−.03	.87 .03	.44 .06	.35 .05	−.03 .08	.28	4.81	5.92	1.11
1967	5.30	4.91	.95	.29	.24	.03	5.03	.94	.30	.26	−.01	.88 .03	.44 .05	.35 .05	−.01 .08	.32	4.33	5.80	1.47
1968	5.96	5.18	.95	.37	.28	.09	5.14	.94	.38	.30	.06	.88 .04	.50 .06	.39 .05	.06 .08	.42	4.40	6.02	1.62

142

(MAX.), and range of the individual stochastic replications—are shown in the last four columns.

Several general tendencies in the figures and the tables are apparent. Most striking is closeness of the deterministic solution and the stochastic mean, a result also reported for the Brookings Model by Nagar [60]. The resolution of the large computer-drawn graphs frequently did not permit the two time paths to be distinguished, even for the interest rates which have substantial variability. It seems that, at least so far as the first moment of the stochastic solutions is concerned, the nonlinearity of the FMP model is of little consequence.

Both of these paths track the actual path remarkably well in the 52-quarter dynamic simulation. There is a persistent tendency, however, to underestimate the amplitude of relative peaks and troughs and, also, the fit of the interest rates deteriorates noticeably in the last four or five quarters. (The last eight quarters of the simulation are beyond the period over which the model was estimated.) Still, the actual time path generally falls well within the range of values observed in the 25 stochastic replications.

A third tendency is quite expected—the increase in magnitude with time in the standard deviation and the range of the stochastic solutions. This follows from the accumulation of errors due to the presence of a large number of lagged endogenous variables in the model. We would not expect to observe this in the one-period simulation of section 3.3 where lagged endogenous variables are reset each period to their historical values. It is interesting, though, to point out that, even here in dynamic simulation, the phenomenon is far from a strict rule. It is not apparent for the short rate and only moderately noticeable for the long rate. Further, the increases in dispersion, where they do occur very visibly (say, for the three GNP variables), are by no means a strict rule; that is, there are fluctuations in the dispersion although it undeniably trends upward. While 25 replications may not be a large enough sample not to attribute these "exceptions" to the drawings of random numbers in those periods, it is more likely that the ultimate effect of shocking the model depends critically on the values of the exogenous variables in a particular quarter and the current state of the system. In a completely linear difference equation model with additive disturbances, we could show that the *only* source of variation in the tendency for measures of dispersion to increase would be the particular drawings of random numbers. In a stable model, we would expect the variance to approach a limit asymptotically. In the FMP model, on the other hand, this variation is induced more by nonlinearities of various sorts affecting the way the model responds to all exogenous influences and its current state.

Another general observation tends to support the contentions of the previous paragraph. The time paths of the minimum and maximum of the stochastic replications are not at all symmetrically situated about the mean. This is especially evident for real GNP and the deflator but it is true also for the interest rates, although somewhat hidden by the greater variability in these latter two series.[12]

Turning to the individual series, we can also make a number of interesting observations. For nominal GNP and based on the RMSE and MAE, the stochastic mean tracks the historical path better than the deterministic solution, although, as already noted, the two solutions are quite close to each other. Over the first half of the period, the stochastic mean also had smaller bias (|ME|). Over the 52 quarters, the RMSE of both paths rise very slowly from the neighborhood of 4 to about 11, the MAE from about 3 to 10—a creditable performance.

The four goodness-of-fit measures were calculated in a similar manner for each individual stochastic solution and the mean and standard deviation of these are reported. Obviously, the mean of the individual ME must be identical to the ME of the stochastic mean. The other three measures involve more than linear operators, though, and no such equivalence is observed. Because we, in effect, algebraically cancel errors in calculating the stochastic mean, the average of the individual RMSE and MAE must exceed the corresponding RMSE and MAE, respectively, of the stochastic mean.[13] This all hints at another problem with deterministic simulation *even in linear systems*. If the stochastic nature of the system is vital to a problem under investigation and the problem includes measures of performance—say, for social welfare—which are nonlinear, we may still require stochastic simulation! The separation principle of taking expectations first (deterministic solution in a linear system or mean stochastic solution) and then evaluating the nonlinear function will not in general[14] be equivalent to taking the expectation of the function of individual stochastic replications. Thus, in questions of macroeconomic stabilization where it is essential to confront the policy decision maker with an uncertain environment, the use of deterministic simulation for evaluating alternative policies according to some utility function involves certain distortions. We must judge these distortions from two points of view: the social-welfare loss of misspecification, evaluated relative to benchmarks like the costs of other approximations that modeling involves; and the nonnegligible additional costs of stochastic simulation, especially given that statistical tests of results are only approximate.[15]

As pointed out earlier, we note that the stochastic mean comes with a standard deviation, whereas no measures of confidence are possible in deterministic simulation. Since the set of replications, we hope, constitutes a random sample, we can calculate the standard deviation of the mean stochastic solution by dividing the standard deviation of the individual replications by the square root of the number of replications. For example, in the first row of Table 3–1, the stochastic mean of nominal GNP in 1956: IV is 435.1 and its standard deviation will be $5.2/\sqrt{25}$ or approximately 1.0. Similarly, we could calculate the standard deviation for the ME of the mean stochastic solution, but not for the deterministic solution. In 1956 again, the ME of the stochastic mean is -2.8 with a standard deviation of $2.7/\sqrt{25}$ or approximately 0.5. It should be apparent that the "randomness" of the mean stochastic solution is a function of the number of replications. With enough replications, it does converge in probability to the true mean (assuming the specification is correct), which can be calculated in principle—say, by a Taylor series approximation—but is rarely done so for obvious reasons. The standard deviation of the individual replications is most useful as the basis for tests of model validity. As we have mentioned, we do not perform tests of this particular type here.

Table 3–2 and Figure 3–2b clearly indicate that the result obtained for nominal GNP—that the stochastic mean tended to be a better predictor than the deterministic solution—is not true in general. In the case of the GNP deflator, the deterministic solution outperforms the stochastic mean over most of the sample period, though by a very small margin. Another observation from the table is that although the RMSE or MAE of the stochastic mean are fairly stable (i.e., do not trend upward) for the last 12 of 13 rows in the table, the RMSE of the individual stochastic solutions increase sharply with time. Further, although the ME of the stochastic mean is always positive, a glance at the rising standard deviation of the individual ME indicates immediately that many of the individual replications do not share this attribute of their mean. In 1968: IV, for example, the standard deviation of the ME (0.6) is $0.9(=4.4/\sqrt{25})$. This discrepancy is confirmed by the dispersion statistics in the table and Figure 3–2a. The marked skewness of the stochastic solutions of the GNP deflator could be due to the fact that the price mechanism in the model is a principle area of nonlinearity.

In the case of real GNP, the stochastic mean is clearly a better predictor than the deterministic solution. Here, too, the stability of the RMSE and MAE over time hides the increasing dispersion in the stochastic solutions evident from looking at the measures averaged over individual replications or Figure 3–3a. This dispersion affects not only the means of the measures but also their standard deviations. It is, in fact, disturbing to find the range in real GNP as high as $200 billion and the standard deviation on the order of $40 billion. Since the skewness of real GNP seems to be opposite in direction to that observed for the GNP deflator, we did not see this effect in their product, nominal GNP.

The striking observation about the interest-rate graphs in Figures 3–4a and 3–5a is the manner in which the jaggedness of the minimum and maximum reflects movements in the mean; since these two curves are envelopes of the individual replications, much smoother series might have been expected. For both interest-rate series, we also find that there is no general conclusion as to which of the deterministic solution and the stochastic mean is the better predictor of the actual; again the differences are small, anyway. Over most of the sample period the RMSE and MAE for the two paths are fairly stable. This is confirmed by looking at those measures for the individual replications, the dispersion statistics, and Figures 3–4a and 3–5a. Both interest rates deteriorate in fit in the last part of the post-estimation period. Finally, the short rate solutions exhibit many of the same, unfortunate, characteristic "spiking" noted in the Monetary Sector simulations of Chapter 1.

3.3 One–Period Simulation Results

The experiments and calculations of the previous section are repeated but all simulations are now one-period. This enables us to learn more about the (one-quarter-ahead) forecasting performance of the model; but, of course, most of the dynamic elements of the structure are no longer apparent. The same uniform random numbers are used to generate the stochastic disturbances, so that all differences between the results of this section and the last are due solely to the resetting, each period, of lagged endogenous variables to their historical values.

Figures and Tables 3–6 to 3–10 correspond to last section's Figures and Tables 3–1 to 3–5, respectively. One change is made in Figures 3–6a, 3–7a, and 3–8a. Dispersion of the individual stochastic solutions was too small for the resolution of the computer-drawn graphs. On these three figures of the GNP variables, only the mean, minimum, and maximum appear; the one-standard-deviation band around the mean has been suppressed. The tables and figures are left for the reader to peruse. A very few general conclusions are offered, though, highlighting some differences from those of the preceding section.

The stochastic mean and deterministic solution are even closer than they were in dynamic simulation. What was said about the ex post prediction performance of the deterministic solution in Chapter 2, thus, holds true here for both time paths. The reader who is interested in a criterion of forecasting performance other than squared error— such as analysis of turning points—may find the "b" parts of the five figures instructive since no graphs of this type were presented there. As before, historical values generally fall within the range of stochastic solutions; the notable exceptions are the interest rates in the latter part of the postestimation period. The range of one-period simulations, of course, is much smaller than that of dynamic simulations.

There are no discernible trends in the dispersion statistics. A useful piece of information that comes out of these dispersion statistics is a measure of the variability induced in the five variables by stochastic simulation. For nominal GNP, GNP deflator, real GNP, long-term interest rate and short-term interest rate we find the standard deviations of stochastic solutions to be on the order of 3.5, 0.2, 3.5, 0.10 and 0.23, respectively; variation in these numbers from quarter to quarter of 20 percent is not uncommon. For the five variables (in the same order), the ranges are on the order of 13, 0.7, 14, 0.40, and 0.90, respectively. These numbers represent the way the system of equations dissipates the normally distributed intercorrelated shocks added to 59 different equations each quarter.

As we also noted in the last section, the mean of the individual RMSE and MAE exceed the RMSE and MAE of the mean stochastic solution. There are no significant trends here in any of these statistics for any of the variables. Real and nominal GNP did perform

Figure 3-6a. Mean, Minimum, and Maximum of Stochastic One-Period Solutions: Nominal GNP.

Figure 3–6b. Actual, Deterministic One-Period Solution, and Mean Stochastic One-Period Solution: Nominal GNP.

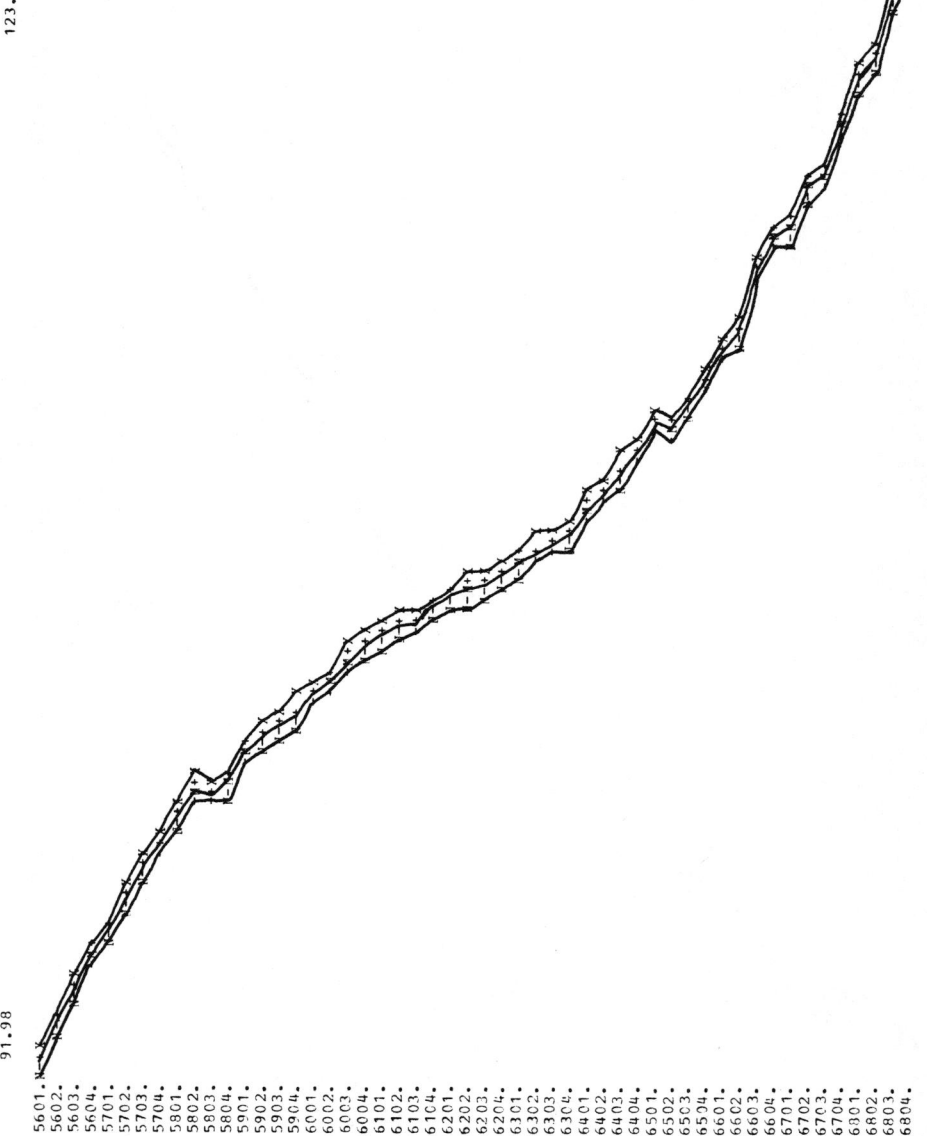

Figure 3–7a. Mean, Minimum, and Maximum of Stochastic One-Period Solutions: GNP Deflator.

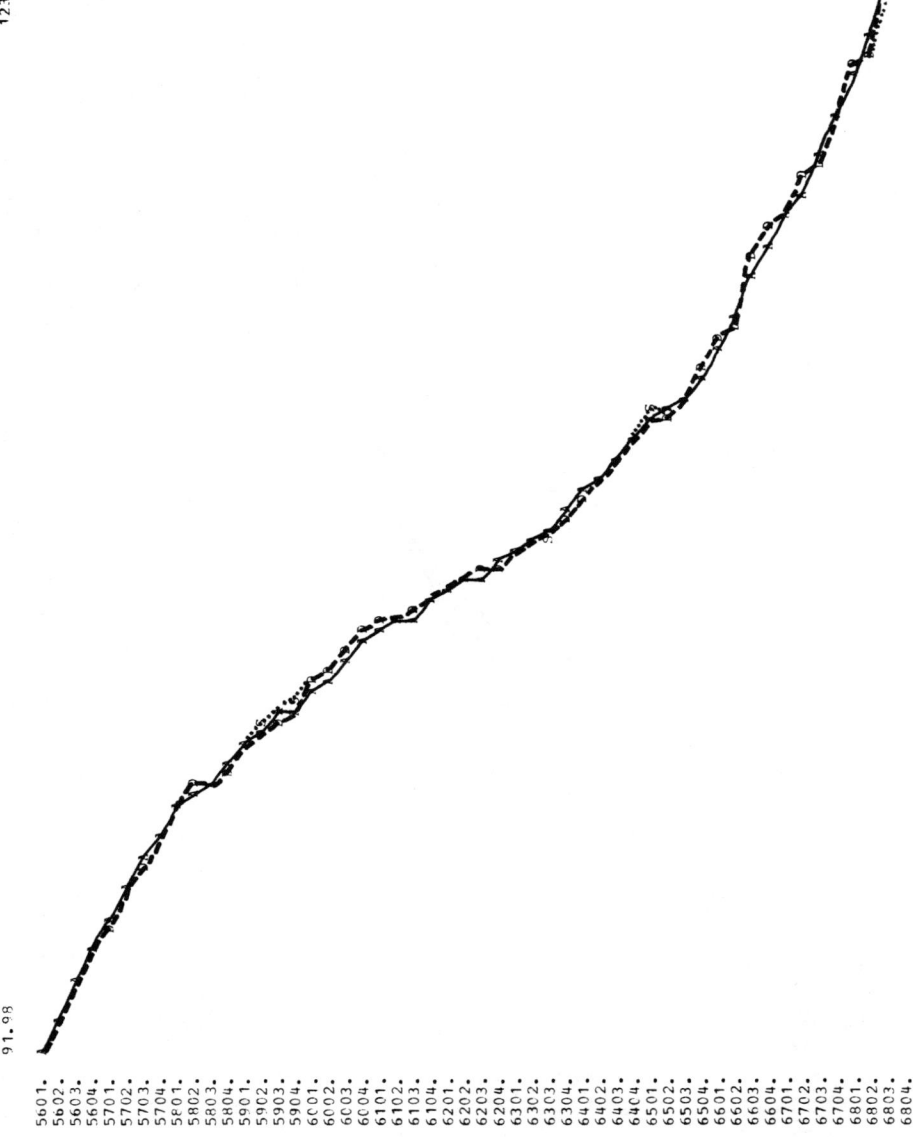

Figure 3-7b. Actual, Deterministic One-Period Solution, and Mean Stochastic One-Period Solution: GNP Deflator.

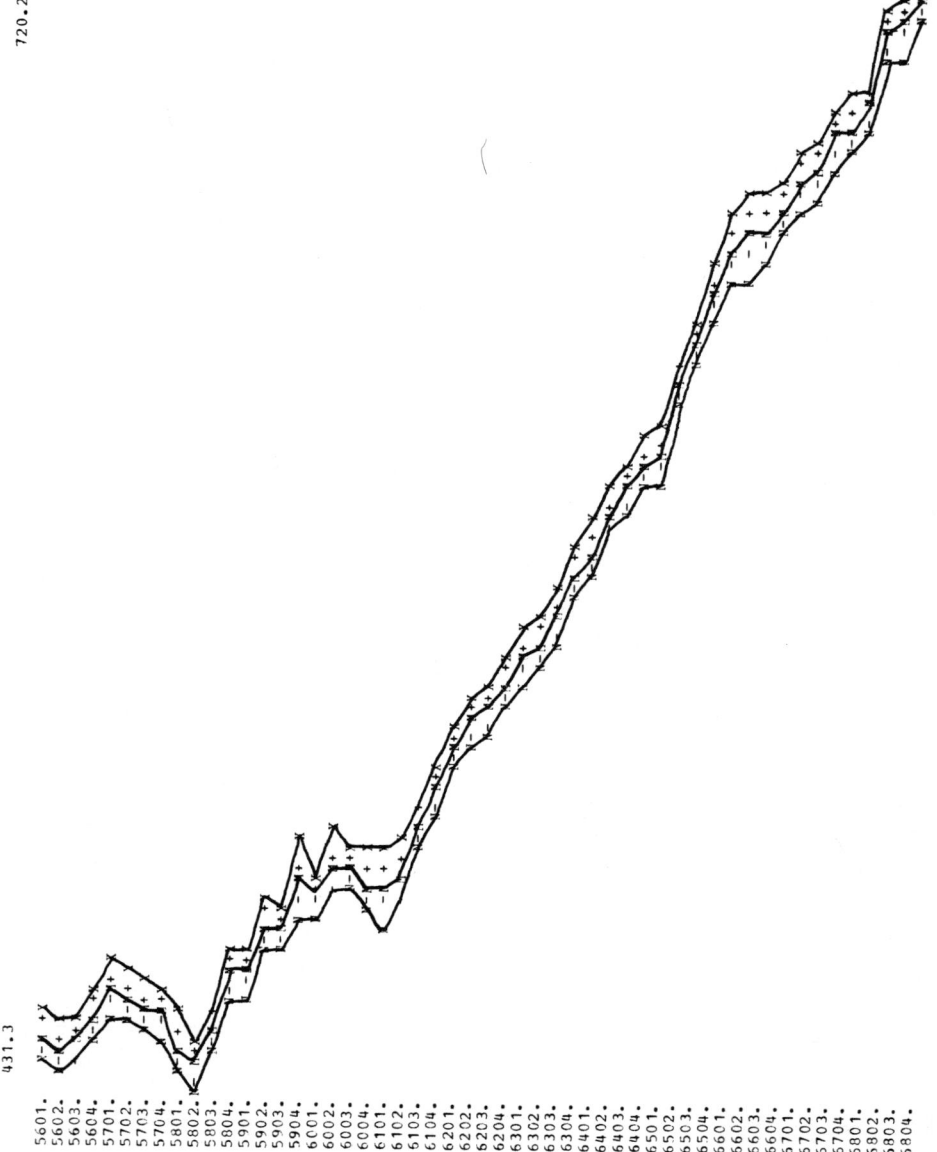

Figure 3–8a. Mean, Minimum, and Maximum of Stochastic One-Period Solutions: Real GNP.

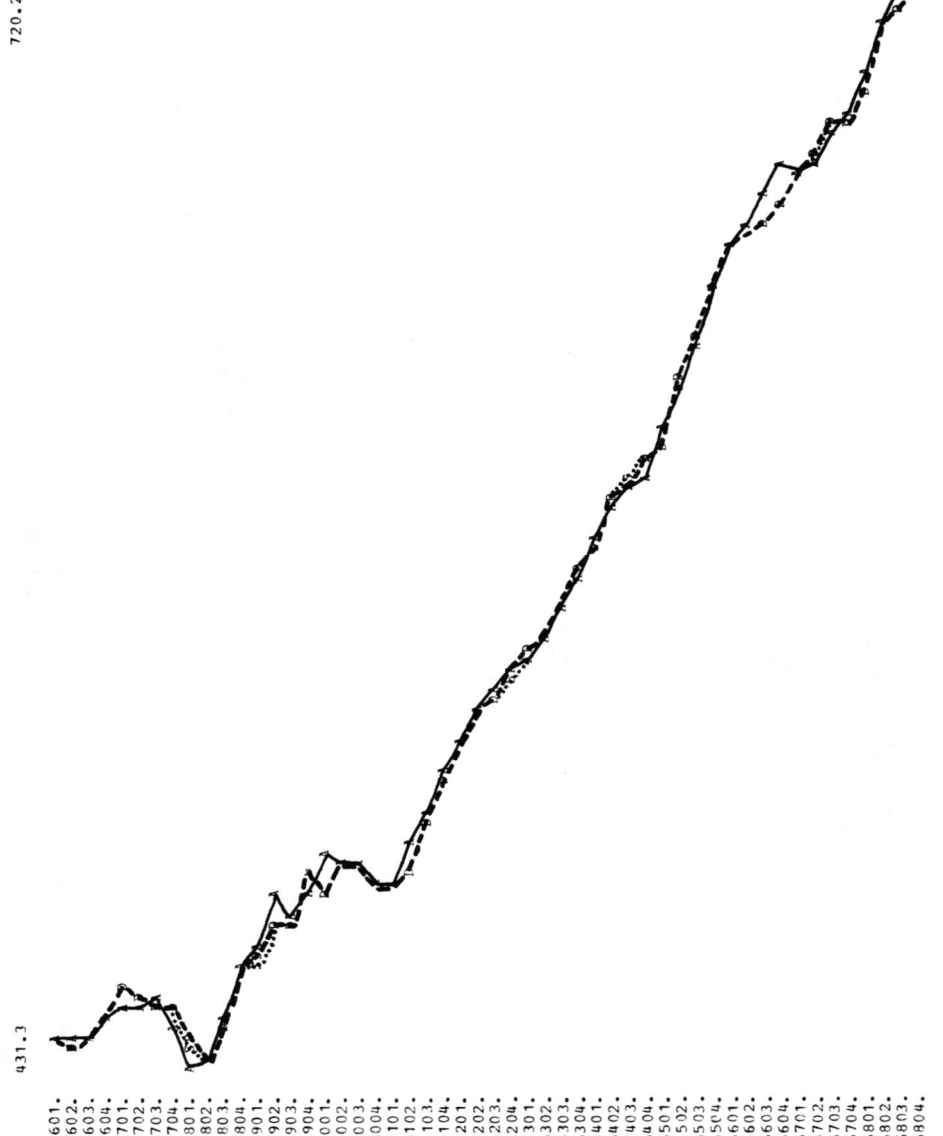

Figure 3-8b. Actual, Deterministic One-Period Solution, and Mean Stochastic One-Period Solution: Real GNP.

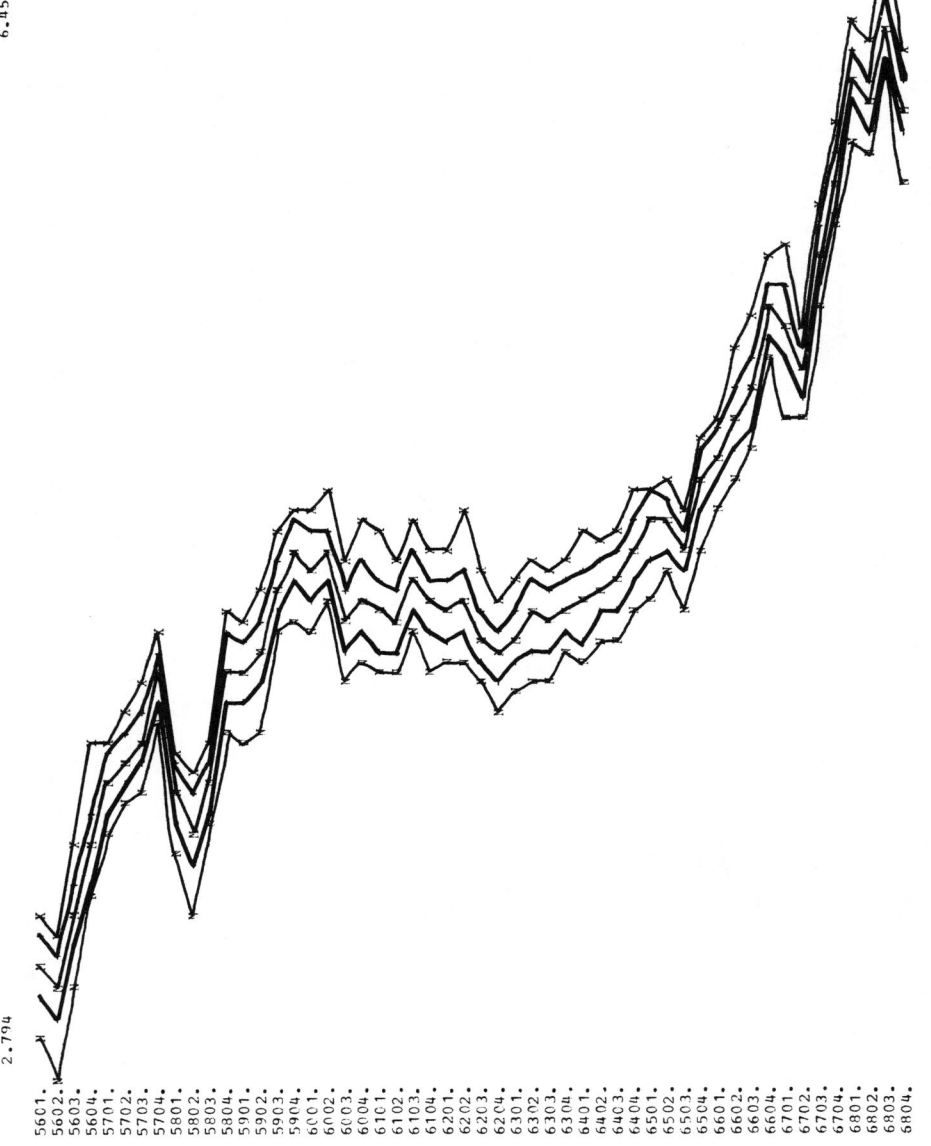

Figure 3-9a. Mean, Standard Deviation, Minimum, and Maximum of Stochastic One-Period Solutions: Long-Term Interest Rate.

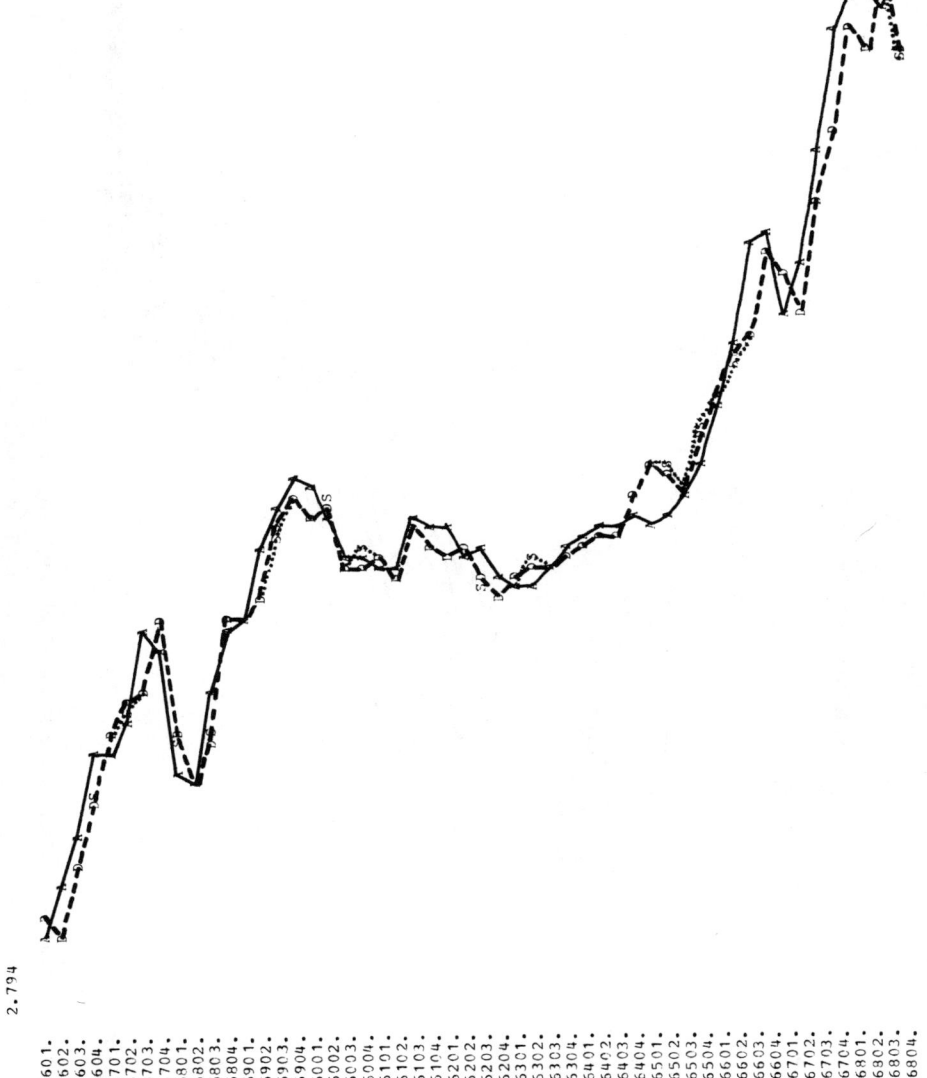

Figure 3-9b. Actual, Deterministic One-Period Solution, and Mean Stochastic One-Period Solution: Long-Term Interest Rate.

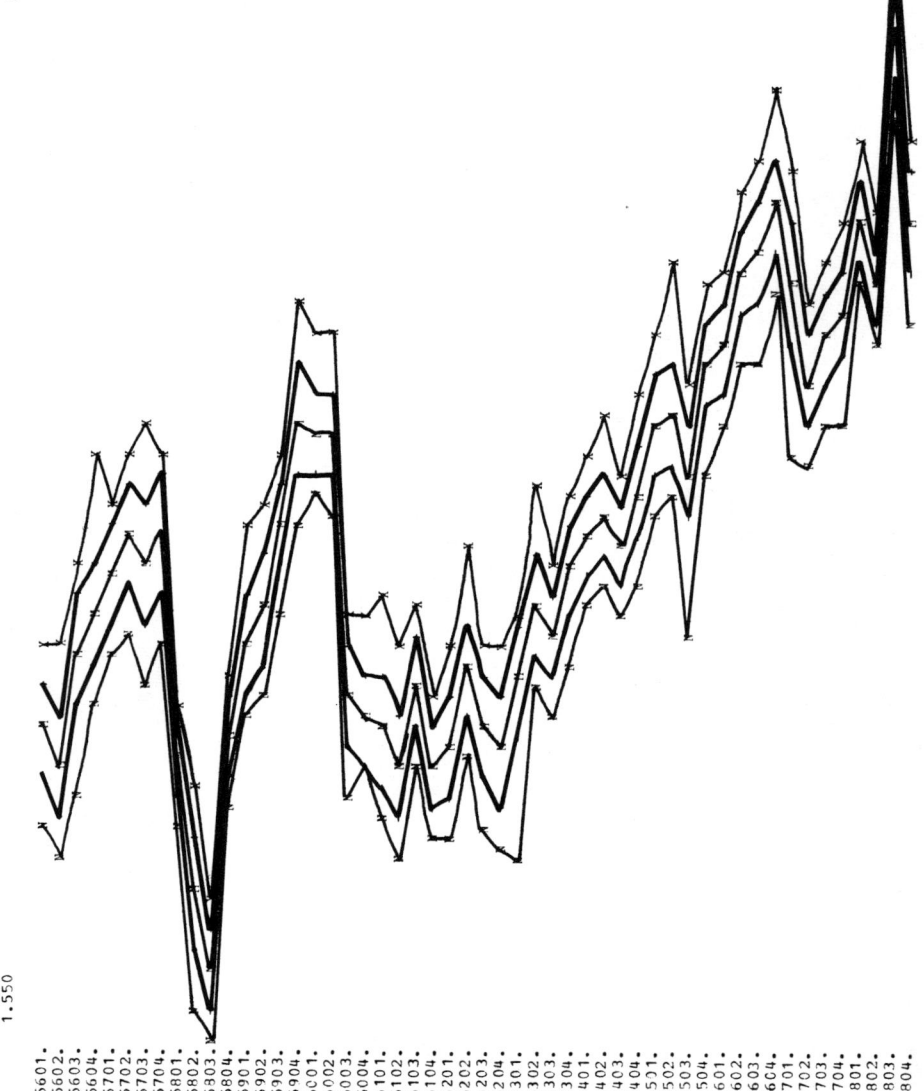

Figure 3–10a. Mean, Standard Deviation, Minimum, and Maximum of Stochastic One-Period Solutions: Short-Term Interest Rate.

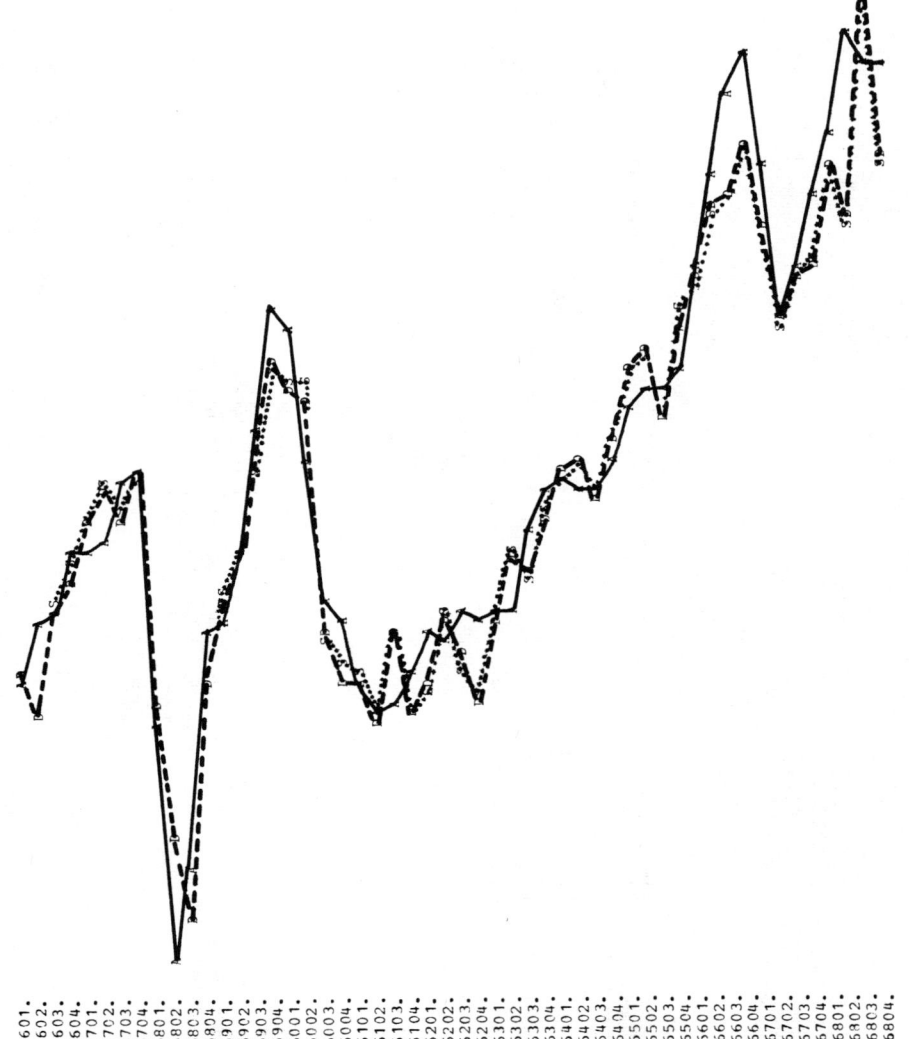

Figure 3–10b. Actual, Deterministic One-Period Solution, and Mean Stochastic One-Period Solution: Short-Term Interest Rate.

TABLE 3-6 One-Period Simulation Summary: Nominal GNP

Year (4th Qtr.)	Actual	Deterministic Solution				Mean Stochastic Solution					Individual Replication: Goodness-of-Fit							Individual Replications: Distribution			
											CORR.		RMSE		MAE		ME		STD.			
		SOLN.	CORR.	RMSE	MAE	ME	SOLN.	CORR.	RMSE	MAE	ME	μ	σ	μ	σ	μ	σ	μ	σ	DEV.	MIN.	MAX.	RANGE
1956	429.5	429.4	.98	1.7	1.3	0.8	429.5	.97	2.2	1.7	1.1	.94	.05	3.3	.9	2.9	1.0	1.1	1.4	3.4	422.9	435.6	12.7
1957	441.5	444.6	.98	2.5	2.0	0.2	444.7	.98	2.4	2.1	0.2	.97	.02	3.5	.9	3.0	.9	0.2	1.0	2.8	438.7	450.6	11.9
1958	464.4	463.8	.98	2.9	2.3	0.1	462.7	.98	2.7	2.3	0.2	.97	.02	3.8	.8	3.2	.7	0.2	0.6	2.9	457.5	468.7	11.2
1959	490.5	495.3	.99	3.4	2.7	0.5	495.2	.99	3.3	2.8	0.7	.99	.01	4.4	.7	3.6	.6	0.7	0.6	4.1	487.2	504.8	17.6
1960	503.3	503.5	.99	3.6	2.8	0.7	504.8	.99	3.6	3.0	0.7	.99	.00	4.6	.7	3.8	.6	0.7	0.6	3.9	498.0	512.8	14.6
1961	537.7	535.0	.99+	3.6	2.9	0.9	534.5	.99+	3.5	3.0	1.0	.99	.00	4.7	.5	3.8	.5	1.0	0.6	3.3	529.6	539.0	9.4
1962	572.0	570.0	.99+	3.4	2.7	1.0	569.3	.99+	3.4	2.9	1.1	.99+	.00	4.6	.5	3.7	.5	1.1	0.5	3.3	563.3	576.5	13.2
1963	605.8	605.8	.99+	3.2	2.5	1.0	606.5	.99+	3.2	2.6	1.0	.99+	.00	4.5	.5	3.6	.4	1.0	0.4	2.7	601.2	611.7	10.5
1964	645.1	549.1	.99+	3.2	2.4	0.7	649.5	.99+	3.2	2.6	0.7	.99+	.00	4.5	.4	3.6	.4	0.7	0.5	3.3	644.0	656.2	12.2
1965	710.0	710.1	.99+	3.1	2.3	0.7	711.1	.99+	3.2	2.6	0.6	.99+	.00	4.5	.4	3.6	.4	0.6	0.4	3.2	703.3	717.2	13.9
1966	768.2	762.5	.99+	3.1	2.4	0.9	761.8	.99+	3.3	2.6	0.8	.99+	.00	4.6	.5	3.7	.4	0.8	0.4	3.6	754.8	769.0	14.2
1967	811.0	808.8	.99+	3.1	2.3	0.7	807.7	.99+	3.2	2.6	0.7	.99+	.00	4.6	.4	3.7	.3	0.7	0.4	4.4	801.9	817.9	16.0
1968	887.4	880.4	.99+	3.3	2.6	1.1	880.2	.99+	3.5	2.8	1.1	.99+	.00	4.8	.4	3.9	.3	1.1	0.4	3.6	874.6	889.0	14.4

TABLE 3-7 One-Period Simulation Summary: GNP Deflator

Year (4th Qtr.)	Actual	Deterministic Solution					Mean Stochastic Solution					Individual Replication: Goodness-of-Fit								Individual Replications: Distribution			
		SOLN.	CORR.	RMSE	MAE	ME	SOLN.	CORR.	RMSE	MAE	ME	CORR. μ	σ	RMSE μ	σ	MAE μ	σ	ME μ	σ	STD. DEV.	MIN.	MAX.	RANGE
1956	95.4	95.5	.99+	.2	.1	.1	95.4	.99+	.2	.1	.1	.99	.01	.2	.1	.2	.1	.1	.1	.2	95.1	95.7	.6
1957	98.5	98.5	.99+	.2	.1	.1	98.5	.99+	.2	.1	.1	.99+	.00	.2	.0	.2	.0	.1	.1	.2	98.2	98.7	.5
1958	100.6	100.4	.99+	.2	.1	.1	100.3	.99+	.2	.2	.1	.99+	.00	.3	.0	.2	.0	.1	.0	.2	99.8	100.6	.8
1959	102.1	102.1	.99+	.2	.1	.1	102.2	.99+	.2	.1	.0	.99+	.00	.2	.0	.2	.0	.0	.0	.2	101.8	102.8	1.0
1960	104.0	104.2	.99+	.2	.1	.0	104.2	.99+	.2	.2	.0	.99+	.00	.3	.0	.2	.0	.0	.0	.2	103.8	104.5	.7
1961	105.1	105.1	.99+	.2	.1	.0	105.2	.99+	.2	.2	.0	.99+	.00	.3	.0	.2	.0	.0	.0	.1	104.9	105.4	.5
1962	106.3	106.1	.99+	.2	.1	.0	106.2	.99+	.2	.2	.0	.99+	.00	.3	.0	.2	.0	.0	.0	.1	105.8	106.5	.7
1963	107.8	107.3	.99+	.2	.2	.0	107.3	.99+	.2	.2	.0	.99+	.00	.3	.0	.2	.0	.0	.0	.2	107.0	107.6	.6
1964	109.6	109.7	.99+	.2	.1	.0	109.7	.99+	.2	.2	.0	.99+	.00	.3	.0	.2	.0	.0	.0	.1	109.4	110.0	.6
1965	111.5	111.7	.99+	.2	.1	.0	111.7	.99+	.2	.2	.0	.99+	.00	.3	.0	.2	.0	.0	.0	.1	111.4	112.0	.6
1966	115.2	115.7	.99+	.2	.2	.0	115.7	.99+	.2	.2	.0	.99+	.00	.3	.0	.2	.0	.0	.0	.2	115.4	116.1	.7
1967	118.9	119.0	.99+	.2	.2	.0	119.0	.99+	.2	.2	.0	.99+	.00	.3	.0	.2	.0	.0	.0	.2	118.5	119.2	.7
1968	123.5	123.5	.99+	.3	.2	.0	123.5	.99+	.2	.2	.0	.99+	.00	.3	.0	.2	.0	.0	.0	.1	123.3	123.8	.5

TABLE 3-8 One-Period Simulation Summary: Real GNP

Year (4th Qtr.)	Actual	Deterministic Solution					Mean Stochastic Solution					Individual Replication: Goodness-of-Fit							Individual Replications: Distribution			
		SOLN.	CORR.	RMSE	MAE	ME	SOLN.	CORR.	RMSE	MAE	ME	CORR. μ σ	RMSE μ σ	MAE μ σ	ME μ σ				STD. DEV.	MIN.	MAX.	RANGE
1956	450.3	449.8	.79	1.9	1.5	0.6	450.0	.72	2.5	1.9	1.0	.54 .35	3.9 1.0	3.4 1.1	1.0 1.6				4.1	443.4	458.1	14.7
1957	448.2	451.4	.84	2.6	2.3	-0.2	451.5	.87	2.7	2.4	-0.2	.76 .12	4.0 1.0	3.4 1.0	-0.2 1.1				3.1	445.0	456.4	11.4
1958	461.6	462.1	.90	2.9	2.4	-0.3	461.3	.92	2.8	2.3	-0.2	.83 .07	4.1 .8	3.4 .8	-0.2 .7				3.2	455.2	468.0	12.8
1959	480.4	485.1	.97	3.3	2.8	0.2	484.7	.97	3.3	2.9	0.4	.94 .02	4.6 .8	3.8 .7	0.4 .7				4.5	476.5	495.5	19.0
1960	483.7	483.3	.98	3.6	2.9	0.6	484.4	.98	3.6	3.0	0.7	.96 .01	4.8 .8	3.9 .6	0.7 .7				4.0	477.6	494.0	16.4
1961	511.7	508.8	.99	3.7	3.0	1.0	508.1	.99	3.7	3.1	1.0	.98 .01	4.9 .6	4.0 .6	1.0 .6				3.3	502.8	513.5	10.7
1962	538.3	537.2	.99	3.5	2.8	1.0	536.3	.99	3.5	2.9	1.1	.99 .00	4.8 .5	3.9 .5	1.1 .5				3.2	530.0	543.3	13.3
1963	562.1	564.5	.99+	3.3	2.6	0.8	565.2	.99+	3.3	2.7	0.9	.99 .00	4.7 .5	3.8 .5	0.9 .4				2.9	559.3	570.6	11.3
1964	588.5	591.7	.99+	3.2	2.5	0.6	592.2	.99+	3.3	2.6	0.6	.99+ .00	4.7 .5	3.7 .4	0.6 .5				3.3	586.2	599.4	13.2
1965	636.6	635.9	.99+	3.2	2.5	0.6	636.7	.99+	3.4	2.7	0.6	.99+ .00	4.7 .4	3.8 .4	0.6 .4				3.0	629.4	643.6	14.2
1966	667.1	659.0	.99+	3.4	2.7	0.9	658.4	.99+	3.6	2.8	0.9	.99+ .00	4.9 .4	3.9 .4	0.9 .4				3.3	651.3	664.9	13.6
1967	681.8	679.6	.99+	3.3	2.6	0.8	679.2	.99+	3.5	2.7	0.8	.99+ .00	4.9 .4	3.9 .4	0.8 .4				4.2	673.6	689.6	16.0
1968	718.4	712.8	.99+	3.5	2.7	1.0	712.7	.99+	3.7	2.9	1.1	.99+ .00	5.0 .4	4.0 .3	1.1 .4				3.2	706.8	720.2	13.4

TABLE 3-9 One-Period Simulation Summary: Long-Term Interest Rate

Year (4th Qtr.)	Actual	Deterministic Solution					Mean Stochastic Solution					Individual Replication: Goodness-of-Fit								Individual Replications: Distribution			
		SOLN.	CORR.	RMSE	MAE	ME	SOLN.	CORR.	RMSE	MAE	ME	CORR. μ	σ	RMSE μ	σ	MAE μ	σ	ME μ	σ	STD. DEV.	MIN.	MAX.	RANGE
1956	3.68	3.51	.90	.14	.13	.09	3.55	.92	.12	.12	.09	.87	.08	.16	.04	.13	.03	.09	.05	.11	3.39	3.89	.50
1957	4.00	4.11	.94	.13	.12	.04	4.11	.95	.12	.11	.04	.92	.02	.15	.02	.12	.02	.04	.03	.08	3.94	4.26	.32
1958	4.09	4.13	.93	.12	.11	.02	4.12	.94	.11	.10	.03	.91	.02	.14	.02	.12	.02	.03	.03	.12	3.92	4.31	.39
1959	4.57	4.51	.97	.11	.10	.04	4.50	.97	.11	.09	.04	.95	.01	.14	.02	.12	.02	.04	.03	.10	4.28	4.65	.37
1960	4.32	4.29	.97	.11	.09	.04	4.35	.98	.10	.09	.04	.96	.01	.14	.02	.11	.02	.04	.02	.11	4.16	4.61	.45
1961	4.41	4.35	.98	.10	.08	.04	4.34	.98	.09	.08	.03	.96	.01	.13	.02	.11	.01	.03	.02	.09	4.13	4.51	.38
1962	4.26	4.17	.98	.10	.08	.04	4.17	.98	.09	.08	.04	.95	.01	.13	.01	.11	.01	.04	.02	.09	3.99	4.36	.37
1963	4.33	4.30	.98	.09	.08	.03	4.32	.98	.09	.07	.03	.95	.01	.13	.01	.10	.01	.03	.02	.08	4.17	4.47	.30
1964	4.43	4.51	.98	.09	.07	.03	4.52	.98	.08	.07	.03	.95	.01	.13	.01	.11	.01	.03	.02	.10	4.30	4.70	.40
1965	4.61	4.70	.97	.09	.08	.02	4.73	.97	.09	.07	.01	.95	.01	.13	.01	.11	.01	.01	.02	.10	4.50	4.88	.38
1966	5.38	5.30	.98	.10	.08	.02	5.29	.98	.10	.08	.02	.96	.01	.14	.01	.11	.01	.02	.02	.08	5.14	5.48	.34
1967	6.04	5.68	.98	.11	.09	.03	5.69	.98	.11	.09	.03	.97	.01	.15	.01	.12	.01	.03	.02	.10	5.55	5.91	.36
1968	6.24	5.97	.99	.12	.09	.04	5.94	.99	.12	.09	.04	.98	.00	.15	.01	.12	.01	.04	.02	.09	5.71	6.12	.41

TABLE 3-10 One-Period Simulation Summary: Short-Term Interest Rate

Year (4th Qtr.)	Actual	Deterministic Solution					Mean Stochastic Solution					Individual Replication: Goodness-of-Fit							Individual Replications: Distribution			
		SOLN.	CORR.	RMSE	MAE	ME	SOLN.	CORR.	RMSE	MAE	ME	CORR. μ σ		RMSE μ σ		MAE μ σ		ME μ σ		STD. DEV.	MIN.	MAX.	RANGE
1956	3.63	3.48	.74	.22	.16	.14	3.57	.75	.22	.14	.10	.62	.24	.31	.09	.25	.07	.10	.13	.25	3.14	4.36	1.22
1957	3.99	3.98	.88	.19	.14	.05	3.96	.88	.20	.14	.02	.77	.10	.31	.06	.26	.05	.02	.10	.28	3.44	4.36	0.92
1958	3.21	2.99	.93	.24	.19	.02	2.98	.93	.25	.19	.00	.88	.05	.34	.05	.28	.04	.00	.08	.20	2.66	3.27	0.61
1959	4.76	4.52	.95	.22	.17	.03	4.51	.95	.23	.18	.02	.90	.03	.33	.04	.26	.04	.02	.07	.27	4.00	5.09	1.09
1960	3.27	3.01	.95	.23	.18	.05	3.08	.95	.24	.19	.03	.90	.03	.33	.04	.27	.03	.03	.06	.21	2.84	3.55	0.71
1961	3.06	2.83	.95	.22	.18	.04	2.84	.94	.23	.19	.02	.89	.03	.33	.03	.27	.03	.02	.06	.20	2.52	3.18	0.66
1962	3.26	2.90	.94	.23	.19	.06	2.93	.93	.24	.20	.05	.88	.03	.33	.03	.27	.03	.05	.06	.26	2.49	3.43	0.94
1963	3.91	3.78	.94	.22	.18	.05	3.79	.93	.23	.19	.04	.87	.03	.33	.03	.27	.03	.04	.06	.20	3.32	4.16	0.84
1964	4.06	4.15	.94	.21	.17	.04	4.18	.93	.22	.18	.03	.88	.03	.32	.03	.25	.03	.03	.05	.21	3.70	4.62	0.92
1965	4.47	4.68	.95	.21	.17	.03	4.77	.94	.22	.18	.02	.89	.03	.31	.03	.25	.03	.02	.04	.20	4.27	5.15	0.88
1966	6.00	5.53	.97	.23	.18	.05	5.54	.96	.24	.19	.04	.93	.02	.33	.03	.26	.03	.04	.04	.22	5.11	6.06	0.95
1967	5.30	4.98	.97	.23	.18	.06	5.02	.97	.23	.19	.05	.94	.01	.32	.03	.26	.03	.05	.04	.21	4.48	5.46	0.98
1968	5.96	5.48	.97	.26	.20	.08	5.45	.97	.27	.21	.07	.94	.01	.35	.03	.28	.02	.07	.04	.24	4.97	5.84	0.87

according to these statistics a little better in the first couple of years than for most of the sample period and the long-term interest rate did a little poorer. These were minor variations and are certainly attributable to the specifics of the periods involved. Furthermore, when there is no cumulative process to tracking errors, we expect those average measures computed over a few periods to be more variable than those averages computed over more periods. For all five variables, in fact, the standard deviations of the individual RMSE and MAE decline almost monotonically through time. This is consistent with the stability of the averages.

3.4 Estimation of Reduced-Form Equations

The dynamic simulation output, almost one-quarter million values of endogenous variables, is an extremely valuable resource. Assume, for the moment, that the FMP model as estimated represents a true model of the U.S. economy, that this is the structure that econometricians have long sought. The simulation output can then be viewed as twenty-five realizations of the economic variables, twenty-five sets of data. Back in the real world, economists get only one realization and one set of the data. To evaluate their methodology, econometricians have more and more been turning to Monte Carlo methods in which they write down a "true" model, generate data, and use these data and their knowledge of the "true" system to compare alternative techniques. The problem with this approach has always been that the final inferences to be drawn are severely conditioned; the scope and generality of conclusions are usually strictly limited by the model the investigator specified, the range of parameters used, and so on. The simulation output data set here is not completely free of these problems; but the model and the parameters were not chosen for any specific Monte Carlo study, nor even for any such study at all. The system generating the data is orders of magnitude larger and broader than the models employed in the usual Monte Carlo study. This section takes advantage of these properties and describes one particular Monte Carlo experiment.

The issue we comment on here is the reliability and stability of so-called reduced-form models. We detect a movement back towards very small and very simple econometric models after the "equations race" of the 1960s. The St. Louis Federal Reserve Bank "Monetarist" Model, in particular, has received extremely wide attention by economists not only in academic institutions but also in business.[16] The model rests on the principle that it is sufficient to concentrate on those endogenous variables ultimately affected by exogenous variables and, without specifying the intermediate paths and economic mechanisms, to fit stable statistical relationships using no advanced econometric techniques.

The equation examined is the monetarist, "expenditure" reduced-form equation, expressing the change in nominal GNP as a distributed lag on current and past changes in the money supply and federal expenditures. In particular, we write

$$\Delta Y = a + \sum_{i=0}^{n_m} m_i \Delta M_{-i} + \sum_{i=0}^{n_e} e_i \Delta E_{-i} + \varepsilon \qquad (3.10)$$

where

ΔY = change in nominal GNP

ΔM_{-i} = change in money stock in current quarter ($i=0$) or in ith past quarter ($i=1, 2, ..., n_m$)

ΔE_{-i} = change in "high-employment" federal expenditures in current quarter ($i=0$) or in ith past quarter ($i=1, 2, ..., n_e$)

n_m, n_e = maximum lag for ΔM and ΔE, respectively

m_i, e_i = lag coefficients (obtained by regression) for ΔM and ΔE, respectively

a = constant

ε = disturbance term

Actually, this is not really a reduced-form equation in the strict sense of the term. According to the accepted econometric definition, a reduced-form equation is one in which an endogenous variable of a structural model is expressed in terms of the predetermined variables of the model—and predetermined variables include not only exogenous variables but also lagged endogenous variables. The monetarists' rather imprecise formulation of the economic structure that leads to equation (3.10) does not suggest any a priori reasons for the exclusion of lagged values of nominal GNP or other endogenous variables. We can interpret their meaning in the most favorable light by specifying that any lagged endogenous variables that would occur have been eliminated by solving recursively, leading to a distributed lag formulation on exogenous variables only. Strictly speaking, this yields what is usually called a structural model's "final-form" equation or, alternatively, a "fundamental dynamic equation." Having been permitted this bit of pedantry, we shall resume using the now common misnomer because there are more important points to be made.

We ask under what circumstances can an equation of this type possess stable, reliable statistical estimates for the coefficients m_i and e_i. First, the equation must contain truly exogenous regressors. Chapter 1 goes to great length to explain that the money stock is not exogenous and that a more reasonable choice of the exogenous instrument of open-market operations is unborrowed high-powered money or, if we abstract from changes in the demand for currency, unborrowed reserves. Admittedly, there have been periods where the short-term rate of interest is also a reasonable choice, but, over the sample period of estimation of equation (3.10), the money supply certainly does not qualify. The force of this argument is that inclusion of ΔM in (3.10) violates the assumption of the classical linear regression model because it is bound to be not statistically independent of the disturbance term of that equation. As the evidence in Chapter 1 further demonstrates, there is bound to be a direct effect of Y on M through the demand-for-money function. Second, unless the economic structure implicit behind (3.10) is linear, the coefficients m_i and e_i will not be constant through time, but rather functions of the variables and even disturbances of the model. Third, and related to the previous point, is the absence of any effect of initial conditions. ΔM and ΔE are constrained to have the same effect on ΔY regardless of the state of the economy, and, further, this effect is symmetric with respect to the signs of both ΔM and ΔE. Fourth, and in many ways most important, there are many other exogenous variables, fiscal and monetary, that ought to be included in the equation; their omission will result in specification biases in the estimated coefficients. We have a compounding of problems too, in that, to the extent ΔM is endogenous, the joint effects of other exogenous variables on ΔY and ΔM tend toward an overestimation of the influence of ΔM on ΔY in (3.10). This is a rather loose statement, but certainly it is to be expected that some of the omitted fiscal variables cause positively correlated movements in ΔM and ΔY.

A more complete analysis of this and the other problems is given in Modigliani [55], where some challenging empirical evidence is also offered.[17] Briefly, equation (3.10) was estimated on data based on dynamic simulation output of the FMP model and the coefficients shown to bear reasonable resemblance to those based on historical data. Yet, when the coefficients were used to calculate the effect on ΔY over time of a particular given time path of ΔE, the effect was shown to be totally dissimilar to the results of a policy simulation of the model for the same path of ΔE. In other words, the equation based on model output could not reproduce the implications of the model, as we would expect of a properly specified reduced-form equation of a linear structural model.

To extend this analysis here is beyond the scope of this chapter. We offer simply some evidence and comments on the practice of estimating (3.10) (or any equation of this sort containing endogenous variables on both sides of the equal sign). In particular, (3.10) is estimated on the simulation output of the model, both deterministic and stochastic. Modigliani indicates his presentation was "basically in the spirit of a Monte Carlo experiment"; what was lacking was the characteristic randomization and the replication to reduce sampling error. Our experiments earlier in this chapter, provide us this capability. Since the computations that follow were actually undertaken quite independently of Modigliani's paper, our results are based on a specification of (3.10) different in detail from his. The decision had been made to have our estimation procedure conform as closely as possible to that of Andersen and Carlson [4]. Specifically, the m_i and e_i were chosen to lie along fourth-degree polynomials,[18] with n_m and n_e set to 4 and the polynomials constrained at both endpoints. Thus, three degrees of freedom are used up in fitting each five-period lag structure; there is more flexibility for the coefficients in this specification than in the one used by Modigliani, which involved a third-degree unconstrained polynomial over eight periods.[19]

The data used for estimation were the deterministic and 25 stochastic dynamic solutions of ΔY and ΔM, plus the St. Louis Fed's series for ΔE. A series for ΔE could conceptually be calculated directly from the FMP data; we did not do so but we did establish that such a series would be completely exogenous for our version of the FMP model and not change from one stochastic replication to another.[20] The period of estimation was the same as the simulation period, 1956: I to 1968: IV.

Since M was not featured in the figures and tables of the last two sections, a few words on its behavior are in order. Our comments can be limited to the demand-deposit component of the money supply since currency was taken to be exogenous, as explained in section 3.1. In dynamic stochastic simulation, this variable was reasonably well behaved. It did not exhibit the great dispersion of the GNP deflator or real GNP; nor did it display the marked deterioration at the very end of the sample period as did the short rate. (The error in the money market seems to have been absorbed largely by the market price rather than the quantity.) The stochastic mean and the deterministic solution were very close to each other and tracked the actual series well. RMSE and MAE were around 1.8 and 1.4 at the *end* of the simulations. Increases in dispersion did occur but not at all monotonically. The range rose from 3.7 to 10 in 1968:IV and the standard deviation increased from 0.9 to 2.7, with larger values for both measures somewhere along the way. The mean of the RMSE and MAE of the individual stochastic solutions exceeded the same measures for the stochastic mean by about 50 percent, not the 300 percent exhibited by the GNP deflator. From one-period stochastic simulations, we note that the standard deviation induced in demand deposits and, hence, in the stock of money was of the order of 0.6 for most of the sample, but about 0.7 for the last 2 years.

Estimation results are summarized in two figures and one table. Figure 3–11 displays the estimated lag structures for ΔM and ΔE, the former in the top part of the figure, the latter in the bottom half. Coefficients estimated on deterministic solution data are joined by a solid line; the means of coefficients estimated on the data sets provided by the individual stochastic solutions are joined by a dashed line; and, for purposes of comparison only, the coefficients corresponding to historical data are also shown and are joined by a dotted line. Modigliani found reasonable similarity between the pattern of coefficients based on a deterministic solution and that based on historical data. This is no way at odds with the divergence apparent in Figure 3–11, at least for ΔE, since, as contrasted with his procedure, the versions of the FMP model used were very different; the estimation period was not the same; ΔE was defined differently; and our lag polynomials were of higher order, constrained at the endpoints and restricted to a much shorter lag. Although M and Y deterministically simulated values are highly correlated (over 0.99) with actual values, their first differences exhibit lower correlation; this creates the observed divergence. A much more significant conclusion to be drawn from Figure 3–11 rests on the relationship

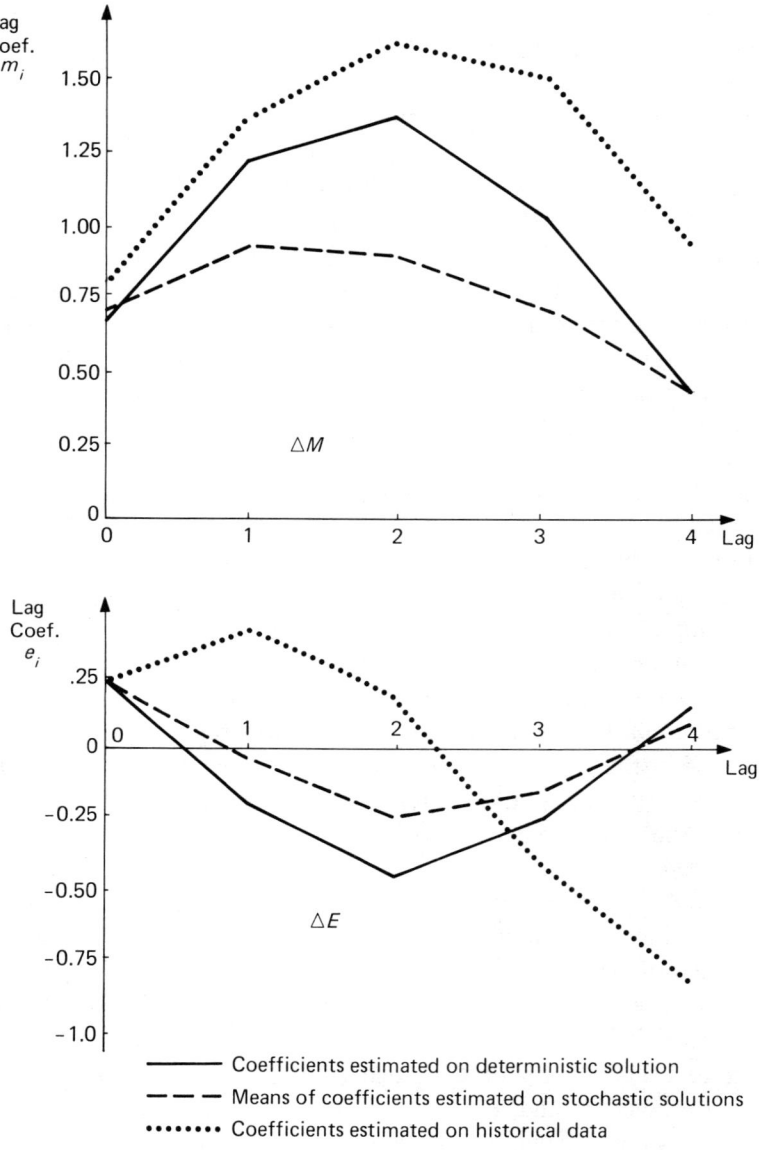

Figure 3-11. Estimated Lag Structures for ΔM and ΔE.

of the dashed and solid lines. Basically, the means of coefficients estimated on individual stochastic solution data are less in absolute value than those based on the deterministic solution; alternatively, estimation based on deterministic solutions overstates the importance of both right-hand-side variables. In the classical, linear, two-variable, single-equation model with errors of measurement in the only regressor, it is well known that the slope coefficient is biased toward zero; errors in the dependent variable, however, become impounded in the residual variance only. In the case of (3.10) we have many regressors and, relative to the deterministic case, the "Almonized" or "scrambled" synthetic variables corresponding to ΔM are noisy; those for ΔE are not. Nevertheless, the general tendency is that the lag coefficients for both variables are closer to zero for the stochastic system. Estimation based on deterministic simulation data, while damning to currently practiced reduced-form methodology from Modigliani's evidence, does not go far enough in pointing out the dangers of including endogenous variables on the right-hand side of an equation. If ΔY were the only endogenous variable in the equation, the fact that it is noisy relative to the deterministic case would *not* by itself lead to significant differences between the deterministic coefficients and the mean of the stochastic ones.[21] The attenuation effect of the errors-in-variable model dominates here the effect of our previously hypothesized positive correlation between ΔM and the disturbances of (3.10).

Further detail of the estimation can be gained from Table 3-11. Here the deterministic coefficients (with estimated standard errors) are shown with the means and standard deviations of the stochastic coefficients. For comparative purposes, the coefficients based on actual data (with estimated standard errors) for the same period are included along with the Andersen and Carlson coefficients.[22] Note that the actual variation in the coefficients is always greater than that predicted by the estimated standard errors of the deterministic coefficients.

A measure of the dispersion in lag coefficients over the 25 stochastic replications is provided in Figure 3-12, the "a" part for ΔM and the "b" part for ΔE. Histograms depict the variation in each estimated coefficient. Note that, although the vertical scale is the same for each coefficient (representing the number of coefficients lying in an interval), the horizontal scale is not; the approximate range of each coefficient was divided into nine equal intervals for

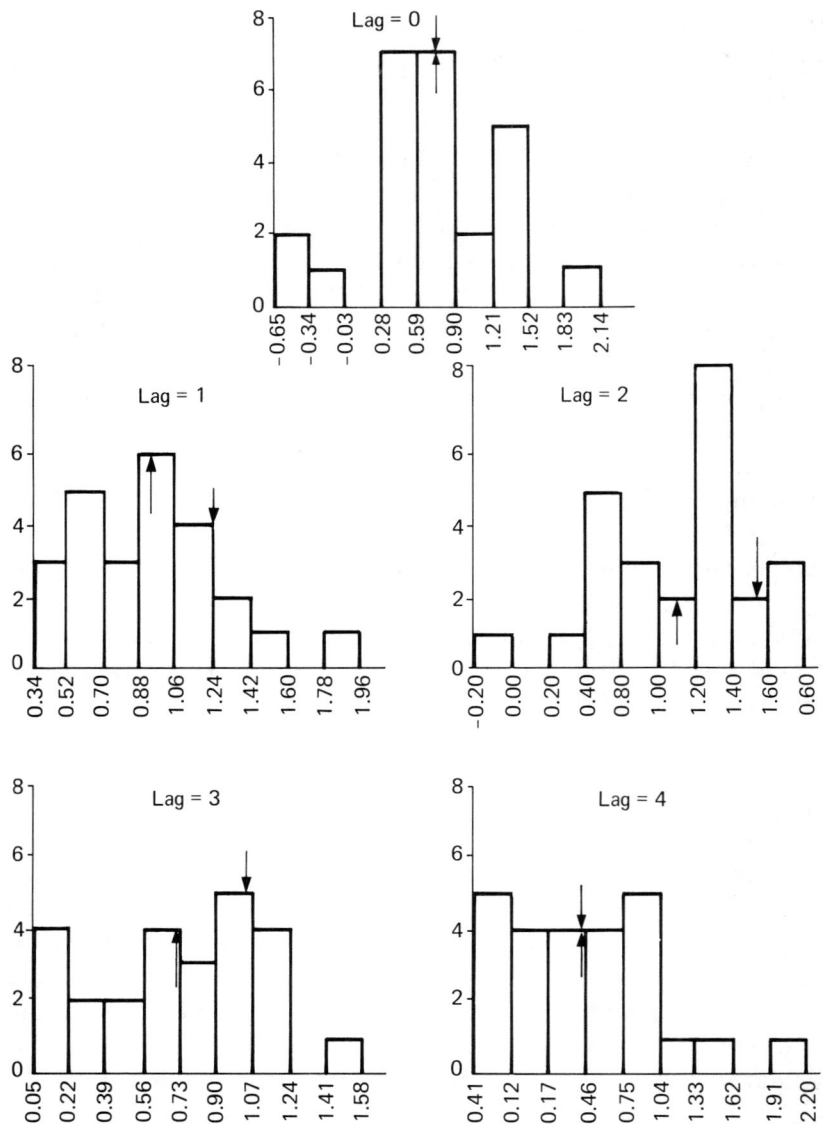

Figure 3-12a. Distribution of Estimated Lag Coefficients for ΔM.

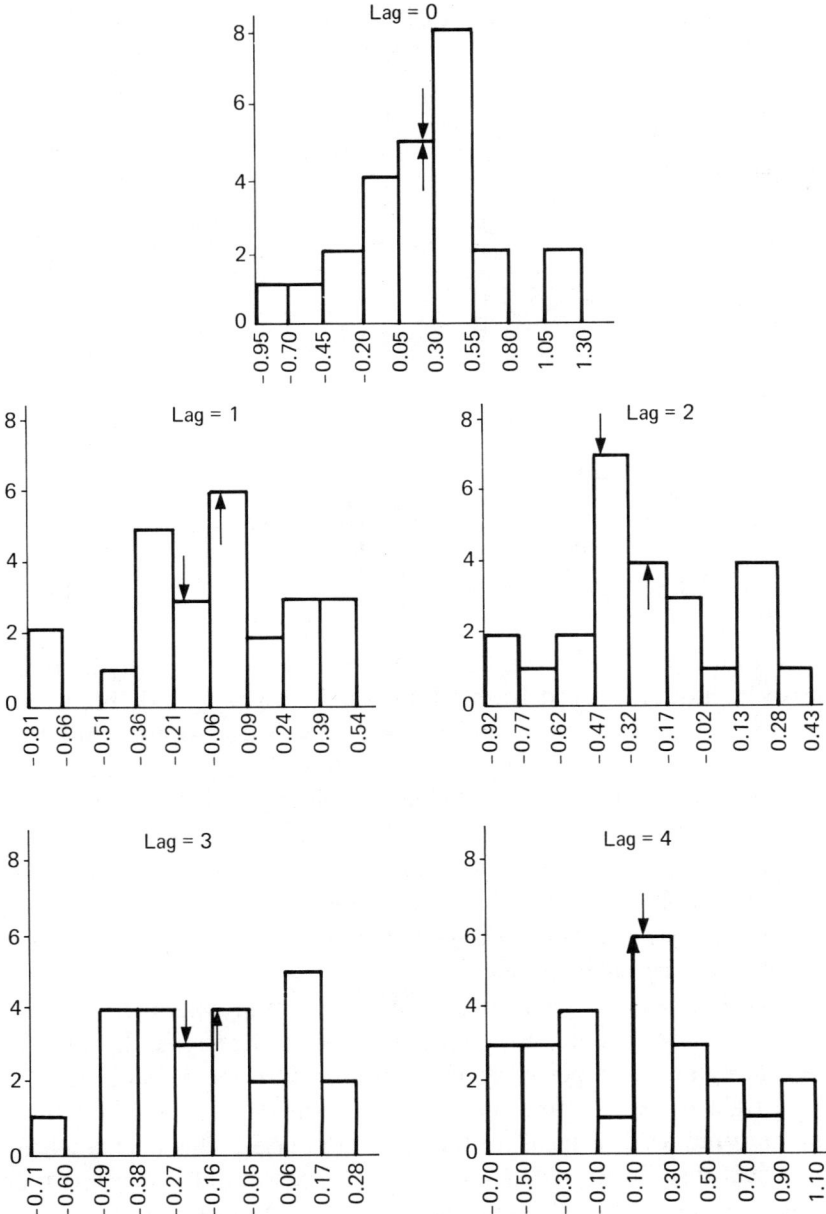

Figure 3-12b. Distribution of Estimated Lag Coefficients for ΔE.

TABLE 3-11 Estimated Lag Coefficients for ΔM and ΔE

Statistic	Deterministic Solution		Individual Stochastic Solutions		Actual		Andersen and Carlson
	Coef.	SE	Mean Coef.	Std. Dev. of Coef.	Coef.	SE	Coef.
ΔM							
0	0.68	.41	.70	.60	0.81	.44	1.22
−1	1.23	.29	.92	.37	1.37	.26	1.80
−2	1.37	.34	.89	.42	1.62	.36	1.62
−3	1.04	.30	.72	.39	1.49	.26	0.87
−4	0.44	.43	.44	.63	0.95	.45	0.06
Sum	4.76		3.67		6.24		5.57
ΔE							
0	.22	.29	.23	.47	.23	.26	.56
−1	−.19	.20	−.04	.34	.41	.18	.45
−2	−.44	.24	−.24	.34	.18	.23	.01
−3	−.25	.18	−.15	.26	−.40	.17	−.43
−4	.15	.29	.10	.48	−.78	.27	−.54
Sum	−.51		−.10		−.36		.05

each plot. Also shown on the histograms are the mean (by a small arrow pointing upward from within the histogram) and the deterministic estimate (by a small arrow pointing downward onto the histogram). A rough analysis shows that the three intermediate deterministic coefficients for ΔM are much more in the right tail of the stochastic distribution than are those for ΔE in the left tail. Our intuition suggests this is the natural consequence of ΔM being noisy and ΔE not. Table 3-11 and especially Figure 3-12 indicate that the coefficients estimated on stochastic simulation data are quite sensitive and do not appear to be stable.

This obviously preliminary foray into estimation experiments based on model simulation data suggests a few conclusions. If we are estimating an improperly specified reduced-form equation in which some right-hand-side variables are endogenous, stochastic simulation data are required to measure the resulting biases. This is true when the structure is linear; if it is not linear, then we should also expect the estimated coefficients to be unstable. We do not answer the question here, though, of whether or not we can recapture the implications of a structural model by estimating a reduced-form equation. Stochastic simulation data are also useful if we are estimating a structural equation as part of a Monte Carlo experiment (for example, one designed to test alternative simultaneous equations estimators). Much careful planning has to be given to the selection of experimental parameters such as the number of replications. The "irregularities" of the histograms of Figure 3–12 may as well be from too few sample points as much as nonlinearities in the structure producing the trial data. Finally, the likely possibility of skewed and "irregular" distributions of estimated coefficients suggests that measures other than simply means and standard deviations be calculated and analyzed.[23]

Notes

[1] An example is the study of Adelman and Adelman [1] whose purpose it was to demonstrate the *possibility* of cyclical behavior in economic variables induced by random shocks.

[2] A sixth reason, involving nonlinear functions of simulation results, is not widely recognized and is discussed and illustrated in section 3.2.

[3] Knuth [47], vol. 2, pp. 82–97, describes a spectral test for evaluating the randomness of computer-generated sequences based on all possible n-tuples that appear over the cycle length of the generator. The generator of Payne et al. was tested along with a well-known alternative by Lewis, Goodman, and Miller [51]. The tabulation below suggests the apparent superiority of the one used here. The reader should see Knuth [47] for a full interpretation of these results, but essentially a score of less than 0.1 is bad, of 0.1 to 1 is good, and greater than 1 is excellent.

n-tuple	Payne et al.	Lewis et al.
2	2.44	0.41
3	0.47	0.50
4	3.71	1.08
5	4.94	3.21
6	0.81	1.72

I am indebted to Professor Gordon Sande of the University of Chicago for helpful discussions of these alternatives and his calculation of these scores for me.

[4] Normality was not, of course, a necessary assumption for the methods used to estimate the model.

[5] Two other methods have been used to generate normal pseudo-

random numbers from uniform ones. The most common is based on summing 12 random numbers (and subtracting the constant, 6) and relying on the operation of the central limit theorem; the other uses a transformation based on the inverse Gaussian distribution function.

[6] Nagar [60] describes an alternative method which requires that the sample covariance matrix of regression residuals be nonsingular. In large models, the number of equations usually exceeds the number of observations and one has to impose constraints on the covariance matrix of generated structural disturbances (such as block-diagonality) in order to use his method.

[7] The FMP model has not yet been estimated with a consistent method; the calculated residuals, however, are the only estimates we have of the structural disturbances, inconsistent or not.

[8] In a sense, these experiments are best referred to as "solutions" since "simulations" connotes the varying of parameters, exogenous variables, etc.

[9] A summary table of these means and variances was distributed during a talk on some of the material in sections 3.1 to 3.3, presented by the author at the Midwest Model Users Conference at the Chicago Federal Reserve Bank in December 1969.

[10] See Goldberger, Nagar, and Odeh [37].

[11] These are the same five variables that we concentrated on in Chapter 2. Results for the larger set reported there are available from the author. The absence of the unemployment rate is due to exogenization of that segment of the model for the simulations reported in this chapter.

[12] In future studies of this sort, given the evidence of this asymmetry in the distribution of the individual solutions, other measures of dispersion, such as the semi-interquartile range, should be calculated.

[13] This happens for essentially the same reason that $|a|+|b| \geqslant |a+b|$.

[14] An exception in decision theory is the set of circumstances which leads to a certainty equivalence approach.

[15] See section 4.3 and 4.4.

[16] See Andersen and Carlson [4].

[17] See especially pp. 65–74.

[18] See Almon [3] or Cooper [19].

[19] Modigliani chose the longer lag structure because his aim was to validate the computed multiplier effect of (3.10) against that of the FMP model. Since he knew that the model implied much longer lags than those chosen by Andersen and Carlson he was giving the

reduced-form methodology an "edge."

[20] Specifically, we could compute the series from

$$\frac{E2 \times E75}{100} + E35 + E78 + E18 + E34 + E36 + \text{function of time}$$

The E-numbered variables are all exogenous and defined in the Glossary and Coding Sheets for version 4.1. The "function of time" is a linear trend used by St. Louis FRB to proxy for unemployment insurance benefits at full employment. Essentially, the computation is equivalent to taking the national income budget, subtracting the one endogenous component—unemployment insurance benefits—and adding back a linear function of time. Some trial regressions showed that estimates of (3.10) were fairly insensitive to the exact choice of the linear trend. The expenditure deflator was endogenized in later versions of the model so that ΔE could no longer be classified as completely exogenous.

[21] The first and last coefficients do not really differ as the intermediate ones do. This is likely a consequence of the endpoint constraints.

[22] The latter are estimated over 1953:I to 1969:IV; the others from 1956:I to 1968:IV, as stated earlier in the text.

[23] For the estimates here, we have also computed many of the statistics suggested by Tukey [78] such as medians, trimeans, midmeans, midspreads, etc. Our purpose in this section was mainly a demonstration of feasibility and so these are not discussed.

4 Policy Analysis: Simulation of Monetary Rules

4.1 Constant-Growth-Rate, Proportional, and Derivative Rules

The investigations reported in this chapter are directed to the question of the type of monetary rule which should be used if a rule is to be adopted for monetary policy. The rule usually considered in discussions of "rules versus discretion" is that of steady growth of the money supply, as, for example, in Culbertson [24], Friedman [33, 34], and Sayers [69]. One set of arguments concerns "rules versus discretion" itself: For instance, it is argued that both inertia and political factors frequently prevent changes in monetary policy which are clearly called for by the behavior of the economy; and that the goals of a discretionary policy may be diverted from stabilization to other targets (such as the pegging of bond yields). The second set of arguments concerns the rule that should be adopted if a monetary rule is to be used: the argument here is that changes in the money stock take effect on target variables with long and variable lags so that any countercyclical stabilization policy, discretionary or not, is likely to be destabilizing. Accordingly, it is argued, a constant-growth-rate rule should be used.

However, results in control theory, introduced to economics by Tustin [80], Phillips [66], and Holt [42], and investigated more recently by others suggest that rules in which policy variables are automatically adjusted in response to deviations of target variables from desired levels (proportional controls) and in response to the rate of change of target variables (derivative controls) can be stabilizing relative to a constant growth rate rule. Whether such controls pro-

---

This chapter is the result of collaboration with Stanley Fischer and represents an edited, partial reproduction of Cooper and Fischer [20, 21, 22]. Computation was financed in part by National Science Foundation grants GS 2607 and GS 29711.

duce significant gains in stability in models of the economy is not, however, a trivial question, for these models may have characteristics—such as very long lags—which make the gain from use of feedback controls of little significance. For instance, it will be seen, in our simulations, that proportional controls do not lead to sizable increases in stability. The monetary policies considered in this chapter are automatic control rules rather than discretionary policies; the results we present thus bear on questions raised in the second set of arguments mentioned above.

We report here the results of simulations of monetary rules in the FMP model for the period 1956: I through 1968: IV. The simulations are directed to the question of whether, in this model, for the period covered, the variability of the rates of inflation and unemployment produced under a constant-growth-rate rule can be reduced by following some simple rule of the Phillips type. Although feedback control rules of the sort employed here are not in general optimal controls,[1] for they do not take advantage of any forecasts that are available, they have the significant advantage of simplicity. The computational difficulties of finding the optimum controls in a large nonlinear model like the FMP model have led us instead to search, within a restricted class of controls, for rules which improve upon that most frequently suggested—that of a constant growth rate. We also wish to use policies that can be applied in different econometric models representing prevalent views about the working of the economy.

The FMP model is used for a number of reasons: First, careful attention has been paid to monetary factors in its construction; second, it is a model in which the lags in the effects of monetary policy are long;[2] and third, the effects of monetary policy vary over the cycle and with changes in other exogenous variables in this model.[3]

Before proceeding to a description of our study, we discuss briefly earlier work on rules by Bronfenbrenner [11, 12] and Modigliani [56]. The methodology used by both of these authors requires the assumption that velocity would have followed its historical path whatever monetary rule had been used. A target money supply —which would have produced full employment with price stability— is calculated for each period, and each of the various rules is evaluated by measures which are functions of the difference between the target money supply and the money supply resulting from application of a rule. The results are in general inconclusive. The major weaknesses of the studies—which were duly noted by the authors—stem from the fact that there was no way of discovering how unemployment and inflation would have behaved over time had the rules been followed consistently for long periods. It was this weakness that led Modigliani to doubt that "a test [of the constant-growth-rate rule] can ever be performed from historical data."[4] The most important respect in which our study differs from theirs is that we can, with the help of a structural model, examine the behavior of unemployment and inflation resulting from application of our rules over long periods.

In the policy simulations reported in this chapter all exogenous variables other than monetary ones have been set at their historical levels. In addition, in sections 4.1 and 4.2 the stochastic specification of the FMP model has been suppressed in that all error terms in the behavioral equations have been set at zero; that is, our simulations are deterministic and not stochastic. Changes in exogenous variables, including fiscal variables, do shock the model in each period in our simulations and provide fluctuations with which monetary policy has to contend. Further, some of the effects one would hope to capture through stochastic simulations are undoubtedly present in our simulations because of the endogenous variability of money multipliers. The fact that we do not consider fiscal policy rules does not reflect a view—certainly incorrect in the FMP model—that fiscal policy has no effect; it reflects, rather our desire to concentrate here on the issue of a monetary rule.

The money supply—in these simulations, currency plus demand deposits ($M1$)—has been determined by following a variety of rules. The breakdown into currency and demand deposits is determined endogenously. It has been noted that the money supply itself was an endogenous variable in the estimation of the model; the exogenous monetary variables were unborrowed high-powered money, the required reserve ratios, and the discount rate. We have allowed the discount rate and reserve ratios to take their historical levels and have made unborrowed high-powered money endogenous. Thus, one of the by-products of our simulations is the level of unborrowed high-powered money that would have been needed—according to the model—to produce the requisite money supply in each period.[5]

From 1956: I on, the money supply is controlled by a feedback control rule of the Phillips [66] or Holt [42] type. In particular,

TABLE 4-1 Simulations

Simulation No.	Parameter Values Used							Results						
	a_1	a_2	a_3	a_4	a_5	a_6	a_7	$\Delta P/P$ μ	$\Delta P/P$ σ	u μ	u σ	$\Delta MD/MD$ μ	$\Delta MD/MD$ σ
1a	.005							.0047	.0028	.0524	.00849	.0041	.0012
1b	.0075							.0055	.0026	.0493	.00737	.0071	.0011
1c	.01							.0062	.0026	.0466	.00719	.0099	.0011
1d	.0125							.0071	.0029	.0446	.00862	.0127	.0011
2	.01	1.00						.0067	.0027	.0450	.00895	.0092	.0036
3	.01		.0062	.40				.0067	.0025	.0465	.00966	.0097	.0051
4	.01	0.25	.0062	.10				.0063	.0025	.0463	.00720	.0099	.0011
5	.01	1.00						.0064	.0024	.0460	.00699	.0098	.0014
6	.01		.0062	.40		1.00		.0068	.0026	.0449	.00849	.0091	.0054
7	.01	0.50			.0466		.40	.0066	.0024	.0467	.00901	.0100	.0055
8	.01		.0062		.0466	1.00	.40	.0064	.0024	.0456	.00705	.0097	.0038
9	.01	0.50		.20	.0466	1.00	.40	.0065	.0023	.0460	.00715	.0099	.0031
10	.01	0.25	.0062	.20	.0466	1.00	.40	.0066	.0023	.0460	.00830	.0096	.0054
11	.01	0.50	.0062	.10	.0466	1.00	.40	.0065	.0023	.0458	.00681	.0098	.0040
12	.01		.0062		.0466	1.00	.40	.0064	.0023	.0457	.00676	.0098	.0040
13	.01	0.50		.20		1.00	2.00	.0065	.0022	.0460	.00699	.0099	.0042
14	.01		.0062			2.00	2.00	.0064	.0021	.0458	.00593	.0105	.0104
15	.01	0.50		.20	.0466	2.00	3.00	.0064	.0021	.0461	.00603	.0105	.0107
16	.01	0.50	.0062			3.00	4.00	.0064	.0021	.0457	.00550	.0107	.0155
17	.01	0.50	.0062			4.00	3.00	.0064	.0020	.0456	.00516	.0109	.0207
18	.01					3.00	3.00	.0065	.0021	.0455	.00569	.0109	.0153
19	.01	0.50	.0062	.20	.0466	3.00	3.00	.0063	.0021	.0460	.00559	.0105	.0160
20	.005	0.50	.0047			3.00	3.00	.0050	.0023	.0511	.00619	.0052	.0151

$$\frac{M_t - M_{t-1}}{M_{t-1}} = a_1 - a_2 \left(\frac{P_{t-1} - P_{t-2}}{P_{t-2}} - a_3 \right) + a_4(u_{t-1} - a_5)$$

$$- a_6 \left(\frac{P_{t-1} - P_{t-2}}{P_{t-2}} - \frac{P_{t-2} - P_{t-3}}{P_{t-3}} \right) + a_7(u_{t-1} - u_{t-2})$$

$$a_i \geq 0, \quad i = 2, 4, 6, 7$$

where P is the GNP deflator and u the unemployment rate.[6] The parameter a_1 is the "average" or "design" growth rate of the monetary aggregate M; a_2 and a_4 are proportional control parameters calling for adjustments in the rate of growth of M when the rates of inflation or unemployment deviate from their respective targets a_3 and a_5; a_6 and a_7 are derivative control parameters calling for adjustments in the rate of growth of M when the rates of inflation or unemployment are themselves changing, regardless of their relation to their respective targets.[7]

We do not use formal optimality criteria in our exploration of the results produced in different regions of the parameter space; our search procedure in this paper is a heuristic one. Implicitly, we are trying to find the tradeoffs between the means and standard deviations of the rates of inflation and unemployment which are implied by the structure of the model. Our search procedure assumes that any rule which produces a lower standard deviation in both variables for given means is to be preferred to one which has higher standard deviations, but we are not more explicit than this about the utility function of the policy maker.

The values of the parameters $a_1 \cdots a_7$ used in the policy simulations are indicated in Table 4–1. Blanks represent zeroes. The means and standard deviations of the rates of inflation and unemployment for the simulations are also presented in Table 4–1. In addition, the mean and standard deviation of the quarterly rate of change in demand deposits is shown in the last two columns. We concentrate on demand deposits both because these constitute the major part of *M1* and because, as explained in Chapter 1, they are more important than currency in the causal structure of the model.

We proceed now to a description of the rules tested and of our search procedure. Runs 1a–1d are four constant-growth-rate rules in which all parameters but a_1 are set at zero. In the four runs a_1 was allowed to take the values .005, .0075, .01, and .0125, corresponding approximately to annual growth rates of 2–5 percent.

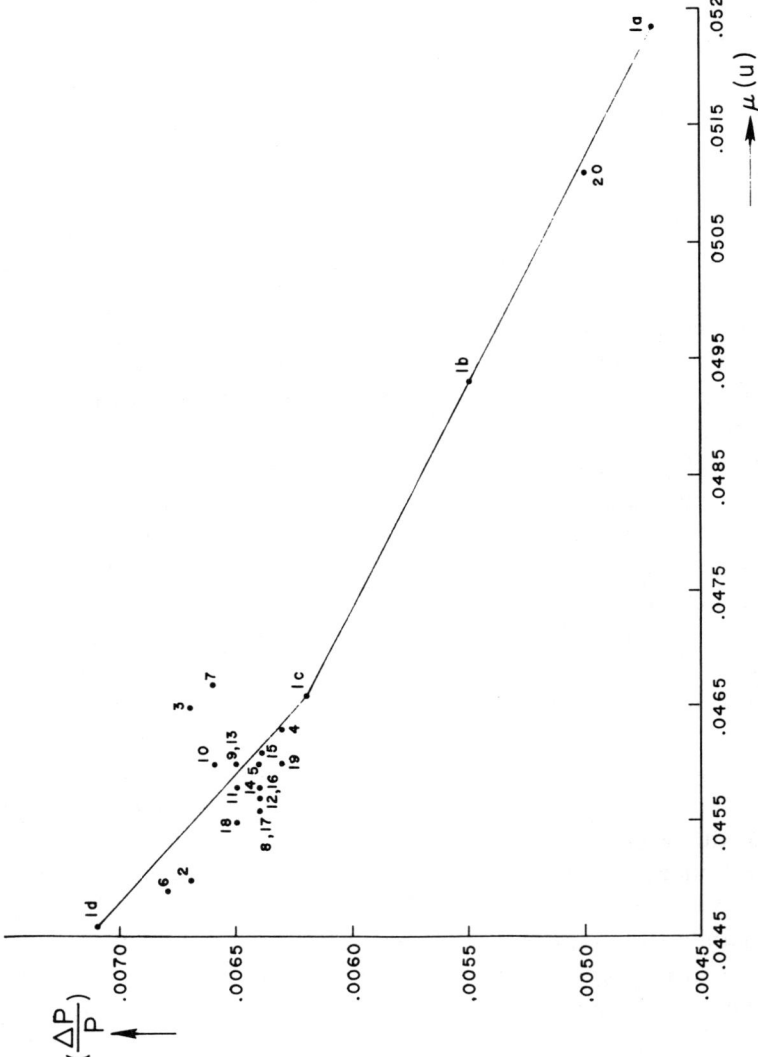

Figure 4-1. Mean Quarterly Rates of Inflation and Unemployment for Simulations 1 to 20.

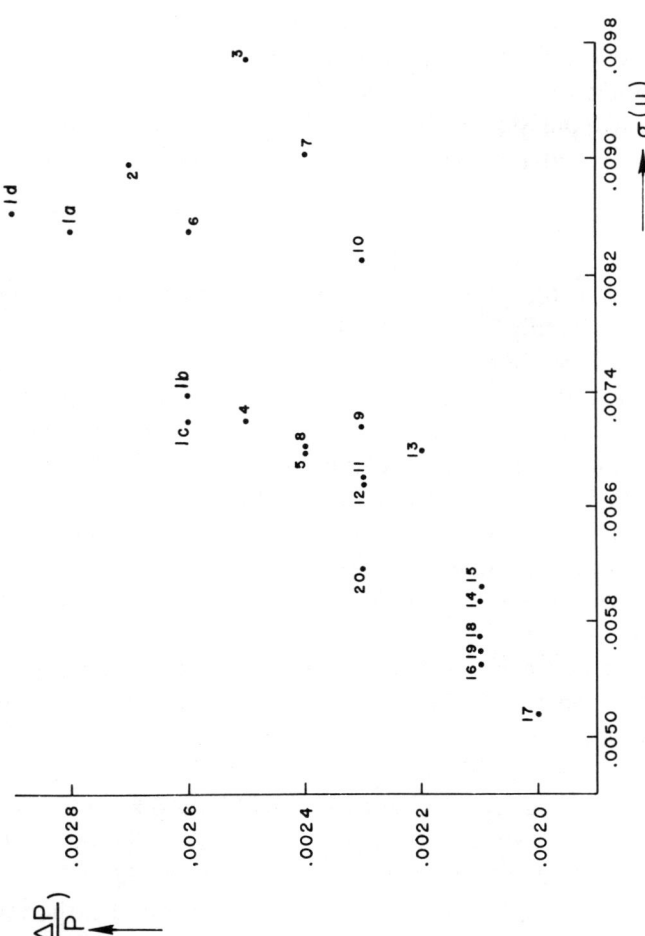

Figure 4-2. Standard Deviations of the Quarterly Rates of Inflation and Unemployment for Simulations 1 to 20.

The mean rates of inflation and unemployment in these simulations are plotted in Figure 4–1, and the corresponding standard deviations may be read off from Table 4–1 and Figure 4–2.[8] We assumed that the choice of a point on the "Phillips curve" in Figure 4–1 would give us consistent values of a_1, a_3, and a_5 to use in the rule and that we could then vary a_2, a_4, a_6, and a_7 in an attempt to reduce the variability of the rates of inflation and unemployment about the means a_3 and a_5.[9]

We chose the means corresponding to the 4 percent constant-growth-rate rule for a_3 and a_5 and plot the means for the simulations 2 to 19 in Figure 4–1. While the means did in fact change between the various simulations, usually in the direction of a higher mean rate of inflation and a lower mean rate of unemployment, these changes were not large. We did not think it worthwhile to attempt to correct a_1 to ensure that the mean rates of inflation and unemployment were exactly the same for every simulation, nor are we sure this could have been done. Through an iterative procedure, we might also have adjusted the rule so that the realized growth rate of M was exactly a_1; this, too, would hardly merit the expense.

One further comment is in order on the points a_1, a_3, and a_5. Since, in the long run, the FMP model basically exhibits the neutrality of money, we should expect an annual rate of growth of $M1$ of 4 percent to lead to about a 1 percent annual rate of inflation, assuming the annual rate of growth of real output to be about 3 percent. Thus, in steady state, we should have a lower rate of inflation and a higher rate of unemployment than the 2.5 percent and 4.66 percent represented by a_3 and a_5, respectively. Furthermore, although the annual "design" rate of growth of $M1$ is varied in runs 1a to 1d from 2 percent to 5 percent, the mean annual rate of inflation changes only by about 1 percent. Although the simulations were run over 52 quarters, the maximum lags in some equations are about one-third this length. Add to this the great variability of the exogenous variables and we must conclude that the steady state has not been reached. Our approach, however, is to attempt to analyze the question of rules over a specific historical period, accepting as given the values taken by other exogenous variables.

Once the values of a_1, a_3, and a_5 had been chosen we proceeded to use a variety of proportional and derivative controls on the rates of inflation and unemployment in an attempt to reduce the standard deviations of these variables. Earlier experiments had led to the conclusion that strong proportional controls would be destabilizing. That this indeed is the case may be seen from runs 2 and 3. In run 2, a quarterly rate of inflation of 1 percent above the "target" rate of 0.62 percent implies a zero growth rate of money: this rule leads to a small increase in the standard deviation of the rate of inflation and a 25 percent increase in the standard deviation of the rate of unemployment. In run 3, a rate of unemployment 2.5 percent above the "target" of 4.66 percent implies a doubling of the growth rate of money. This rule leads to a slight reduction in the variability of the rate of inflation and an increase of 33 percent in the standard deviation of the rate of unemployment. By contrast, in runs 4 and 5, proportional correction factors of one-quarter the strength of those in runs 2 and 3 led to slightly less variability in the target variables than did the constant-growth-rate rule.

The destabilizing effect of strong proportional controls is presumably due to the lags in the model. When strong proportional controls are used, there are rapid increases in the money supply whenever, say, the unemployment rate is above its target level. When, eventually, the unemployment rate starts falling, it continues falling as the results of earlier monetary policies take effect, while the money supply continues to grow faster than normal (until the unemployment rate falls below its target level). Then, the growth rate of money is reduced in an attempt to move the unemployment rate back up to its target level. This restrictive phase occurs too late to prevent unemployment rates substantially below historical experience.

While strong proportional controls are destabilizing, the use of weak proportional controls improved only slightly on performance under the constant-growth-rate rule; this is evident from the results of runs 4 and 5. Accordingly we proceeded to the addition of derivative controls in which attention is paid to the direction of movement of target variables. Thus, when the economy turns around at any time, monetary policy responds in the next quarter.

When the rate of inflation is increasing (whatever its level) and a_6 is positive, the rate of growth of $M1$ is reduced; similarly, for a falling rate of unemployment and a_7 positive, the rate of growth of $M1$ is reduced. It became clear from runs 6 and 7 that the addition of derivative controls on the same variables to which the strong proportional controls had previously been applied reduced the standard deviations of the target variables. But the proportional parameters of $a_2 = 1.00$ and $a_4 = 0.40$, which had been used in runs 2 and 3, still appeared to be having a destabilizing effect; this turned out to be the case, as may be seen from the results of runs 8 and 9 where moderate proportional controls were used, and we were once more brought back to the region in which standard deviations were slightly better than those yielded by the constant-growth-rate rule.

Once it became clear that derivative controls of the strength used in runs 6–9 were stabilizing, the questions arose of how far they could be strengthened without becoming destabilizing, and how they should be combined with proportional controls. Runs 10 to 19 were undertaken in an attempt to answer these questions. In run 10, the parameters of runs 8 and 9 were combined giving proportional and derivative control on both $\Delta P/P$ and u. The destabilizing effects of even the moderate proportional controls are reinforcing, producing the net result that run 10 is dominated by run 9 and incomparable with run 8 under our criteria; furthermore, halving the proportional controls of run 10 led to a clear improvement in run 11. In each of runs 12 and 13, then, only one proportional control, but of moderate strength, was retained along with both derivative controls. Both runs 12 and 13 did improve upon runs 8, 9, and 10. Derivative controls were increased in runs 14 and 15, with the result that each run clearly dominated runs 1 to 13. Going further, with proportional control only on the rate of inflation, we increased both of the derivative controls in runs 16 and 17; in the latter run, the very strong derivative controls led to a negative treasury bill rate in one period.

The conclusions that emerge from these runs are that strong derivative controls are stabilizing and that inclusion of a proportional control is of little help—as witness, run 18 in which no proportional controls were used and run 19 in which both proportional controls were used. We found no levels of the derivative parameters that were destabilizing for the unemployment and inflation rates, though the standard deviation of interest rates increased with the standard deviations of $\Delta MD/MD$.

Figures 4–3, 4–4, and 4–5 present the time series of demand deposits (MD), the rate of inflation ($\Delta P/P$), and the rate of unemployment (u) for simulation run 1c, the 4 percent rule. The base-

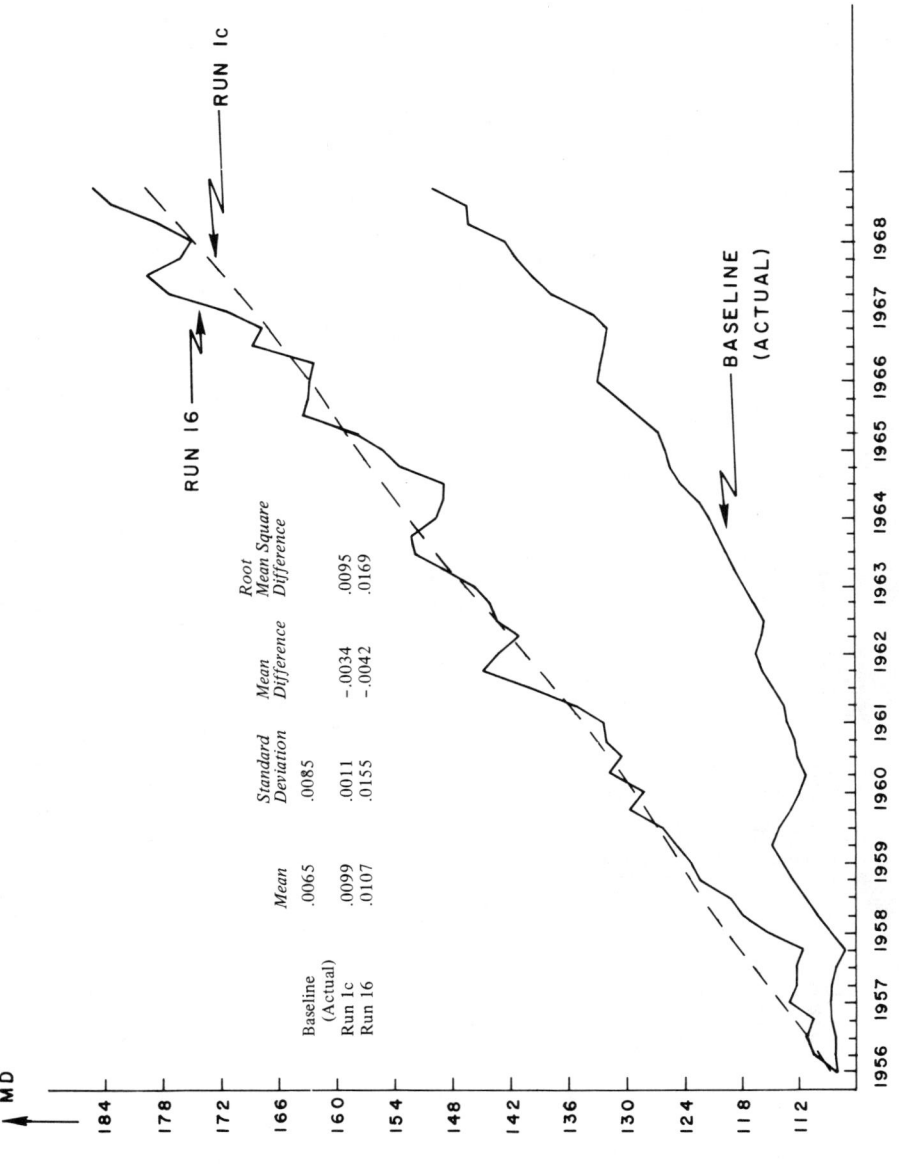

Figure 4-3. Time Paths of Demand Deposits (Statistics on Quarterly Rate of Change of Demand Deposits).

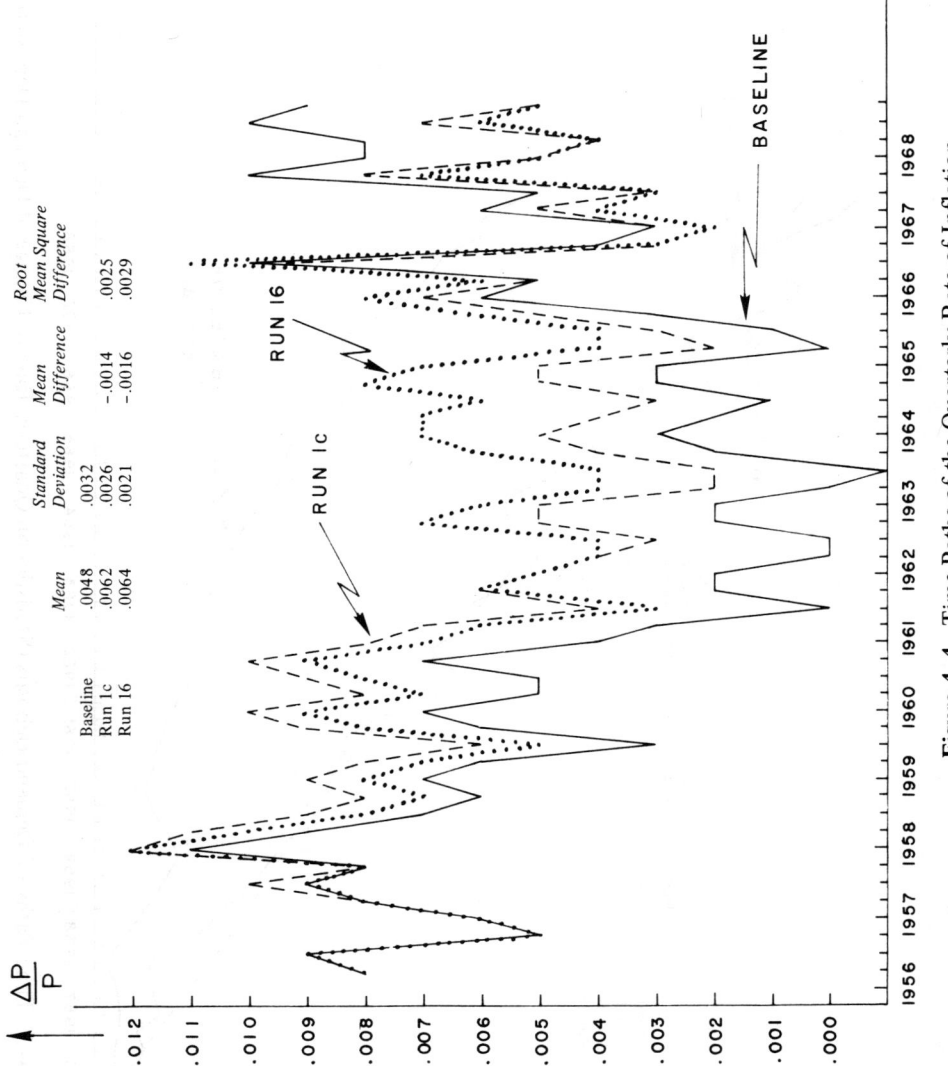

Figure 4–4. Time Paths of the Quarterly Rate of Inflation.

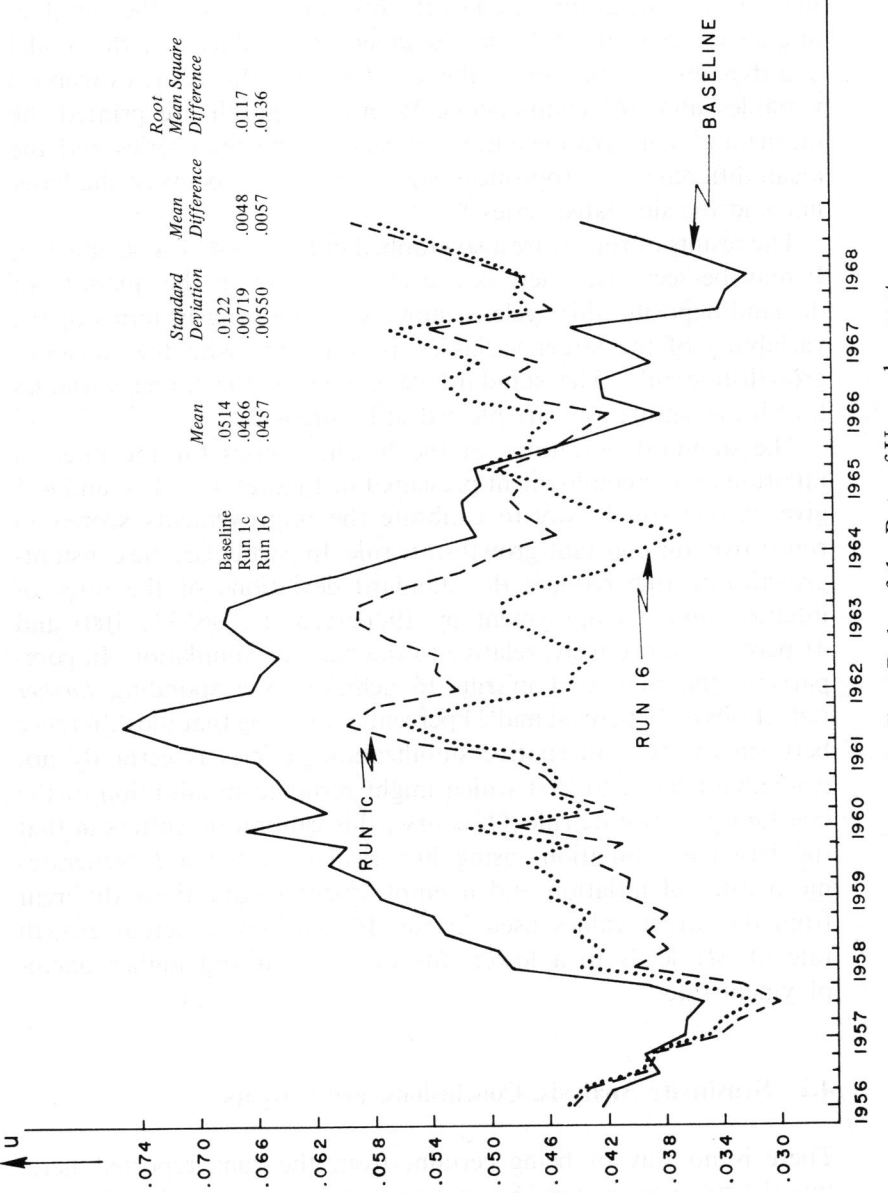

Figure 4-5. Time Paths of the Rate of Unemployment.

189

line series in the graphs are not the historical levels of the variables in question but rather the values which are produced by the model in a dynamic solution given the actual time paths of the exogenous variables and *M1* components. With each graph are printed the means and standard deviations of each of the time series and the mean difference and root mean square difference between the baseline and the simulated series.[10]

The results of run 16 are also graphed in Figures 4–3, 4–4, and 4–5. It may be seen that there is a cyclical pattern in the quantity of demand deposits: this cycle is, however, stabilizing in terms of the variability of the target variables as compared with the constant-growth-rate rule. The standard deviations of the target variables for all the simulations are plotted in Figure 4–2.

The standard deviations of the baseline series for the rates of inflation and unemployment presented in Figures 4–3, 4–4, and 4–5 give us one rough way to calibrate the improvements scored in run 16 over the constant-growth-rate rule. In particular, the constant-growth-rate rule reduces the standard deviations of the rates of inflation and unemployment by 19 percent $(=.06/.32 \times 100)$ and 41 percent, respectively, relative to the baseline simulation. In comparison, the rule used in run 16 achieves corresponding *further* reductions of 19 percent and 24 percent, indicating that the difference between the two alternative stabilization policies is certainly not negligible relative to that which might result from adoption of the constant-growth-rate rule. Of course, this calibration suffers in that the baseline simulation, using historical data for *M1*, generates mean rates of inflation and unemployment substantially different from the target values used in run 16. The lower actual growth rate of *M1* leads to a lower rate of inflation and higher unemployment rate.

4.2 Sensitivity Analysis, Conclusions, and Caveats

There is no way of being certain, from the runs reported here, that the rule used in run 16 is not an improvement on the constant-growth-rate rule only if the other exogenous variables take the values they did for 1956:I to 1968:IV and if the constant growth rate used is 4 percent. As a partial check on this possibility we present in run 20 the results of a simulation in which a_1 was set at .005 (approximately 2 percent per annum); a_3 and a_5 at the appropriate levels; and a_2, a_4, a_6, and a_7 at the levels of run 16. The variability of the rates of inflation and unemployment in run 20 is reduced from the variability in run 1a by about the same percentage as applies between runs 16 and 1c.

As another check, we divided the period in two at 1962: II (i.e., after 26 quarters) and computed the means and standard deviation for these subperiods in runs 1c and 16. These results are presented in Table 4–2. The reduction in standard deviations for the entire period in run 16 over that for run 1c appears to be due largely to a smaller difference in the means in the two subperiods, rather than to marked reductions in variability within each subperiod. The only large reduction in standard deviation obtained is that for the rate of unemployment in the first subperiod. These results do raise the possibility that the results obtained from the monetary rules we have found are dependent on the path of fiscal policy.[11]

In order to be certain that the rule used in run 16, or more generally, rules involving strong derivative controls, will reduce the variability of the rates of inflation and unemployment for other paths of the exogenous variables, simulations in which fiscal parameters change are required. In one preliminary experiment in this direction, we lagged by eight quarters the exogenous variable in the model measuring federal expenditures on goods and services.[12] By the use of proportional and derivative controls, we were able to reduce the variability of rates of inflation and unemployment as compared with the variability under a constant-growth-rate rule. However, the derivative controls used had to be reduced slightly from those of run 16 in order to prevent negative treasury bill rates from occurring.

We have demonstrated that in the context of the FMP model, and given the time paths of other exogenous (including fiscal) variables, a monetary rule using derivative controls—a systematic policy of "leaning against the wind"—would have reduced the variability of the rates of inflation and unemployment over the period 1956:I to 1968:IV as compared with a constant-growth-rate rule—this despite the very long lags in the model. We have also shown that proportional controls, unless used with care, are destabilizing.

One potential difficulty inherent in this type of study, whatever model is used, arises from the possibility that adoption of a rule

TABLE 4-2 Simulation Results for Two Subperiods

Statistic	$\frac{\Delta P}{P}$						u			
	1956: II–1962: II		1962: III–1968: IV			1956: I–1962: II		1962: III–1968: IV	
	Run 1c	Run 16	Run 1c	Run 16		Run 1c	Run 16	Run 1c	Run 16
Mean	.0079	.0073	.0045	.0055		.0432	.0439	.0501	.0475
Standard deviation	.0021	.0020	.0019	.0020		.0077	.0056	.0049	.0049
Root mean square deviation about mean for entire period	.0027	.0022	.0026	.0022		.0084	.0059	.0063	.0053

might modify the behavioral relations of the economy. For instance, it is sometimes argued that adoption of a rule per se would reduce uncertainty and increase the stability of the economy. Insofar as the rules are concerned, it is plausible that our measures of the performance of rules would be correlated with the additional stability induced by the adoption of any rule.

Other limitations on our results and the future research that is indicated are fairly obvious: the results are both model-specific and period-specific. Studies of this sort do require the use of a model, and the significance of our finding that control rules involving strong derivative controls are stabilizing will become greater if it can be shown that the same rule, or one very similar, produces the same effects in other models.[13] Similarly, the possibility that our results are not independent of the values of fiscal policy parameters makes it desirable that similar simulations for a wide range of alternative fiscal policies be carried out. Other questions that arise are those of the appropriate monetary aggregate to use in the rule, and of whether intermediate targets have any place in the rule. Stochastic simulation tests of our hypothesis are also desirable since performance under uncertainty is an important criterion for discriminating between alternative policy regimes; these are carried out in sections 4.3 and 4.4.

We do not claim that our results are an overwhelming demonstration of the inferiority of the constant-growth-rate rule. Our "optimal" rule reduced the standard deviation of the rate of inflation by about 19 percent and the standard deviation of the rate of unemployment by about 24 percent as compared with the constant-growth-rate rule; given that we were working with a model whose structure is, in principle, known, and that we used the model itself in our procedure for finding an "optimal" rule, these reductions are not strikingly impressive. Our results, then, should be regarded as showing that the constant-growth-rate rule performs well, but that there is potential for improving on its performance by use of other very simple monetary rules—particularly those involving strong derivative controls. If it is shown that such rules perform consistently better than the constant-growth-rate rule in other models and for other periods and in a stochastic environment, our belief in that potential will be increased; if not, the case for the constant-growth-rate rule will be strengthened.

4.3 Experimental Design and Explanation of Tests for Stochastic Simulation

In this and the next section, we extend the results of section 4.1 to include stochastic simulation of monetary rules. The reasons for stochastic simulation have already been mentioned briefly in this chapter and in greater detail in section 3.1 We begin with a discussion of the design of our experiments and the nature of the tests we employ. Our results and conclusions are reserved for section 4.4. We indicate there that the conclusions derived from our stochastic simulations of the FMP model differ in some respects from our earlier results based on deterministic simulations.

Because of the expense of stochastic simulations (as compared with deterministic simulations) the use of a search procedure for an "optimal" rule as used in section 4.1 was rejected; besides, our stated purpose here is to find whether there are certain simple monetary rules which outperform constant-growth-rate rules, rather than to find an optimal rule. On the basis of our earlier results, and of preliminary experimentation with stochastic simulations, we set out four alternative policies to be tested. They are summarized in Table 4–3. Rules I, II, and IV correspond to runs 1c, 14, and 16 in section 4.1, respectively.

TABLE 4–3 Parameter Values for Policy Rules

Rule Number	a_1	a_2	a_3	a_4	a_5	a_6	a_7
I	.01	0	0	0	0	0	0
II	.01	.5	.0062	0	0	2	2
III	.01	.5	.0062	.5	.0466	2	2
IV	.01	.5	.0062	0	0	3	3

Rule I is a constant-growth-rate rule; rules II and IV utilize a proportional control on the rate of inflation and derivative controls on both target variables. Rule II was introduced because we were disturbed by the finding in section 4.1 that the derivative control parameters could be continually increased without destabilizing the target variables; we suspected that the values of a_6 and a_7 in rule IV—which was the best of the rules examined in deterministic simulations—might be unduly high. Rule III is the same as II with the addition of a proportional control on unemployment. We were interested here in reexamining our earlier finding that proportional controls, unless used weakly, are destabilizing. The results of preliminary stochastic simulations did not suggest that any of rules II, III, and IV could be immediately rejected as markedly worse than the others.[14]

One other decision was reached as a result of early simulations: the control rule was modified so that no increase in the money supply which pushed the bill rate below 50 basis points was permitted. The equations of the FMP model do not themselves prevent negative bill rates. The rules tested were thus those given in Table 4–3 plus the constraint, in every case, that wherever the rule would have produced a bill rate below .5, the money supply is set at that level which keeps the bill rate at .5.

Each of the four rules was to be used in one deterministic and n replications of stochastic simulations. The initial value of n was chosen to be 10; if, on the basis of these results, further replications were deemed "necessary," then another 10 simulations would be run. An example of such a decision is discussed in the next section. A prior limit of 30 replications was set because of budget restrictions. The large step in sample size, 10, was chosen in a tradeoff between the simulation costs themselves, and the computer and investigator setup costs of running a set of simulations and calculating response statistics. The prior limit of 30 replications was not in fact reached.

An important point in the experimental design is that each policy rule was run on the same set of random numbers; that is, if $n=10$, we used 10 and not 40 sets of random numbers in the simulations. This differs from the strategy of the example of Naylor, Wertz, and Wonnacott [61] where 40 independent sets of random numbers would have been used in our case. Essentially our technique controls for the random number drawing; the errors behave like exogenous terms in the equations and we are examining how the system would behave under the four rules given 10 particular paths for these exogenous terms.[15] We expected—and found—that between-replication variance in the results under a particular rule was large and our technique makes it possible to draw inferences from a smaller number of replications than would be required if the alternative technique were used.[16]

Another measure of variability, which could have been used, is the root mean square error (RMSE) about the respective target levels. The difference between the average RMSE and average standard deviation, both across replications, is due to two terms: first, the bias in the mean from the target levels of the variables, and second, the variability in the means. We chose to work with the standard deviation measure because our main concern is with countercyclical stabilization policy—policies to reduce instability in the economy. It is for this reason, too, that we chose a_3 and a_5—the "target" rates of inflation and unemployment—to lie on the Phillips curve of the model. The results obtained in section 4.1 were not in fact dependent on the particular point chosen on the Phillips curve. However, we have checked that our conclusions would be little affected by use of RMSE rather than standard deviations.[17]

The major part of next section is devoted to an analysis of the output of the stochastic simulations. Five different measures are applied in analyzing the consequences of different policies. They are listed here, and will be referred to henceforth as tests A to E:

- A. Average Standard Deviation (square root of averaged variances) across replications for each policy.
- B. Better-Worse-Tied Paired Comparisons: the results for a pair of policies are compared using each replication as a separate observation. If policy J has lower standard deviations in both target variables than policy j on a particular replication, then J is "better"; if one standard deviation is lower but the other is higher, then we have a "tie." Scores are summed over replications.
- C. Analysis of Variance and F tests on Means.
- D. Tukey's Multiple Comparison of Means.
- E. Dunnett's Comparison of Means with Control Means.

Tests C–E are discussed in the very useful paper by Naylor, Wertz, and Wonnacott [61], which also includes a complete list of references. These tests require some assumptions on the probability distributions of the standard deviations or variances in whose magnitudes we are interested. These distributions are not known to us a priori; they are the results of inputting exogenous variables and normally distributed random numbers into a nonlinear model which generates highly serially correlated endogenous variables. Naylor et al. suggest taking the log of the variance of the target and assuming it to be normally distributed, and we have adopted this procedure.[18] Tests C–E also require the four variances (of the log variances) across replications to be the same under the different policies. We have not tested either of these assumptions, but the analysis of variance is not very sensitive to moderate departures from normality and equality of variances.

Once the transformation of the variances to logs has been carried out, C–E are used to discern which of the policies leads to the lowest mean log variance.[19] Test C is a test of whether the four means (i.e., of log variances) are the same. Tukey's test D is very conservative and allows us to form joint confidence intervals for comparisons between all pairs of policies. Dunnett's test E yields joint confidence intervals for comparisons of the means of the log variances under rules II, III, and IV with those under I (assumed to be a "control").

We continue to rank rules only if performance in terms of both targets is unambiguous; j is preferred to J only if j produces lower standard deviations of both the rates of inflation and unemployment separately. In cases where this method of ranking fails —as would likely be the case when more nearly optimal rules are found—a more complex utility function would be required.

4.4 Results and Conclusions

The output of the simulations is contained in Table 4.4 following. The data presented there are the means and standard deviations of the rates of inflation and unemployment for each policy and for each replication. Replication 0 is a deterministic simulation; replications 11–20 were required as a result of calculations based on the first 10 replications. The reasons for the extra 10 replications will be discussed below.

Test A. The results are summarized in Table 4-5. The mean standard deviations are presented over both 10 and 20 replications for rules I, III and IV.

Several features are immediately apparent. On the basis of stochastic simulation, II, III, and IV clearly dominate I. After 10 replications the relative ranking of III and IV was ambiguous although both dominated II. After 20 replications IV appears to be the

TABLE 4-4 Results of Stochastic Simulations

		I		II		III		IV	
		μ	σ	μ	σ	μ	σ	μ	σ
0	$\Delta P/P$	.0062	.0026	.0064	.0021	.0062	.0023	.0064	.0021
	u	.0466	.0072	.0458	.0059	.0471	.0076	.0458	.0054
1	$\Delta P/P$	.0061	.0052	.0059	.0051	.0061	.0047	.0057	.0050
	u	.0582	.0146	.0588	.0138	.0560	.0120	.0599	.0137
2	$\Delta P/P$	.0053	.0059	.0051	.0065	.0058	.0055	.0048	.0062
	u	.0524	.0158	.0560	.0181	.0537	.0187	.0565	.0173
3	$\Delta P/P$	.0079	.0054	.0070	.0056	.0065	.0036	.0064	.0036
	u	.0463	.0147	.0502	.0160	.0481	.0139	.0463	.0110
4	$\Delta P/P$	.0062	.0038	.0061	.0035	.0055	.0035	.0060	.0034
	u	.0413	.0062	.0409	.0053	.0424	.0057	.0411	.0054
5	$\Delta P/P$	.0062	.0039	.0058	.0039	.0059	.0038	.0054	.0040
	u	.0492	.0097	.0504	.0102	.0508	.0115	.0522	.0104
6	$\Delta P/P$	.0061	.0054	.0059	.0051	.0065	.0044	.0054	.0049
	u	.0578	.0159	.0574	.0142	.0547	.0142	.0602	.0149
7	$\Delta P/P$	.0062	.0048	.0058	.0039	.0053	.0038	.0055	.0040
	u	.0449	.0116	.0443	.0099	.0456	.0104	.0453	.0103
8	$\Delta P/P$	.0091	.0162	.0077	.0058	.0082	.0049	.0074	.0045
	u	.0821	.0390	.0608	.0235	.0525	.0199	.0567	.0196
9	$\Delta P/P$	.0062	.0046	.0058	.0046	.0063	.0048	.0054	.0047
	u	.0532	.0114	.0543	.0109	.0544	.0136	.0565	.0122
10	$\Delta P/P$	.0054	.0074	.0052	.0059	.0056	.0066	.0047	.0067
	u	.0586	.0179	.0556	.0147	.0551	.0159	.0601	.0162
11	$\Delta P/P$	.0051	.0089			.0077	.0119	.0054	.0053
	u	.0598	.0222			.0580	.0234	.0520	.0149
12	$\Delta P/P$	.0056	.0041			.0058	.0032	.0054	.0036
	u	.0485	.0110			.0463	.0079	.0484	.0098
13	$\Delta P/P$	.0067	.0064			.0066	.0038	.0065	.0037
	u	.0515	.0214			.0435	.0135	.0444	.0127
14	$\Delta P/P$	.0056	.0052			.0063	.0038	.0053	.0046
	u	.0566	.0140			.0501	.0116	.0554	.0130
15	$\Delta P/P$	.0053	.0089			.0052	.0079	.0049	.0084
	u	.0757	.0282			.0673	.0228	.0753	.0249
16	$\Delta P/P$	.0097	.0091			.0066	.0031	.0077	.0045
	u	.0433	.0166			.0419	.0093	.0423	.0131
17	$\Delta P/P$	.0061	.0048			.0062	.0048	.0054	.0046
	u	.0468	.0129			.0506	.0160	.0492	.0126
18	$\Delta P/P$	.0060	.0042			.0062	.0041	.0053	.0038
	u	.0485	.0116			.0479	.0130	.0502	.0117
19	$\Delta P/P$	.0072	.0042			.0057	.0041	.0058	.0035
	u	.0442	.0122			.0459	.0098	.0446	.0080
20	$\Delta P/P$	.0071	.0040			.0065	.0046	.0063	.0041
	u	.0470	.0104			.0513	.0147	.0497	.0113

TABLE 4–5 Summary Standard Deviations of Target Variables

Variable	Detail	I	II	III	IV
$\sigma_{\Delta P/P}$	Mean for 10 repl.	.0071	.0051	.0047	.0048
	Mean for 20 repl.	.0068	—	.0052	.0048
	Deterministic	.0026	.0021	.0023	.0021
σ_u	Mean for 10 repl.	.0178	.0145	.0141	.0137
	Mean for 20 repl.	.0174	—	.0146	.0138
	Deterministic	.0072	.0059	.0076	.0054

best policy of those examined. Although not shown, it is also generally true that the variances across replications exhibited the same ranking; in other words not only did rule I have a higher average standard deviation than the other rules, but it also had a somewhat greater dispersion of results.

The deterministic results are also presented for contrast: first, the levels obtained for $\sigma_{\Delta P/P}$ and σ_u are much smaller in the deterministic systems; second, on the basis of the deterministic simulations III appears unworthy of further testing since it is dominated by II and IV. This is one of those cases where the behavior of the stochastic system is different from that of the deterministic system.

Test B. Table 4–6 presents, in sporting-world fashion, the record of the rules under this measure. Each cell contains two entries—the

TABLE 4–6 Better-Worse-Tied Comparisons (of Row Policies with Column Policies)

Rule	II	III	IV
I	3–7–0	1–7–2	3–7–0
		4–13–3	4–15–1
II		3–4–3	4–4–2
III			3–4–3
			7–10–3

upper over 10 replications and the lower over 20. For example, the 3–7–0 in row I, column IV means that rule I was better than IV in 3 of the first 10 replications and worse in 7.

After 10 replications II, III, and IV dominate I but are not distinguishable among themselves. After 20 replications both III and IV dominate I, and IV appears slightly better than III from two viewpoints—comparison of each with I and of III with IV. While this measure does not weight large differences heavily as do quadratic measures, it attaches too much weight to the last decimal place of a standard deviation.

Test C. Detailed results for this and the following tests are presented only for the complete 20 replications on rules I, III, and IV; however, the results for the first 10 replications will be discussed. Table 4–7 presents data for a two-way analysis of variance in the

TABLE 4–7 Two-Way Analysis of Variance

Source of Variation ($x_{ij} \equiv \log \sigma^2$ on ith replication of policy j)	Sum of Squares $\Delta P/P$		Degrees of Freedom	Mean Squares $\Delta P/P$	
	$\Delta P/P$	u		$\Delta P/P$	u
Between replications: $3 \sum_{i=1}^{20} (\bar{x}_{i.} - \bar{x}_{..})^2$	15.3186	25.7092	19	—	—
Between policies: $20 \sum_{j=\text{I, III, IV}} (\bar{x}_{.j} - \bar{x}_{..})^2$	2.5790	0.9796	2	1.2895	.4898
Remainder (error)[a]	7.2838	3.8296	38	0.1917	.1008
Total $= \sum_{i=1}^{20} \sum_{j=\text{I, III, IV}} (x_{ij} - \bar{x}_{..})^2$	25.1814	30.5184	59	—	—

[a] Tukey's test [79] for nonadditivity of the errors was carried out and the null hypothesis of additivity was not rejected.

logs of the variances. The raw data are contained in Table 4–4. The particular analysis of variance model employed can be found in Brownlee [13]—namely, a special case of the two-way mixed model of analysis of variance with one observation per cell.[20] As stated earlier, the between-replications variance is much larger than the between-policies variance and must be extracted before a test on the latter can be performed.

The F ratios for this test—of whether there is any difference between the results of the policies—are 6.74 and 4.86 for the rates of inflation and unemployment, respectively; these are to be compared with the tabulated value of $F_{.95}(2,38)=3.25$. At the 95 percent confidence level, then, the results do not support the null hypothesis of equal target standard deviations for the policies I, III, and IV.

Over the first 10 replications and for 4 policies we could reject the null hypothesis for the rate of inflation at the 95 percent confidence level, but for the unemployment rate the confidence level was only 75 percent.

Test D. This test permits us to form simultaneous confidence intervals on the differences between the policy means (of the log variances). At the 95 percent level of confidence all of the following statements hold:

$$E[x_{ij}-x_{iJ}] \in (\bar{x}_{.j}-\bar{x}_{.J}) \pm q_{.95}(k,\tau)\left(\frac{MS_e}{n}\right)^{1/2}$$

$$i=1,\ldots,n$$
$$j, J=1,\ldots,k \quad j \neq J$$

where
k = number of policies
τ = number of degrees of freedom for the mean square error, MS_e
n = number of replications
and $q_{.95}(k,\tau)$ is tabulated as the Studentized Range Statistic in Winer [82]. Here $\tau=38$, $n=20$, and $k=3$; $q_{.95}(3,38)=3.45$.

Table 4–8 presents the differences between the sample means and the simultaneous 95 percent confidence intervals for the mean differences. As is apparent from the table, the null hypothesis of like means is rejected for policies I and IV on both target variables; the null hypothesis for policies I and III is rejected only for the rate

TABLE 4-8   Simultaneous Confidence Intervals on
Differences in All Means

Target	Rule	III	IV
$\Delta P/P$	I	.43 ±.34	.45 ±.34
u		.21 ±.24	.31 ±.24
$\Delta P/P$	III		.02 ±.34
u			.10 ±.24

of inflation (but almost on the unemployment rate also); III and IV are not significantly different.

Over the first 10 replications the only mean difference that was significantly different from zero at the 95 percent confidence level (in the joint test) was between policies I and III for the rate of inflation; the difference between I and IV was just nonsignificant in both target variables; and II was not close for either target.

Test E. This is less conservative than test D since it assumes that the comparisons to be made are only those in the first row of Table 4-8. Both one- and two-tailed tests are possible. At the 95 percent level of confidence, all of the following statements hold: Either

$$E[x_{ij} - x_{iJ}] \in (\bar{x}_{.j} - \bar{x}_{.J}) \pm d_{.975}(k, \tau) \left(\frac{2MS_e}{n} \right)^{1/2} \quad \text{(two-tailed)}$$

$$E[x_{ij} - x_{iJ}] \in (\bar{x}_{.j} - \bar{x}_{.J}) - d_{.95}(k, \tau) \left(\frac{2MS_e}{n} \right)^{1/2} \quad \text{(one-tailed)}$$

$$i = 1, \ldots, n$$
$$j, J = 1, \ldots, k \quad j \neq J$$

where k, τ, and n are defined as in the Tukey test and $d_.(k, \tau)$ is tabulated as Dunnett's t statistic.[21]

Table 4-9a presents the two-tailed confidence intervals for differences between means of III and IV from the "control" policy I. The one-tailed 95 percent confidence intervals are presented in

TABLE 4–9 Simultaneous Confidence Intervals for
Comparing Means of III and IV with I (Control)

		a				b	
Target	Rule	III	IV	Target	Rule	III	IV
$\Delta P/P$	I	.43 ±.32	.45 ±.32	$\Delta P/P$	I	.43 −.27	.45 −.27
u		.21 ±.23	.31 ±.23	u		.21 −.20	.31 −.20

Table 4–9b. The critical values for d are $d_{.975}(3, 38) = 2.30$ and $d_{.95}(3, 38) = 1.97$.[22]

Table 4–9b indicates that we can reject the null hypothesis that III and IV each have means equal to that of the control in favor of the alternative hypothesis that the mean variance of the control is larger. In Table 4–9a, the null hypothesis is rejected for both targets with IV but only for the rate of inflation with III.

After 10 replications, the two-tailed test rejected the null hypothesis only for the rate of inflation with policy III, although policy IV was close for both targets; the one-tailed test yielded the same results as did the 20-replication two-tailed test above. Policy II did not come close to significance on either target variable, and we accordingly decided to conduct no further simulations using this policy.

Our general conclusion after 10 replications was that on each of the tests A to E, there was a general tendency for III and IV to dominate I but that there were too few sample points to allow strong conclusions. It was accordingly decided to run another 10 replications of rules I, III, and IV.

After 20 replications policy IV shows statistically significant superiority over policy I under the tests D and E; tests A and B provide less formal evidence for this conclusion. Policy III performs only slightly less well than IV, especially with respect to the rate of inflation. Accordingly, no further replications were indicated.[23]

Our results show that there are monetary policy rules which, in the context of the FMP model, would have been stabilizing for the rates of inflation and unemployment over the period 1956: I to 1968: IV, relative to performance under a constant-growth-rate rule. In particular, our stabilizing policy rules require strong elements of derivative control; some proportional correction is also used.

We can make more precise statements about relative variability

TABLE 4–10 Range of Ratios of Standard Deviations

Rule	Target	III	IV
I	$\Delta P/P$	1.04—1.44	1.07—1.48
	u	0.99—1.24	1.04—1.31

under monetary rules in the FMP model. Table 4–10 is an interpretation of our earlier use of Dunnett's two-tailed test in which we have given 95 percent confidence intervals for the ratios of standard deviations under rule I relative to rules III and IV.[24] Interpreting this table, the results say that at the 95 percent confidence level, the reduction in standard deviation from using rule IV rather than rule I in the FMP model is between 7 percent and 32 ($=0.48/1.48 \times 100$) percent on the inflation rate and between 4 percent and 24 percent on the unemployment rate.

It is especially interesting to note that, in the stochastic model, rules III and IV are quite close in performance according to our various tests, yet, on the basis of deterministic simulation, III is clearly dominated by IV. The relative improvement in the performance of III is, we expect, due to a need to change the relative strength of proportional and derivative controls in a stochastic system. Basically, our feedback controls use the level and first difference of a target variable. When random elements are present the level of the target variable becomes "noisy," but the change in the variable could be much more so. Thus relatively more weight should be placed on proportional control—and this is precisely how III differs from IV.

As usual, a number of qualifications are required. First, as noted in section 3.1, we have not made lag coefficients explicitly variable. Second, our simulations have been conducted only over a particular period and we intend, in subsequent studies, carrying out tests of their period specificity. Third, we are also considering alternative search procedures for rules.[25] Nonetheless, we believe that, if a monetary rule is to be adopted, the evidence presented in this study provides substantive reasons to use monetary rules including proportional and derivative controls.

We feel that this conclusion is further supported by our experiments with the St. Louis FRB "Monetarist" model which are reported in Cooper and Fischer [22]. The policy rules are much more effective relative to the constant growth rule in the St. Louis model than in the FMP model. Given that arguments for a constant-growth-rate rule are usually made by monetarists, this is a particularly significant result. We hypothesize that the difference in results is accounted for largely by the relatively more rapid impact of changes in the money stock in the St. Louis model, as evidenced by the time patterns of money multipliers.

Appendix 4A   The Use of the Secant Method in Econometric Models

In working with econometric models, it may be desired to solve for values of policy (instrument) variables which are consistent with specified levels of target variables. Tinbergen's work [74] on economic policy uses such solutions for a variety of linear models. Tinbergen's approach, however, cannot be employed in large nonlinear models such as the FMP model.

A straightforward method of solving for the requisite values of the instrument variables, when the Gauss-Seidel algorithm is used in solving the complete model, is to renormalize the equation of the target variable in terms of the policy variable, in effect making the target variable exogenous and the policy variable endogenous. If the policy variable does not appear in the equation for the target variable, then the equation should be renormalized in terms of one of the right-hand-side endogenous variables. If the original equation for this last endogenous variable contained the policy variable, then one more renormalization (in terms of the policy variable) solves the problem; if it does not, then this equation will also have to be renormalized in terms of one of its right-hand-side endogenous variables, and so on, until the chain of causation leads back to an equation containing the policy variable. When the policy and target variables are, in some sense, far apart—i.e., in different sectors—then the amount of renormalization can be substantial and is usually specific to each pair of policy and target variables. The generalization to more than one target, using more than one instrument, is conceptually straightforward, though we are not sure of its workability.

In applications of automatic feedback controls in the FMP model we used the money supply (M) as the policy variable, although M

was endogenous in the structure of the model and unborrowed reserves plus currency was the open-market policy variable. Given the structure of the monetary sector, it was convenient to renormalize to make M, in effect, an exogenous variable and to generate the appropriate value for unborrowed high-powered money.

An alternative method is available which involves no renormalization but which introduces a difference equation in the policy and target variables into the Gauss-Seidel iterative procedure. For instance, in attempting to solve the FMP model—in the renormalized version in which the money supply was a policy variable—for the value of M that leads to a specific value (u^o) of the unemployment rate (u), we added an equation which is, subject to some qualifications,[26]

$$M = M_{-1} - \left(\frac{M_{-1} - M_{-2}}{u_{-1} - u_{-2}}\right)(u_{-1} - u^o)$$

where the subscripts refer to iteration numbers relative to the current one. M and u then will converge only when $u \approx u^o$ and M is consistent with this value. This method can be generalized to more than one target; the choice of difference equations to introduce into the iteration process would then be affected by considerations similar to those discussed in the "assignment problem" of international trade theory.[27] Alternatively, a "Jacobian" relating every instrument to all targets could be derived from an initial computation and then updated at each iteration.

It turns out that this approach is known as the "secant method" for solving nonlinear equations. It is described, and its relation to the Newton-Raphson method is shown, by Ralston [67]. Its efficiency relative to other methods is discussed by Barnes [8]. For those working with econometric models, however, its chief virtue is that it requires relatively little tinkering with the equations of the model.

In practice, the method works well. Using a secant method we were able to solve the FMP model for values of M that led to specific values of the rates of inflation or unemployment—the renormalization process was not tractable. Although the values of M obtained were often outside feasible regions, this is a result of the structure of the model—especially its long lags in the effects of monetary policy—rather than the secant method. Economists at the

Federal Reserve Bank of Chicago have recently been using our technique successfully over a wide range of instrument variables in the same model.

Notes

[1] For discussion of this topic, see Box and Jenkins [10, ch. 12].
[2] See deLeeuw and Gramlich [26] for a discussion of the timing of effects of monetary policy in the FMP model.
[3] Zecher [83] presents evidence on this point.
[4] See Modigliani [56, p. 219].
[5] We are thus abstracting from the difficulties which face the authorities in achieving a specified level of the money supply—though, in deterministic simulations in the model, no such difficulty arises.
[6] Interest rates or other intermediate targets were not used in the control rule because some exploratory simulations in which the treasury bill rate was stabilized by variations in the money supply indicated that stability of interest rates did not lead to stability in the rates of inflation and unemployment.
[7] Another type of feedback control is the integral control, which is effective in bringing variables back to their target levels; we did not use such controls because of our concentration on the stability of rates of inflation and unemployment rather than on the levels of these rates. Further, preliminary difficulties encountered with strong proportional controls suggested that integral controls might be destabilizing.
[8] One must not assume that, because the mean rate of unemployment falls as a_1 increased from .005 to .0125, the rate itself would show the same pattern in any one quarter. In 1968:IV, for example, runs 1a and 1d led to unemployment rates of 5.7 percent and 6.0 percent, respectively; real GNP was slightly lower in the higher growth rate run, too. The response to any control rule is dependent upon the behavior of exogenous variables and the state of the system.
[9] This approach was suggested by Milton Friedman as a possible way of holding the mean rates of inflation and unemployment constant while examining their variability under different rules.
[10] In Figure 4–3, these statistics are calculated on the quarterly rate of change of demand deposits.

[11] This is not to say that the fact that the means for the subperiods in run 16 are closer together than those in run 1c is of no importance from the viewpoint of reducing variability in the relevant variables over the whole period.

[12] This was almost equivalent to moving the Korean War into the relevant data base and the Vietnam War out of it.

[13] This is the case with the St. Louis FRB model; see Cooper and Fischer [21] and also the end of section 4.4.

[14] The behavior of the money stock under rule IV in a deterministic simulation is presented in section 4.1, where the parameterization of the rules is discussed in detail. An example may help convey the "feel" of the rules used here: suppose that the annual rate of inflation was 4 percent last quarter and 4.5 percent a quarter earlier, while the rate of unemployment has been steady at 6 percent. Then, according to rule III, the money supply should grow at an annual rate of almost 7 percent this quarter.

[15] Our experimental design can be likened to duplicate bridge in which each player is confronted with the same distribution of hands. It is discussed further in section 4.4 under the subheading "Test C."

[16] See Conway [17].

[17] We can provide, upon request, a table which is counterpart to Table 4-5, for example, in the text following.

[18] See also Winer [82] for discussion of "normalizing" transformations.

[19] Since our basic interest is in finding differences in variability produced under the various rules, all our tests are for significance of differences of means, across replications, of log variances.

[20] See, specifically, Brownlee [13, pp. 498–499 and 548–550]. Some authors are wary of the use of this particular model in applications dealing with simulation experiments of this type (see Conway [17] for example). The particular experimental design chosen was necessitated, though, because of its superior efficiency relative to those designs for which the standard one-way analysis of variance is clearly applicable. Other authors, however, do suggest that the tests employed in the text are relevant provided the mean square error and degrees of freedom of the two-way classification replace their one-way counterparts usually found in the multiple comparison formulae (see Wine [81, pp. 407–408]). See also Scheffé [70, pp. 270–271], who discusses the utility of these tests as an approximation under our statistical model.

We feel reasonably confident in our applications here for other reasons. First, the Tukey test is known to be conservative among the various multiple comparison procedures. Second, an even more conservative way of building simultaneous confidence intervals, which is *independent* of our experimental design, is the method described by Miller [54] and applied in Jucker and Gómez [45] for pooling individual t tests with the Bonferroni (or Boolean) inequality; results equivalent to those of Table 4-8 and Table 4-9a in the text were computed and there was no qualitative difference in the conclusions. The latter reference also includes a discussion of the assumptions required for tests C–E to be valid in the experiments reported here.

[21] Naylor et al. [61] err in using $d_{.95}(k, \tau)$ for a two-tailed test at the 95 percent level of confidence. As an example observe the case of $k=2$ where the Tukey and Dunnett tests are identical. This requires $q(2, \tau) = \sqrt{2} d(2, \tau)$; this equality is confirmed in statistical tables where $q_{.95}(2, \tau) = \sqrt{2} d_{.975}(2, \tau) \neq \sqrt{2} d_{.95}(2, \tau)$. The Tukey test, focusing on the range, automatically gives us a two-tailed test on the difference.

[22] The confidence intervals could also be presented in terms of ratios of standard deviations between policies. This is done in the concluding paragraphs of the section.

[23] This is in accordance with our rather loose a priori rule of stopping sampling once clear differences between rule I and other rules were obtained.

[24] See Naylor et al. [61, p. 195] for a similar test.

[25] One possible avenue—that of trying to solve for the path of *M1* which would keep one of our target variables at its desired level—has been explored. We concluded that in the FMP model, given other exogenous variables, no feasible path of the money supply could have kept the unemployment rate constant for 1956: I–1968: IV. The basic reason is that money multipliers are too small, given the fluctuations in other exogenous variables. The method we used for these attempts is outlined in the Appendix to this chapter.

[26] Actual implementation should take into account: (i) the presence of a damping factor in the solution process, (ii) the ordering of the equations for the target and instrument variables, (iii) the balance of the convergence criteria on the target and instrument variables, and (iv) a constraint on the value of the quotient term in the added equation.

[27] See Mundell [59].

References

1) Adelman, Irma, and Frank L. Adelman, "The Dynamic Properties of the Klein-Goldberger Model." *Econometrica* (October 1959): 596–625.
2) Allais, M. F. C. "A Restatement of the Quantity Theory of Money." *American Economic Review* (December 1966): 1123–1157.
3) Almon, Shirley. "The Distributed Lag Between Capital Appropriations and Expenditures." *Econometrica* (January 1965): 178–196.
4) Andersen, L. C., and K. M. Carlson. "A Monetarist Model for Economic Stabilization." *Federal Reserve Bank of St. Louis Review* 52, 4 (April 1970): 7–25.
5) Anderson, R. L. "Distribution of the Serial Correlation Coefficient." *Annals of Mathematical Statistics* 13, 1 (1942).
6) Ando, A., and Franco Modigliani. "Velocity and the Investment Multiplier." *American Economic Review* (September 1965): 693–728.
7) Ando, Albert, and Franco Modigliani. "Econometric Analysis of Stabilization Policies." *American Economic Review, Papers and Proceedings* (May 1969): 296–314.
8) Barnes, J. G. P. "An Algorithm for Solving Non-linear Equations Based on the Secant Method." *Computer Journal* (April 1965): 66–72.
9) Baumol, W. J. "The Transactions Demand for Cash." *Quarterly Journal of Economics* (November 1952): 545–554.
10) Box, G. E. P., and G. M. Jenkins. *Times Series Analysis: Forecasting and Control*. San Francisco: Holden-Day, 1970.
11) Bronfenbrenner, Martin. "Statistical Tests of Rival Monetary Rules." *Journal of Political Economy* (February 1961): 1–14.
12) Bronfenbrenner, Martin. "Statistical Tests of Rival Monetary Rules: Quarterly Data Supplement." *Journal of Political Economy* (December 1961): 621–625.
13) Brownlee, K. A. *Statistical Theory and Methodology in Science and Engineering*, 2nd ed. New York: Wiley, 1965.
14) Brundy, J. M., and D. W. Jorgensen. "Efficient Estimation of

Simultaneous Equations by Instrumental Variables." *The Review of Economics and Statistics* (August 1971): 207–224.

15) Brunner, K., and A. H. Meltzer. "Predicting Velocity: Its Implications for Theory and Policy." *Journal of Finance* (May 1963): 319–354.

16) Chow, G. "On the Long-Run and Short-Run Demand Function for Money." *Journal of Political Economy* (April 1966): 111–131.

17) Conway, R. W. "Some Tactical Problems in Digital Simulation." *Management Science* (October 1963): 47–61.

18) Cooper, J. Phillip. "Stochastic Reserve Losses and Expansion of Bank Credit: Note." *American Economic Review* (September 1971): 741–745.

19) Cooper, J. Phillip. "Two Approaches to Polynomial Distributed Lags Estimation: An Expository Note and Comment." *The American Statistician* (June 1972): 32–35.

20) Cooper, J. Phillip, and Stanley Fischer. "Simulation of Monetary Rules in the FRB-MIT-Penn Model." *Journal of Money, Credit and Banking* (May 1972): 384–396.

21) Cooper, J. Phillip, and Stanley Fischer. "Stochastic Simulation of Monetary Rules in Two Macroeconometric Models." *Journal of the American Statistical Association* (December, 1972): 750–760.

22) Cooper, J. Phillip, and Stanley Fischer. "The Use of the Secant Method in Econometric Models." *Journal of Business* (April 1973): 274–277.

23) Cooper, J. Phillip, and Charles R. Nelson. "The *Ex Ante* Prediction Performance of the St. Louis and FRB–MIT–Penn Econometric Models." CMSBE Report 7236, University of Chicago, 1972. (Mimeographed.)

24) Culbertson, John M. "Friedman on the Lag in Effect of Monetary Policy." *Journal of Political Economy* (December 1960): 617–621.

25) de Leeuw, Frank. "A Model of Financial Behavior." *The Brookings Quarterly Econometric Model of the United States*. Edited by J. S. Duesenberry et al. Chicago: Rand-McNally, 1965.

26) de Leeuw, Frank, and Edward M. Gramlich. "The Channels of Monetary Policy: A Further Report on the Federal Reserve–MIT Model." *Journal of Finance, Papers and Proceedings* (May 1969): 265–290.

27) de Leeuw, Frank, and Edward M. Gramlich. "The Federal Reserve–MIT Econometric Model." *Federal Reserve Bulletin* (January 1968): 11–40.
28) Duesenberry, J. S.; G. Fromm; L. E. Klein; and E. Kuh, eds. *The Brookings Model: Some Further Results*. Chicago: Rand-McNally, 1969.
29) Dutta, M., and E. Lyttkens. "Iterative Instrumental Variables Method and Estimation of a Large Simultaneous System." Discussion Paper No. 7, Bureau of Economic Research, Rutgers University, 1970.
30) Enzler, J. J., and H. O. Stekler. "An Analysis of the 1968–69 Economic Forecasts." *The Journal of Business* (July 1971): 271–281.
31) Friedman, B. "The Demand for Money: Testing a Neo-Fisherian Approach." Unpublished paper presented at the meetings of the Econometric Society, December 1966.
32) Friedman, Milton. "The Demand for Money: Some Theoretical and Empirical Results." *Journal of Political Economy* (August 1959): 327–351.
33) Friedman, Milton. *A Program for Monetary Stability*. New York: Fordham University Press, 1960.
34) Friedman, Milton. "The Lag in Effect of Monetary Policy." In *The Optimum Quantity of Money and Other Essays*. Chicago: Aldine, 1969.
35) Fromm, Gary, and Lawrence E. Klein. "Solutions of the Complete System." *The Brookings Model: Some Further Results*. Edited by J. S. Duesenberry, et al. Chicago: Rand-McNally, 1969.
36) Geisel, M. S. "Comparing and Choosing Among Parametric Statistical Models: A Bayesian Analysis with Macroeconomic Applications." Ph. D. dissertation, University of Chicago, 1970.
37) Goldberger, A. S.; A. L. Nagar; and H. S. Odeh. "The Covariance Matrix of Reduced Form Coefficients and of Forecasts for a Structural Model." *Econometrica* (October 1961): 556–573.
38) Goldfeld, S. *Commercial Bank Behavior and Economic Activity*. Amsterdam: North-Holland, 1966.
39) Goldfeld, S., and E. Kane. "The Determinants of Member Bank Borrowing." *Journal of Finance* (September 1966): 499–514.

40) Gordon, Robert J. "Large-Scale Econometric Models: An Introduction and Appraisal for Noneconometricians." University of Chicago, 1970. (Mimeographed.)
41) Hester, D., and J. Pierce. "Cross-section Analysis and Bank Dynamics." *Journal of Political Economy* (July/August 1968), Part II, 755–776.
42) Holt, Charles C. "Linear Decision Rules for Economic Stabilization and Growth." *Quarterly Journal of Economics* 76, 1 (February 1962): 20–45.
43) Howrey, E. Philip, and H. H. Kelejian. "Simulation Versus Analytical Solutions." In *The Design of Computer Simulation Experiments*. Edited by Thomas H. Naylor. Durham, N.C.: Duke University Press, 1969.
44) Jaffee, Dwight M., and Franco Modigliani. "A Theory and Test of Credit Rationing." *American Economic Review* (December 1969): 850–872.
45) Jucker, James V., and Jorge G. Gómez. "Policy-Comparing Simulation Experiments: Design and Analysis." Working Paper HBS 70–18, Graduate School of Business Administration, Harvard University, 1970.
46) Klein, L. R. *An Essay on the Theory of Economic Prediction.* Helsinki, 1968.
47) Knuth, Donald E. *Seminumerical Algorithms.* Vol. 2 of *The Art of Computer Programming.* Reading, Mass.: Addison-Wesley, 1969.
48) Laidler, D. "The Rate of Interest and the Demand for Money—Some Empirical Evidence." *Journal of Political Economy* (December 1966): 543–555.
49) Latane, H. A. "Cash Balances and the Interest Rate—A Pragmatic Approach." *Review of Economics and Statistics* (September 1954): 456–461.
50) Latane, H. A. "Income Velocity and the Interest Rate—A Pragmatic Approach." *Review of Economics and Statistics* (November 1960): 445–449.
51) Lewis, P. A. W.; A. S. Goodman; and J. M. Miller. "A Pseudo-Random Number Generator for the System/360." *IBM Systems Journal* 8, 2, (1969): 136–146.
52) McCarthy, Michael D. "Some Notes on the Generation of Pseudo Structural Errors for Use in Stochastic Simulation Studies." Unpublished. University of Pennsylvania, 1969.

53) Meigs, A. James. *Free Reserves and the Money Supply*. Chicago: University of Chicago Press, 1962.
54) Miller, Rupert G., Jr. *Simultaneous Statistical Inference*. New York: McGraw-Hill, 1966.
55) Modigliani, Franco. "Monetary Policy and Consumption: Linkages via Interest Rate and Wealth Effects in the FMP Model." *Consumer Spending and Monetary Policy: The Linkages*. Boston: The Federal Reserve Bank of Boston, 1971.
56) Modigliani, Franco. "Some Empirical Tests of Monetary Management and of Rules Versus Discretion." *Journal of Political Economy* (June 1964): 211–245.
57) Modigliani, Franco; Robert H. Rasche; and J. Phillip Cooper. "Central Bank Policy, the Money Supply and the Short-Term Rate of Interest." *Journal of Money, Credit and Banking* (May 1970): 166–218.
58) Modigliani, Franco, and Richard Sutch. "Innovation in Interest Rate Policy." *American Economic Review* (May 1966): 178–197.
59) Mundell, Robert A. *International Economics*. New York: Macmillan, 1968.
60) Nagar, A. L. "Stochastic Simulation of the Brookings Econometric Model." *The Brookings Model: Some Further Results*. Edited by J. S. Duesenberry, et al. Chicago: Rand-McNally, 1969.
61) Naylor, T. H.; K. Wertz; and T. Wonnacott "Some Methods for Evaluating the Effects of Economic Policies Using Simulation Experiments." *Review of the International Statistical Institute* (1968), 184–200.
62) Nelson, C. R. *The Term Structure of Interest Rates*. New York: Basic Books, 1972.
63) Nelson, Charles R. "The Prediction Performance of the FRB-MIT-Penn Model of the U.S. Economy." *American Economic Review* (December 1972): 902–917.
64) Orr, D., and W. G. Mellon. "Stochastic Reserve Losses and Expansion of Bank Credit." *American Economic Review* (September 1961): 614–623.
65) Payne, W. H.; J. R. Rabung; and T. P. Bogyo. "Coding the Lehmer Pseudorandom Number Generator." *Communications of the ACM* (February 1969): 85.
66) Phillips, A. W. "Stabilization Policy in a Closed Economy." *Economic Journal* (June 1954): 290–323.

67) Ralston, Anthony. *A First Course in Numerical Analysis.* New York: McGraw-Hill, 1965.
68) Rasche, Robert H., and Harold T. Shapiro. "The FRB-MIT Econometric Model: Its Special Features." *American Economic Review, Papers and Proceedings* (May 1968): 123–149.
69) Sayers, Richard S. "The Theoretical Basis of Central Banking." *Central Banking After Bagehot.* Oxford: Clarendon Press, 1957.
70) Scheffé, Henry. *The Analysis of Variance.* New York: Wiley, 1959.
71) Shull, B. "Report on Research Undertaken in Connection with a System Study: Reappraisal of the Federal Reserve Discount Mechanism." Board of Governors of the Federal Reserve System, 1968.
72) Slutzky, Eugen E. "The Summation of Random Causes as the Source of Cyclical Processes." *Econometrica* (1937): 105–146.
73) Theil, Henri. *Principles of Econometrics.* New York: Wiley, 1971.
74) Tinbergen, Jan. *On the Theory of Economic Policy.* Amsterdam: North-Holland, 1966.
75) Tobin, J. "The Interest Elasticity of Transactions Demand for Cash." *Review of Economics and Statistics* (August 1956): 241–247.
76) Tobin, J. Unpublished Monetary Theory Manuscript, New Haven, 1959, ch. VIII. (Mimeographed.)
77) Tucker, D. P. "Income Adjustment to Money-Supply Changes." *American Economic Review* (June 1966): 431–449.
78) Tukey, John W. *Exploratory Data Analysis.* Limited preliminary edition. Reading, Mass.: Addison-Wesley, 1970.
79) Tukey, John W. "One Degree of Freedom for Non-Additivity." *Biometrics* (September 1949): 232–242.
80) Tustin, A. *The Mechanism of Economic Systems.* London: Heinemann, 1953.
81) Wine, R. Lowell. *Statistics for Scientists and Engineers.* Englewood-Cliffs, N. J.: Prentice-Hall, 1964.
82) Winer, B. J. *Statistical Principles in Experimental Design.* New York: McGraw-Hill, 1962.
83) Zecher, Joseph R. *An Evaluation of Four Econometric Models of the Financial Sector.* Cleveland: Federal Reserve Bank of Cleveland, 1970.
84) Zellner, A. "An Efficient Method of Estimating Seemingly Unrelated Regressions and Tests for Aggregation Bias." *Journal of the American Statistical Association* 57 (1962): 348-368.

85) Zellner, A. "General Description of the Federal Reserve-MIT-Penn Quarterly Econometric Model of the U.S. Economy (Version 4.1–4/15/69)." 1969. (Mimeographed.)
86) Zellner, Arnold. "Implications of the Model-Building Effort for Future Research." *Systems Simulation for Regional Analysis*. Edited by H. R. Hamilton, et al. Cambridge, Mass.: M.I.T. Press, 1969.
87) Zellner, A. *An Introduction to Bayesian Inference in Econometrics*. New York: Wiley, 1971.

Index

Adelman, Frank L., 121, 173
Adelman, Irma, 121, 173
Aggregate money income, 46
Aitken's least squares, 109
Allais, M. F. C., 91
Allais model, 46
American Economic Review, 94
Analysis of variance, 196, 200
Anderson, L. C., 104, 166, 171, 174
Anderson, R. L., 119
Ando, Albert, 7, 8, 52
ARIMA. *See* Integrated autoregressive moving average
Assets, symbols for, 17t
Average Standard Deviation, 196

Balance of payments, 70
Balance sheet, standardized bank, 17t
Banks, earning assets of, 15
  investment portfolio for, 2, 16–20
  monopoly, 25
Banking systems, aggregate, 20
  heavily concentrated, 88
Barnes, J. G. P., 206
Baumol, W. J., 52
Bayesian method, 112
Better-worse-tied comparisons, 196, 199
Bogyo, T. P., 123
Borrowing, aversion to, 37
  cost of, 2, 25–30
  as privilege, 26
Box, G. E. P., 99
Box-Jenkins models, 4
Bronfenbrenner, Martin, 178
Brookings Model, 141
Brownlee, K. A., 201
Brundy, J. M., 93
Brunner-Meltzer model, 46, 47

Carlson, K. M., 104, 166, 171, 174
Certificates of deposit, 53
Charge accounts, 58
Chicago Federal Reserve Bank, 14
Chow, G., 91

Circulation, velocity of, 47
Composite equation, 112
Composite predictions, estimated weights for, 110t, 111t
  policy implications of, 113–115
Composite regressions, 110f
  post-sample errors from, 117t
Computer technology, 12
Confidence intervals, 202t, 203t
Constant-growth-rate, rules for, 6, 177–190, 194, 203, 205
  inferiority of, 193
Consumer price index, 108, 110t, 116t
Controls, derivative, 177, 184, 192, 204
  monetary rule using, 192
  feedback, 207
  integral, 207
  proportional, 177, 178, 181, 184, 192
  destabilizing effect of, 185, 186
Cooper, J. Phillip, 8, 13, 113, 118, 119, 205
Correlation coefficient (CORR), 127
Cost of capital, 8
Credit cards, spread of, 58
Credit rationing, 8
Culbertson, John M., 177
Currency, demand for, 54–57
  supply of, 15. *See also* Money supply
Currency demand estimates, 1955 and 1966, 55t
Currency demand model, refinements of, 57–58
Currency-deposit ratio, 56

Damping factor, 83, 84, 85f, 86, 87, 88
Decision periods, 30
  per unit time, 39
Deflator, GNP, 108, 111t, 116t, 117t, 127
  deviations of stochastic solutions of, 147
  dynamic simulation summary of, 133t
  one-period simulation summary for, 153t
  one-period solutions for, 150f, 151f

219

stochastic dynamic solutions for, 130f, 131f
de Leeuw, Frank, 8, 11, 88
Demand deposit estimates, 49t
Demand deposits, 15, 181
  behavior of, 39
  demand for, 47–51
  dynamic simulation of, 63f, 68f
  increase in, 38
  time paths of, 187f
  time series of, 186
Demand function, 42, 44
Deposit liabilities, new, 78, 80
Deposits, expansion of, 25
  supply of, 28
Deposit supply equation, 27
Derivative rules, 177–190
Deterministic solution, 127, 170
  and stochastic mean, 141
Discount rate, 179
Dunnett, 7
Dunnett's Comparison of Means, 196
Dunnett's statistic, 202
Dunnett's test, 197, 204
Durbin-Watson statistic, 50, 91
Dutta, M., 93
Dynamic simulation, 61
  of demand deposits, 63t, 68f
  error of, 50
  of free reserves, 64f
  root mean square errors of, 62t
  of Treasury Bill Rate, 66f, 69f
Dynamic simulation summary, for
  long-term interest rate, 139t
  real GNP, 138t
  of short-term interest rate, 140t
Dynamic stochastic simulation, 170

Econometric models, secant method in, 205
  simulation technique for, 122
  test of, 115
Econometric Society, 14
Economic policy, study of, 122
Economy, post-Korean War, 7
  U.S., model of, 163
  money supply model for, 2
Endogenous variables, 105t, 106t, 122, 171
  in reduced-form equations, 164
  and stochastic simulation, 172
Enzler, J. J., 118

Equations, final-form, 165
  in FMP Model, 9t
  fundamental dynamic, 165
"Equations race," 163–164
Equilibrium formula, 24
Estimation, methods of, 71
Estimation technique, and money-demand equation, 67
Eurodollar market, of 1969, 93
Excess reserves, 41
Exogenous variables, 24, 70–71, 97, 123
  prediction error of, 104
  in reduced-form equations, 164
  time-paths of, 192
Expenditures, consumer, 116t
  federal, high-employment, 164
  government, 108, 110t

Federal Funds market, 2
  and money supply model, 40–44
  rate of, 26, 89
Federal Reserve, borrowing from, 15
  behavior of, 71
Federal Reserve Board-MIT-Pennsylvania (FMP) model, 1
  aliases of, 13
  automatic feedback controls in, 205
  dynamic simulation output of, 166
  ex ante composites of, 112
  ex ante, serial correlation coefficients for, 106t
  ex post, serial correlation coefficients for, 106t
  linearity of, 5
  monetary rules in, 178
  nonlinearity of, 126, 141
  overview of, 7–11
  predictive performance of, xiii, 3, 97
  sample-period errors of, summary statistics for, 103t
  shocking of, 141
  single-period system properties of, 5
  standard deviations of, 107
  stochastic solutions of, 5
  stochastic specification of, 7, 179
  time period for, 30
  variable coefficients in, 101, 118
Federal Reserve System, 59
  Board of Governors of, 8
Feedback-control rule, 7
Final demand equations, in FMP model, 9t

Financial sector, of FMP model, 1, 10t
Finite maximizing values, 20
Fiscal stabilization policy, 7
Fischer, Stanley, 6, 205
FMP model. *See* Federal Reserve Board-MIT-Pennsylvania model
Forecast, types of, 4
Forecasting, 146
  ex ante, 97, 104
Foreign Reserve banks, foreign bank balances at, 92
Free reserve estimates, 36t
Free reserves, 62
  dynamic simulation of, 64f
  equilibrium value of, 32
  lagged, 67
  mathematical expectation of, 18
  positive, 40
Friedman, B., 91
Friedman, Milton, 52, 177, 207
Friedman model, 46, 47, 91
Fromm, Gary, 95
Fudge factors, 97

Gaussian distribution function, 174
Gauss-Seidel algorithm, 205
Gauss-Seidel iterative method, 123, 206
Gauss-Seidel method, 5, 80, 81, 82, 86, 87, 88
Gauss-Seidel simulation, 3
Geisel, M. S., 112
Goldfeld, S., 15, 88
Goodman, A. S., 173
Goodness of fit, 48, 142
  criteria for, 13
  measures of, 127
  tests for, 4
Gordon, Robert J., 8
Gradual adjustment model, 92
Gramlich, Edward M., 8, 11
Gross national product (GNP), 59
  FMP predictions of, 102
  nominal, 110t, 116t, 117t, 127
    change in, 164
    deviations of stochastic solutions of, 147
    dynamic simulation summary of, 132t
    lagged values of, 164
    one-period simulation summary for, 152t
    one-period solutions for, 148f, 149f
  stochastic dynamic solutions for, 128f, 129f
  stochastic mean of, 142, 143
  real, 11, 104, 110t, 111t, 116t, 117t, 127
    deviations of stochastic solutions of, 147
    dynamic simulation summary of, 138t
    model for, 101
    one-period simulation summary for, 158t
    one-period solutions for, 154f, 155f
    stochastic dynamic solutions for, 134f, 135f
    stochastic mean of, 146

Hester, D., 88
Histograms, 171, 173
Historical value, 127
Holt, Charles C., 119, 177, 179
Households, demand equation, 48
  net wealth of, 11
Howrey, E. Philip, 121
Hypothesis, "static," 22

IBM 360, 65, 123
Income, aggregate money, 46
  distribution of, 9t
  per capita real, 46
Index, consumer price, 108, 110t, 116t
Inflation, quarterly rates of, 182f, 183f, 184
  time paths of, 188f
  rate of, 185, 186, 192, 202
  stabilization of, 203
  standard deviations of, 190
  target rate of, 196
Integrated autoregressive moving average (ARIMA), 99, 116, 118
  coefficients of, 111
  ex ante composites of, 112
  and FMP model, 104
  for FMP variables, 100t–101t
  predictions, 102, 111, 116
  serial correlation coefficients for, 106t
  standard deviations of, 107
Interest rate, 110t
  determination of, 58–71
  long-term, 111t, 116, 117t, 127
    deviations of stochastic solutions of, 147

221

dynamic simulation summary for, 139t
one-period simulation summary, 159t
one-period solutions for, 156f, 157f
St. Louis model for, 113
stochastic dynamic solutions, 136f, 137f
short-term, 39, 71, 110f, 111t, 116t, 117t
deviations of stochastic solutions of, 147
dynamic simulation summary of, 140t
one-period simulation summary for, 162t
stochastic dynamic solutions for, 144f, 145f
stochastic one-period solutions for, 160f, 161f
standard deviation of, 186
Inventory investment, nonfarm, 110t, 116t
Investment, aggregate, 22
aggregate demand for, 20
Investment portfolio, 23
for aggregate banking system, 20
profitable level of, 17

Jaffee, Dwight M., 8
Jenkins, G. M., 99
Joint estimates, 107–113
Jorgenson, D. W., 93

Kane, E., 88
Kelejian, H. H., 121
Keynesian expenditure model, 114
Klein, Lawrence E., 95
Klein, Laurence R., 93
Klein-Goldberger model, 121
Knuth, Donald E., 173
Korean War, 7, 208
Koyck variables, 54

Labor market, in FMP model, 10t
Lag coefficients, 164
estimated, 168f, 169f, 172
Lag structures, estimated, 167f
Laidler, D., 91
Latane, H. A., 91
Least squares composite, 114
Least squares estimates, simulation of, 61–65

Least squares estimator, 3
Legal reserve releases, 34
timing of, 35–37
Lending, return from, 25–30. *See also* Borrowing
Lending policy, optimality of, 74
Lewis, F. A. W., 173
Liabilities, symbols for, 17t
Liquidity trap effects, 51
Loans, commercial, 16
end-of-quarter stock of, 34
expansion of, 25
Logarithmic-trigonometric transformation, 123
Long-run demand equation, 45
Loss function, 119
Lyttkens, E., 93

MAE. *See* Mean absolute error
Market clearing condition, 43
Market instruments, short-term, 35
Massachusetts Institute of Technology, 7
McCarthy, Michael D., 124
ME. *See* Mean error
Mean absolute error (MAE), 127, 142, 147
standard deviations of, 163
stochastic mean of, 143
stochastic solutions for, 170
Mean error (ME), 142
stochastic mean of, 143
Meigs, A. James, 88
Mellon, W. G., 16, 88, 94
Midwest Model Users Conference, 14, 174
Miller, J. M., 173
Model-building, strategy of, 11–13
Models, econometric, 1
linear structural, reduced-form equation of, 166
permanent income, 46–47
Modigliani, France, 2, 8, 13, 52, 53, 91, 91, 165, 166, 170, 174, 178, 179
Monetarist model, St. Louis Federal Reserve Bank, 164
Monetary aggregate, growth rate of, 181
Monetary policy, channels of, 8
instruments of, 59
Monetary rules, adoption of, 204
stochastic simulation, 194
Monetary sector, equations of, 58t

of FMP model, 1
Monetary variables, measurement of, 35
Money, demand for, 44–58
   growth rate of, 185
   neutrality of, 184
   stock of, determination of, 58–71
      change in, 164
Money multipliers, time patterns of, 205
Money supply (MI), demand-deposit component of, 60f
   determination of, 179
   expanding of, xiv
   in FMP model, 205
   hypothesis, 33
   mechanism, 15–39
Money supply model, and Federal Funds market, 40–44
Monopoly bank formula, 24
Monte Carlo experiments, 6
Monte Carlo methods, 163, 166, 172
Moody's AAA corporate band rate, 118
MPS model, 120

Nagar, A. L., 141, 174
Naylor, T. H., 195, 196
Nelson, Charles R., 4, 13, 99, 113, 118, 119, 120
Neo-Fisherian model, 44
Newton-Raphson method, 206
New York Stock Exchange, 98
Nonlinear function, expectation of, 122
Nonlinearity, 126, 141
Normality, 173

Okun's law, 104
One-period simulation summary, for GNP deflator, 153t
   for long-term interest rate, 159t
   for nominal GNP, 152t
   for real GNP, 158t
   for short-term interest rate, 162t
One-period solutions, for GNP deflator, 150f, 151f
   for long-term interest rate, 156f, 157f
   for nominal GNP, 148f, 149f
   for real GNP, 154f, 155f
Open-market operations, 1
Optimal credit, Orr and Mellon model of, 3
"Optimal" rule, 193
   search procedure for, 194

Orr, D., 16, 88, 94
Orr and Mellon model, 3, 72, 73, 79

Payne, W. H., 123, 173
Phillips, A. W., 177, 179
Phillips rule, 178
Pierce, J., 88
Pigou-Latane form, 45
Policy maker, 114, 115
Policy rules, parameter values for, 194
Portfolio, adjustment of, 32
Portfolio behavior, xiii
Post-sample errors, summary statistics for, 116t
Predictions, composite, 107–113
   time series, 98
Predictive performance, ex ante, 97
   one-quarter-ahead sample-period, 97–107
   post-sample, 115–118
Prices, in FMP model, 10t
Probability hypothetical graph of, 21f
Profit function, expected, 73–80
Profits, expected, 19, 79
Proportional rules, 177–190

Rabung, J. R., 123
Ralston, Anthony, 206
Rasche, Robert H., 2, 8, 13
Real income, effects of, 52, 57
Reduced-form equations, estimation of, 163–173
Reduced-form models, 163
Renormalization, 205
Reserve ratios, 179
Reserve release term, 33
Reserves, required, definition of, 27
   violation of, 78
   surplus, 19
   target free, 25–30
   unborrowed, 24
RMSE. *See* Root mean square error
Root mean square error (RMSE), 101, 102, 104, 105, 116, 127, 142, 147, 196
   post-sample period, 120
   standard deviations of, 163
   stochastic mean of, 143
   stochastic solutions for, 170
Rules, proportional, 177–190
   ranking of, 197

Rules vs. discretion controversy, 6

St. Louis Federal Reserve Bank, 6
    Econometric Model of, 104, 113, 118, 208
    "Monetarist" model of, 205
Sample-period errors, ARIMA, 105t
Sande, Gordon, 173
Savings deposits, household, 48
Sayers, Richard S., 177
Scaling factors, 123
Secant method, 205, 206
Sensitivity analysis, 190–194
Separation principle, 142
Serial correlation, 107
Shapiro, Harold T., 8
Short-term assets, available returns on, 45
Shull, Bernard, 37
Simulation, of monetary rules, 177–209
    one-period, 146–163
    stochastic, xiv, 5, 198, 121–126, 193, 194–197
    techniques, 11–12
Single-equation properties, of FMP model, 13
Single equations, 107–113
    root mean square errors of, 62t
Slutzky, Eugen E., 121
Spiking phenomenon, 65, 70
Stability, investigation of, 82
Stabilization, as goal, 177
    macroeconomic, 142
Stabilizing policy, 203
Standard deviations, 192
    range of ratios of, 204
Stekler, H. O., 118
Stochastic dynamic solutions, for GNP deflator, 130f, 131f
    for long-term interest rate, 136f, 137f
    for nominal GNP, 128f, 129f
    for real GNP, 134f, 135f
    for short-term interest rate, 144f, 145f
Stochastic equations, 125
Stochastic mean, 127
    and deterministic solution, 147
Stochastic one-period solutions, for short-term interest rate, 160f, 161f
Stochastic processes, 98
Stochastic simulation, xiv, 5
    results of, 198
    techniques, 121–126
    tests for, 193, 194–197
Stochastic system, and deterministic system, 199
Stock adjustment delay, 54
Studentized Range Statistic, 201
Supply of deposits, for aggregate banking system, 20
Supply function, for Federal Funds, 42
Supply of money, expanding of, xiv.
    See also Money supply
Sutch, R., 53, 91
Synthetic variables, 171

Target variables, standard deviations of, 199
Taxes, in FMP model, 9t
Taylor series approximation, 143
Theil's inequality coefficients, 102
Tinbergen, Jan, 12, 205
Tinbergen diagrams, 108
Time deposits, changes in, 32
    volatility of, 22
Time paths, 127
    of demand depostis, 187f
    expected values of, 122
    of quarterly rate of inflation, 188f
    of rate of unemployment, 189f
Time-series models, 4, 99, 113
Tobin, J., 16, 52
Tracking errors, 163
Transfers, in FMP model, 9t
Treasury bill rate, 108, 116t
    behavior of, 65
    dynamic simulation of, 66f, 69f
    short-run elasticity of, 67
Tukey, John W., 7, 175
Tukey's Multiple Comparison of Means, 196
Tukey's test, 197, 209
Tustin, A., 177
Two-stage least squares technique, (TSLS), 93

Unemployment, mean quarterly rates of, 182f
    mean rates of, 184
    quarterly rates of, 183f
    rate of, 108, 110t, 111t, 116t, 117t, 186, 192
    FMP model for, 113
    standard deviations of, 190

time path of, 189f
target rate of, 196
U.S. Treasury, cash balance of, 71
deposits held by, 59
Unit period, generalization to, 30–35

Variable coefficients, 101
Variance, analysis of, 196, 200
Velocity, definition of, 47
Vietnam War, 7, 208

Wealth, 8
Wealth account, transactions on, 53
Wertz, K., 195, 196
Winer, B. J., 201
Wonnacott, T., 195, 196

Zellner, A., 8, 14, 109u 112
Zellner across-equation, 4

About the Author

J. Phillip Cooper received the B.Com. in commerce and finance from the University of Toronto in 1965 and the Ph.D. in economics from the Massachusetts Institute of Technology in 1972. He is assistant professor at the Graduate School of Business, University of Chicago, and director of quantitative analysis at Dynamics Associates in Cambridge, Massachusetts. Dr. Cooper has been a consultant to a number of corporations, research institutions, and federal government agencies and was vice president of Synergy, Inc., a Washington, D.C. econometric consulting firm. He has developed a computer language for sophisticated economic and statistical analysis called *Econometric Software Package* (ESP), which has been distributed to over forty universities and corporations. Dr. Cooper is the author or coauthor of numerous articles on econometrics and monetary theory in professional business and economic journals.

LIBRARY OF DAVIDSON COLLEGE

Books on regular loan may be checked out for **two weeks**. Books must be presented at the Circulation Desk in order to be renewed.

A fine of **five cents** a day is charged after date due.

Special books are subject to special regulations at the discretion of library staff.